T0222306

Pillars of Computing

Gerard O'Regan

Pillars of Computing

A Compendium of Select, Pivotal Technology Firms

 Springer

Gerard O'Regan
Technical Trainers College
Riyadh, Saudi Arabia

ISBN 978-3-319-21463-4   ISBN 978-3-319-21464-1 (eBook)
DOI 10.1007/978-3-319-37006-4

Springer Cham Heidelberg New York Dordrecht London
© Springer International Publishing Switzerland 2015
Softcover re-print of the Hardcover 1st edition 2015

Printed on acid-free paper

Springer International Publishing AG Switzerland is part of Springer Science+Business Media (www.springer.com)

To Xiao Yun
For friendship and special memories
of Malaysia

Preface

Overview

The objective of this book is to consider a selection of technology firms that have made important contributions to the computing field. The goal is to provide a brief introduction to each selected company and to give a concise account of its key contributions.

It is not feasible, due to space constraints, to consider all of those technology firms that merit inclusion, and the selection chosen inevitably reflects the bias of the author. It is the author's aspiration that the reader will be stimulated by the selection and will gain an insight into the work done by these important technology firms.

Organization and Features

The selection of computer firms is presented in alphabetical order starting with Adobe Systems and ending with Zuse KG. The contributions of 35 companies are considered, and the technology firms considered may be classified into several categories such as those that produced earliest computers; firms that produced the mainframe and minicomputers of the 1960s and 1970s; those companies focused on the semiconductor sector; firms that developed home and personal computers as well as those that produced operating systems and applications for these machines; those companies that were active in the telecommunications field; organizations whose research has made major contributions to the computing fields; e-commerce companies; social media companies; enterprise computing companies; and so on.

We discuss early players in the computer field such as EMCC/Sperry/Unisys, Leo Computers, and Zuse KG. EMCC was founded by John Mauchly and Presper Eckert in 1947, and they were the designers of the ENIAC and EDVAC computers. EMCC was later taken over by Sperry which was later taken over by Unisys. Leo Computers was one of the earliest British computer companies, and it's LEO I computer was based on the EDSAC computer, which was developed at the University of Cambridge. Zuse KG was one of the earliest computer firms, and it was founded by Konrad Zuse in Germany shortly after the end of the Second World War.

We consider companies such as IBM, Amdahl, and Digital that have made important contributions to the mainframe and minicomputer fields. IBM has a long and distinguished history, and we consider a selection of its contribution including the development of SAGE, the System 360 family of computers, and the development of the personal computer. Amdahl became a major competitor to IBM in the mainframe market, and it was founded by Gene Amdahl who was a former IBM employee and the chief architect of the IBM System 360 project. Digital produced the popular PDP minicomputers as well as the VAX series of mainframes.

We present a selection of companies that made important contributions to the semiconductor field, including Intel, Texas Instruments, and Motorola. Intel was founded by Robert Noyce and Gordon Moore, and it developed the first microprocessor, the Intel 4004, in the early 1970s. The microprocessor was a revolution in computing, and Intel's continuous innovation has led to more and more powerful microprocessors. Motorola made important contributions to the semiconductor field, including its well-known 68000 microprocessor.

We discuss companies that were active in developing home and personal computers, as well as those firms that developed applications and games for these machines. Our selection includes Sinclair Research, a British company which produced the Sinclair ZX Spectrum; Commodore Business Machines, which produced the Commodore PET and Commodore 64 machines; Apple, which has made major contributions to the computing field; Atari, which was active in developing arcade games and later games for home computers; IBM, which developed the IBM personal computer; and Dell, which remains a major manufacturer of personal computers. We discuss the contributions of Digital Research, which developed the CP/M operating system, and the many contributions of Microsoft to the computing field.

We discuss some of the contributions important research centers such as Bell Labs, Xerox PARC, and the Software Engineering Institute. Bell Lab's inventors developed information theory and cryptography, coding theory, the Unix operating system and the C programming language, the transistor, and the Analogue Mobile Phone System. Xerox PARC's inventions include the Xerox Alto personal computer, which was a GUI mouse-driven machine which had a major impact on the design of the Apple Macintosh. Xerox PARC also invented the Ethernet technology; the Smalltalk object-oriented programming language; and the laser printer. The Software Engineering Institute has been active in developing state-of-the-art software process maturity models such as the CMMI to assist software development organizations to create best-in-class software.

We discuss the important contributions of Ericsson and Motorola in the telecommunications field. Ericsson developed the first digital exchange, the AXE system, for fixed-line telephony, and its modular design eased Ericsson's transition to the mobile field. Motorola was the leader in first-generation mobile telephony, but it failed to adapt rapidly enough to the later generations of mobile.

We consider SAP's contributions in the enterprise software market, and its software is widely used around the world. It is used to manage business operations and customer relations. Oracle is a world leader in relational database technology, and its software products have changed the face of business computing. It is also involved in the enterprise software market.

We consider the achievements of e-commerce companies such as Amazon and eBay, as well as the browser wars between Microsoft and Netscape. Amazon is a pioneer in online retailing, and it offers the world's largest selection of books, compact disks, DVDs, electronics, computer software, and toys. eBay manages the online auction and shopping site "ebay.com," and it provides a virtual market place for the sales of goods and services between individuals.

We consider the contributions of social media companies such as Facebook and Twitter. Facebook is the leading social networking site in the world, and its mission is to make the world more open and connected. It helps its users to keep in touch with friends and family and to share their opinions on what is happening around the world. Twitter is a social communication tool that allows people to broadcast short messages. It acts as the "SMS of the Internet," and it allows its users to send and receive short 140-character messages called "tweets." Finally, other companies discussed are Adobe, Cisco, Google, HP, and Unimation.

Audience

This book is suitable for computing students who are interested in knowing about the role played by the various technology firms that have shaped the computing field. It will also be of interest to general readers curious about the work done by contemporary and historical technology firms.

Acknowledgments

I am deeply indebted to friends and family who supported my efforts in this endeavor. I would like copyright owners for permission to use their images. The author believes that all of the required permissions have been obtained, but in the unlikely event that an image has been used without the appropriate authorization, please contact the author so that the required permission can be obtained.

I would like to pay special thanks to Xiao Yun (to whom this book is dedicated) for being in my life during the happy time that I spent in Malaysia in 2011. It was my privilege to have shared special times with her, and I wish her every joy and happiness for the future.

I would like to express my thanks to the team at Springer for their professional work, and I would like to especially thank Wayne Wheeler for his help and support over the years. I must also thank Simon Rees for his consistent professional support.

I would like to thank all copyright owners for permission to use their images. The author believes that all of the required permissions have been obtained, but in the unlikely event that an image has been used without the appropriate authorization, please contact the author so that the required permission can be obtained.

Cork, Ireland   Gerard O'Regan
2015

Contents

List of Figures

Chapter 1
Background

1.1 Introduction

Computers are an integral part of modern society, and new technology has transformed the world we live in. Communication today may be conducted using text messaging, email, mobile phones and video calls over the Internet using Skype. In the past, communication involved writing letters, sending telegrams or using home telephones. Today, communication is instantaneous between people, and the new technology has transformed the world into a global village. The developments in computers and information technology have allowed business to be conducted in a global market.

A computer is a programmable electronic device that can process, store and retrieve data, with the data being processed by a set of instructions termed a *program*. All computers consist of two basic parts, namely, *hardware* and *software*. The hardware is the physical part of the machine, and a digital computer contains memory for short-term storage of data or instructions, a central processing unit for carrying out arithmetic and logical operations, a control unit responsible for the execution of computer instructions in memory and peripherals that handle the input and output operations. The underlying architecture is referred to as the *von Neumann architecture*, and it is named after John von Neumann who was a famous Hungarian/American mathematician who made fundamental contributions to mathematics and computing. Software is a set of instructions that tells the computer what to do, and it is created by one or more programmers. It differs from hardware in that it is intangible.

The original meaning of the word *computer* referred to someone who carried out calculations rather than an actual machine. The early digital computers built in the 1940s and 1950s were enormous machines consisting of several thousand vacuum tubes.[1]

---

[1] The Whirlwind computer (developed in the early 1950s) occupied an entire building. One room contained the operating console consisting of several input and output devices.

© Springer International Publishing Switzerland 2015
G. O'Regan, *Pillars of Computing*, DOI 10.1007/978-3-319-21464-1_1

They typically filled a large room or building, but their computational power was a fraction of the power of the computers used today.

There are two distinct families of computing devices, namely, *digital computers* and the historical *analog computer*. These two types of computer operate on quite different principles, and the earliest computers were analog not digital.

The representation of data in an analog computer reflects the properties of the data that is being modelled. For example, data and numbers may be represented by physical quantities such as electric voltage in an analog computer, whereas in a digital computer a stream of binary digits is employed for the representation.

A digital computer is a sequential device that generally operates on data one step at a time. The data in a digital computer are represented in binary format, and the binary number system employs just two digits: namely, 0 and 1. A single transistor has two states, i.e. on and off, and a transistor is used to represent a single binary digit. Several transistors are used to represent larger numbers.

Early computing devices include the slide rule and various mechanical calculators. William Oughtred and others invented the slide rule in 1622, and this device allowed multiplication and division to be carried out significantly faster than calculation by hand. Blaise Pascal invented the first mechanical calculator, the Pascaline, in 1642, and this machine could add or subtract two numbers. Multiplication or division could then be performed by repeated addition or subtraction.

Leibniz[2] invented a mechanical calculator called the *Step Reckoner* in 1672, and this was the first calculator that could perform all four arithmetic operations, i.e. addition, subtraction, multiplication and division.

James Thompson (who was the brother of the famous physicist, Lord Kelvin) did early work on analog computation in the nineteenth century. He invented a integrator, which was used in mechanical analog devices, and he worked with Kelvin to construct a device to perform the integration of a product of two functions.

The operations in an analog computer are performed in parallel, and they are useful in simulating dynamic systems. They have been applied to flight simulation, nuclear power plants and industrial chemical processes.

Vannevar Bush and others developed the first large-scale general-purpose mechanical analog computer, the differential analyser (Fig. 1.1), at the Massachusetts Institute of Technology in the late 1920s. Bush's differential analyser was designed to solve sixth-order differential equations by integration, using wheel-and-disc mechanisms to perform the integration. It allowed integration and differential equation problems to be solved more rapidly.

The machines consisted of wheels, discs, shafts and gears to perform the calculations, and a considerable effort was required by the technicians to set up the machine to solve a particular equation. The differential analyser contained 150 motors and miles of wires connecting relays and vacuum tubes.

Data representation in an analog computer is compact, but it may be subject to corruption with noise. A single capacitor can store one continuous variable in an

---

[2] Leibniz is credited (along with Newton) with the development of the calculus.

Fig. 1.1 Differential analyser at Moore School of Electrical Engineering, University of Pennsylvania

analogue computer, whereas several transistors are required to represent a variable in a digital computer. Analog computers were replaced by digital computers after the Second World War.

1.2 Digital Computers

Early digital computers used vacuum tubes to store binary information. A vacuum tube could represent the binary value "0" or "1". However, the tubes were large and bulky and generated a significant amount of heat. This led to problems with their reliability, and air conditioning was employed to cool the machine.

Shockley and others invented the transistor in the 1950s (see Chap. 7), and they replaced vacuum tubes. Transistors are small and consume very little power. The resulting machines were smaller, faster and more reliable.

Integrated circuits were introduced in the 1960s (see Chap. 32), and a massive amount of computational power may be placed in a very small chip. Integrated circuits are small and consume very little power, and they may be mass-produced to a very high-quality standard. Billions of transistors may be placed on an integrated circuit.

The development of the microprocessor (see Chap. 20) allowed a single chip to contain all of the components of a computer from the CPU and memory to input and output controls. The microprocessor could fit into the palm of the hand, whereas the early computers filled an entire room.

The fundamental architecture of a computer has remained basically the same since von Neumann and others proposed it in the 1940s. It includes a central processing unit, the control unit, the arithmetic logic unit, an input and output unit and memory.

1.3   Hardware and Software

Hardware is the physical part of the machine. It is tangible and may be seen and touched. It includes the historical punched cards and vacuum tubes, transistors and circuit boards, integrated circuits and microprocessors. The hardware of a personal computer includes a keyboard, network cards, a mouse, a DVD drive, hard disc drive, printers, scanners and so on.

Software is intangible in that it is not physical, and instead it consists of a set of instructions that tells the computer what to do. It is an intellectual creation of the programmer or a team of programmers. There are several types of software such as system software and application software.

The *system software* manages the hardware and resources and acts as an intermediary between the application programs and the computer hardware. This includes the UNIX operating system, the various Microsoft Windows operating systems and the Mac operating system. There are also operating systems for mobile phones, video games and so on. *Application software* is designed to perform a specific application such as banking, insurance or accounting.

Early software consisted of instructions in machine code that could be immediately executed by the computer. These programs were difficult to read and debug. This led to the development of assembly languages that represented a particular machine code instruction by a mnemonic, and the assembly language was translated into machine code by an assembler. Assembly languages were an improvement on machine code but were still difficult to use. This led to the development of high-level programming languages (e.g. FORTRAN and COBOL) where a program was written in the high-level language and compiled to the particular code of the target machine.

1.4   Pillars of Computing

The objective of this book is to give a concise account of the contributions of a selection of those technology companies that have made important contributions to the computing field. It is not feasible, due to space constraints, to consider all those firms that merit inclusion, and the selection chosen inevitably reflects the bias of the author.

The selection is presented in alphabetical order, and the contributions of 35 technology companies are discussed. The first firm discussed is Adobe Systems, and the last company presented is Zuse KG. The account of each technology company provides a concise summary of its key contributions.

The companies may be classified into several categories such as those that produced early computers, firms that produced mainframe and minicomputers, those companies focused on the semiconductor sector, firms that developed home and personal computers, those who were active in the telecommunications field, e-commerce companies, social media companies, enterprise software companies and so on.

We discuss early players in the computer field such as EMCC/Sperry/Unisys, LEO Computers and Zuse KG. EMCC was founded by John Mauchly and Presper Eckert in 1947. It was later taken over by Sperry which was later taken over by Unisys. LEO Computers was one of the earliest British computer companies, and it's LEO I Computer was based on the EDSAC computer developed at the University of Cambridge. Zuse KG was one of the earliest computer firms, and it was founded by Konrad Zuse in Germany shortly after the end of the Second World War.

We consider companies such as IBM, Amdahl and Digital that have made important contributions to the mainframe and minicomputer fields. IBM has a long and distinguished history, and we consider a selection of its contribution including its development of SAGE, the System 360 family of computers, and the IBM personal computer. Amdahl became a major competitor to IBM in the mainframe market, and it was founded by Gene Amdahl, who was a former IBM employee. Digital produced the popular PDP minicomputers as well as the VAX series of mainframes.

We present a selection of companies that made important contributions to the semiconductor field, including Intel, Texas Instruments and Motorola. Intel developed the first microprocessor, the Intel 4004, in the early 1970s. The invention of the microprocessor was a revolution in computing, and it led to the development of home and personal computers; Intel's continuous innovation has led to more and more powerful microprocessors. Motorola made important contributions to the semiconductor field, and its well-known 68000 microprocessor was released in 1979.

We discuss companies that were active in developing home and personal computers, as well as those firms that developed applications and games for these machines. Our selection includes Sinclair Research, a British company which produced the Sinclair ZX Spectrum; Commodore Business Machines, which produced the Commodore PET and Commodore 64 machines; Apple, which has made major contributions to the computing field; Atari, which was active in developing arcade games and later games for home computers; IBM, which developed the IBM personal computer; and Dell, which remains a major manufacturer of personal computers. We discuss the contributions of Digital Research which developed the CP/M operating system for microprocessors and the many contributions of Microsoft to the computing field.

We discuss some of the contributions of important research centres such as Bell Labs, Xerox PARC and the Software Engineering Institute. Bell Lab's inventors developed information theory and cryptography, coding theory, the transistor, UNIX and the C programming language and the analog mobile phone system. Xerox PARC's inventions include the Xerox Alto personal computer which was a GUI mouse-driven machine which had a major impact on the design of the Apple Macintosh. Xerox PARC also invented Ethernet technology, the Smalltalk object-oriented programming language and the laser printer. The Software Engineering Institute has been active in developing state-of-the-art software process maturity models such as the CMMI to assist software development organisations in creating best-in-class software.

We discuss the important contributions of Ericsson and Motorola in the telecommunications field. Ericsson developed the first digital exchange (the AXE system) for fixed-line telephony, and the modular design of the AXE system eased Ericsson's transition to the mobile field. Motorola was the leader in first-generation mobile telephony, but it failed to adapt rapidly enough to the later generations of mobile.

We consider SAP's contributions in the enterprise software market, and its software is widely used by companies around the world to manage their business operations and customer relations. Oracle is a world leader in relational database technology, and its software products have changed the face of business computing. It is also involved in the enterprise software market.

We consider the achievements of e-commerce companies such as Amazon and eBay, as well as the browser wars between Microsoft and Netscape. Amazon is a pioneer in online retailing, and it offers the world's largest selection of books, compact discs, DVDs, electronics, computer software and toys. eBay manages the online auction and shopping site *ebay.com*, and it provides a virtual market place that allows buyers and sellers to come together and to negotiate on the price of a good or service.

We consider the contributions of social media companies such as Facebook and Twitter. Facebook is the leading social networking site in the world, and its mission is to make the world more open and connected. It helps its users to keep in touch with friends and family, and it allows them to share their opinions on what is happening around the world. Twitter is a social communication tool that allows people to broadcast short messages. It is often described as the *SMS of the Internet*, and it allows its users to send and receive short 140-character messages called *tweets*. Finally, other companies discussed are Adobe, Cisco, Google, HP and Unimation.

Chapter 2
Adobe Systems

Adobe Systems is an American multinational software company that is well known for its creativity and multimedia software products. It created the popular portable document format (PDF), and its Adobe Creative Suite is a collection of Adobe applications including Acrobat, Photoshop and so on, which is used for graphic design, video editing and web development applications.

Adobe Systems was founded by Charles Geschke (Fig. 2.1) and John Warnock (Fig. 2.2) in Silicon Valley in 1982, and the name *Adobe* was taken from the name of a Californian stream, *Adobe Creek* near Los Altos in California. The stream ran near to John Warnock's house in Los Altos. Today, the company has annual revenues of approximately $4 billion, with net income of approximately $300 million. It employs over 10,000 people around the world, with offices in the United States, Europe and Asia.

Geschke and Warnock were former employees of Xerox PARC, and Geschke had founded PARC's Imaging Science Laboratory in the late 1970s, where he directed research activities in graphics and image processing. He hired John Warnock, and they worked together on a page description language (PDL), which provided a way to describe complex forms such as type interfaces electronically. This language evolved to become the *Interpress* language, which was a design language to process graphic images for graphics printing. It was used on the newly developed PARC laser printer. However, Geschke and Warnock were unable to convince Xerox management of the commercial potential of the Interpress graphics language for controlling printing, and both of them left Xerox PARC to cofound Adobe Systems, with the goal of exploiting this new technology.

Adobe Systems initially intended building a powerful printer, but it decided instead to create tools for printer manufacturers to control these printers. They created a language called *PostScript* in 1984, which evolved from the existing Interpress language that Warnock and Geschke had developed at Xerox PARC. PostScript was similar but simpler than Interpress, and the Apple LaserWriter was the first printer to employ PostScript. This led to the first desktop publishing system, and it allowed users to print documents as they appeared on the screen electronically. PostScript

© Springer International Publishing Switzerland 2015
G. O'Regan, *Pillars of Computing*, DOI 10.1007/978-3-319-21464-1_2

Fig. 2.1 Charles Geschke
(Courtesy of Adobe
Systems)

Fig. 2.2 John Warnock
(Courtesy of Adobe
Systems)

was machine independent and very flexible, and it soon became the language of choice for graphical printing applications.

Adobe introduced the Adobe Illustrator in the mid-1980s, and this was a vector-based drawing program for the Apple Macintosh. It helped to popularise PostScript-enabled printers, and shapes could be drawn with more accuracy than the existing MacDraw Macintosh drawing program.

Adobe introduced Photoshop, its famous graphical editing program, for the Macintosh, in 1989, and this product soon dominated the market. The company introduced its well-known portable document format (PDF) and the associated Adobe Acrobat Reader and Writer software in the early 1990s. Acrobat is used to view or modify PDF files, and PDF documents are used throughout the world as a common medium for electronic documents. There is now an international standard for electronic documents (ISO 32000-1:2008), and this standard specifies a digital form for representing electronic documents. The standard is independent of the environment in which the document is created, viewed or printed.

Adobe has acquired a number of companies to expand its desktop publishing product offerings. It acquired Frame Technology Corporation in 1995, and Adobe FrameMaker is now one of its products. It acquired its rival Macromedia in 2005, and this has enabled Adobe to add products such as Adobe ColdFusion, Adobe Dreamweaver and Flash to its product portfolio. ColdFusion is a rapid application development platform for web development; Adobe Dreamweaver is a web design and development tool; and Adobe Flash is a multimedia platform for creating vector graphics, animation, games and internet applications that can be played and executed on Adobe's Flash Player. Flash movies are in the SWF format ("ShockWave Flash" movies).

Adobe's products have been criticised for having security vulnerabilities, and hackers have exploited these weaknesses to gain unauthorised access to computers. Its Flash Player has been criticised for having performance, memory and security problems. For more information on Adobe, see [Pfi:02].

2.1 Printing and PostScript

Printers were initially designed to print character output from the given ASCII input text, and the characters were difficult to change as they were generally stamped onto the typewriter keys. The technology changed to some extent with the introduction of dot matrix printers, as the characters on these printers were drawn as a series of dots, as defined by a font table inside the printer.

As dot matrix printers evolved, they began to include built-in fonts which the user could select. Dot matrix printers also allowed the user to print raster graphics where the graphics were interpreted by the computer and sent as a series of dots to the printer.

Plotters were special printers used for printing vector graphics, and they were used in applications such as computer-aided design (CAD) to print the designs of machines and ships. Plotters operate by moving a pen or other instruments across a piece of paper, and they are *vector graphics* devices rather than the *raster graphics* devices that are used on dot matrix printers. Plotters can draw complex line art including text but do so slowly because of the movement of the pen. Plotters offered an efficient way to produce very large drawings and high-resolution vector-based artwork, and they used the printer control language HP-GL. Today, plotters are mainly obsolete and have been replaced by large inkjet printers.

Laser printers combine the best features of printers and plotters in that they offer high-quality line art and they are able to generate pages of text and raster graphics. However, a laser printer has an additional capability in that it can position text and high-quality graphics on the same page.

PostScript is more than a printer control language in that it is a complete programming language in its own right. PostScript programs are typically produced by other programs and not by humans. Applications can transform a document into a PostScript program, and the execution of the program results in the printing of the original document.

The early PostScript printers required significant processing power, and they were often more powerful than the machines that they were connected to. The advantages of PostScript are that it is device independent, with users no longer tied to a particular manufacturer. Further, the specification of PostScript is freely available, and a manufacturer may buy a license for a PostScript interpreter and use it to build the output for the device.

2.2 Portable Document Format

The invention of the portable document format (PDF) standard for documents was the result of an internal Adobe project that was concerned with the problem of developing a paperless office. The goal of a paperless office was a pet project of Warnock, and the initial objective of the project was to create a file format for documents that would be independent of the particular computer and operating system. It would allow documents spread throughout the company to be displayed on any computer and operating system, and a document that contained text and graphics characters, such as newspapers and magazines, could be viewed on any computer and printed locally.

The Adobe engineers created a new file format called *portable document format* (PDF) and a set of applications to visualise and create these files. Version 1.0 of PDF was announced in late 1992, and Acrobat tools to visualise and create PDF files appeared in mid-1993. Adobe initially charged for both tools, but it later launched the free version of Acrobat Reader.

Adobe was one of the first big users of PDF, and it distributed all documents for developers as PDF files. The introduction of the Internet and World Wide Web in the early 1990s helped to increase the popularity of PDF, and functionality was added to link PDF files to HTML pages and vice versa. Today, PDF files are widely used throughout the world.

2.3 Photoshop

Adobe Photoshop is a raster graphic editor which was initially released in 1990. A raster graphic editor is a computer program that allows users to create and edit images interactively on the computer screen. The user may then save the image in one of the popular *bitmap* or *raster* formats such as JPEG, PNG or GIF. Adobe Photoshop rapidly became the industry standard in digital colour editing.

A raster image is made up of rows and columns of dots, called *pixels*, and it is the standard form used on a digital camera where the digital photo is represented pixel by pixel. *Vector graphics* (vector images) are created mathematically using geometrical formulae, and they are used in graphic design to represent complex geometric patterns, technical illustrations and so on.

The initial version of Photoshop was developed by Thomas and John Knoll. Their father was a photo enthusiast who had a darkroom at home, and Thomas Knoll became interested in photography and in image manipulation in the darkroom. This involved balancing the colour and contrasts of photographs.

Thomas was working on a PhD in the processing of digital images, and he was using an Apple Mac Plus to assist him in his work. However, the Mac was unable to display the grey-scale levels in his images, and he wrote a series of routines and image processing tools to address these weaknesses. John Knoll was working at a computer company in California, and they worked together to improve the program. This led to an improved version of the application that became "*ImagePro*" in 1988, and John suggested to Thomas that they turn it into a commercial application. They presented the application to Adobe in late 1988, and a licensing deal was agreed shortly afterwards. Adobe Photoshop 1.0 appeared in early 1990.

A Photoshop file has a default extension of ".PSD", and the file may be exported to other Adobe applications such as Adobe Illustrator and Adobe Premiere Pro. Photoshop includes multiple tools such as selection, cropping, slicing, moving and a pen tool for creating precise paths.

In the past, it was common to say that *A camera never lies*. Well, today we have Photoshop, and so we can potentially produce images of people skiing around the great pyramids as well as many other doctored images. It was, of course, possible for skilled photographers to doctor images prior to the invention of Photoshop, but now it is very easy for anyone with basic computer literacy to create interesting photographs that are a distortion of the actual reality.

Chapter 3
Amazon.com

Amazon.com is an international e-commerce company with headquarters in Seattle in the United States. Amazon is a pioneer in online retailing, and it offers the world's largest selection of books, compact discs, DVDs, electronics, computer software and toys. It has worldwide sales of approximately $74 billion and net income of approximately $275 million. It employs approximately 130,000 people around the world.

E-commerce is a relatively new invention, and it became possible shortly after the invention of the World Wide Web by Tim Berners-Lee [BL:00] in the early 1990s. Exponential growth was predicted for the e-commerce world, with the expectation that e-commerce firms would eventually replace the existing bricks-and-mortar companies. This led to frenzy among investors for the purchase of shareholdings in Internet companies, and this culminated in the dot-com bubble of the late 1990s and the subsequent dot-com crash in 2000 when it was clear that the valuations of these technology companies were unrealistic.

Online shopping was a relatively new phenomenon in the mid-1990s, with only a small number of e-commerce firms existing and only a small percentage of sales conducted online.

Jeff Bezos (Fig. 3.1) saw a business opportunity in this new brave world, and he resigned his job as vice president of a Wall Street firm to set up Amazon.com in 1995. His goal was to create the largest online bookstore in the world, and his plan was to develop a pure e-commerce firm without a physical retail presence. That is, the company would be an online bookstore that would sell books online without a physical bricks-and-mortar presence.

The choice of name for the new company was seen as fundamental to its success. Bezos wanted to build a brand name that would encompass the vision of the company, as well as a name that the public could easily identify with. Several candidate names were considered including "cadabra.com" and "relentless.com".[1] However,

---

[1] The "relentless.com" URL was registered in 1994, and if typed into the Internet today, it takes you to Amazon.com. The name "cadabra.com" was seen as too similar to cadaver and was rejected.

© Springer International Publishing Switzerland 2015   13
G. O'Regan, *Pillars of Computing*, DOI 10.1007/978-3-319-21464-1_3

Fig. 3.1 Jeff Bezos

these names were rejected, and instead the name *Amazon.com*, which refers to the largest river in the world, was chosen. The name "Amazon" emphasised the vision that Bezos had of the company becoming the largest online bookstore in the world.

Amazon's initial business model was unusual in that it did not expect to make a profit for its first 4–5 years of existence. This was quite common among the early e-commerce companies, but the valuations of these companies were unusual in the sense that their valuations took their predicted future profits into account, rather than basing the valuation on the normal accounting practices such as the balance sheet and profit and loss accounts. Bezos was successful in convincing sceptical investors who were obviously interested in a quick return on their investment.

Amazon initially invested heavily in warehouses, advertisement and marketing and in developing an effective e-commerce site with a large catalogue of books. As a pioneer in the world of e-commerce, Amazon strived to set the standard for web businesses. It developed an easy-to-use and customer-friendly website with powerful searching capabilities, shopping cart facilities and a secure payment system.

It initially sold books at a loss by giving discounts of 10–30 % to buyers in order to build up market share and to build a reputable well-known brand. The early focus was to build up the "Amazon.com" brand in the United States and later throughout the world. It also offered an optional giftwrapping of packages, and it allowed customers to write reviews of their purchased products, which other customers could read.

Amazon became a public company in 1997, after just 2 years in business, and 3 million shares were offered at a price of $18.00 per share. Bezos used the proceeds of the successful initial public offering (IPO) to continue with improvements to the company's website and on improvements to the distribution capabilities of the company. It opened new distribution centres around the United States to reduce the time required to fulfil a customer order and in order to serve its customers better.

Amazon's product portfolio has expanded over time to include music, movies, toys, computer software, video games, electronics and household goods. It claims to have the largest selection of products available through its family of websites, and its low-cost model offers customers value for money and convenience. The customer has complete flexibility on when to shop as the website is operational $24 \times 7 \times 365$, and so the customer may search online for the desired product and purchase at a convenient time. The purchased products are delivered directly to the customer's home.

Amazon also provides Internet services such as Amazon Prime which offers free 2-day shipping on retail purchases, on-demand video streaming and free access to the Kindle library. Amazon Web Services (AWS) allows customers to use the Amazon infrastructure to run applications, and it also offers a low-cost file storage web service. It manufactures and sells the Kindle family of tablets which are used for electronic books, games and movies. Today, Amazon sells more Amazon Kindle books than traditional physical books.

Amazon has been highly innovative in the e-commerce world, and it has devised alternate retail strategies by acting as the gateway for other retailers, as well as developing a market place for second-hand goods. This allows Amazon to take a small percentage of these third-party sales, without needing to maintain an inventory of these third-party items. It has also developed an associate model, which allows its associates to receive a commission for purchases of Amazon products made through the associate site.

It has a very large product catalogue, a well-designed website with good searching facilities, good checkout facilities and good order fulfilment. The customer can track the status of the order once it is made until it is delivered. Amazon allows customers to rate the product and to provide feedback, and this is potentially useful to other customers. There have been abuses of the product ratings with rival companies posting negative ratings and comments about their competitor products and authors or companies giving a biased rating of their own products under pseudonyms. For more information about Amazon, see [Sto:14].

3.1 Amazon Web Services

Amazon Web Services (AWS) offers a reliable, scalable, and cost-effective *cloud computing service*. It is a collection of remote computing services (web services) that make up a cloud computing platform, and it was launched by Amazon in 2006. It provides online services for other websites or client-side applications.

These web services provide functionality that is used mainly by other developers, and they provide the user with a large computing capacity via virtual servers. Virtual servers provide a faster and cheaper solution to building computing capability and avoid the necessity of building an expensive physical server infrastructure (i.e. a several physical servers). AWS allows Amazon to earn revenue from its massive investment in server infrastructure.

Amazon Web Services is located in several geographical regions of the United States, Europe, Asia and Australia. Each region has several data centres providing AWS. There have been some outages which have caused major disruptions to Amazon's customers, but the architecture of AWS is designed to prevent outages from spreading to other centres. As of 2014, Amazon operates 1.4 million servers across 28 data centres around the world.

3.2 Kindle

The Amazon Kindle (Fig. 3.2) is a series of e-book readers designed and sold by Amazon. It enables readers to browse, download and read e-books via Wi-Fi (a local area wireless technology) or via Amazon's "Whispernet" network. E-books may be purchased online and downloaded wirelessly, and today there are approximately 3 million books in the Kindle bookstore. The Kindle was originally introduced in late 2007, and today Amazon sells more e-books than physical books.

The Kindle has evolved from the original device that was introduced in 2007, which could hold about 200 books. The Kindle 2 included a text-to-speech option, which allowed the text to be read aloud, and it could hold about 1500 books. An

Fig. 3.2 Amazon Kindle

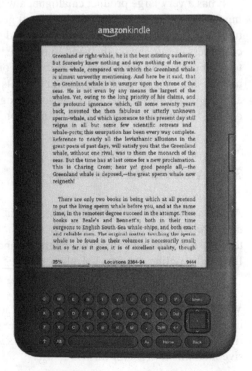

international version of the Kindle 2 became available in late 2009, and the Kindle Fire (an Android-based table) was released in 2011.

Amazon released a *Kindle for PC* application in late 2009, and this free application is available as a download for Microsoft Windows.

3.3 History of E-Commerce

The application of the World Wide Web to commerce and trade was recognised by its inventor, Tim Berners-Lee. He realised that the web offered the potential to conduct business in cyberspace, rather than the traditional approach of buyers and sellers coming together at the market place.

Anyone can trade with anyone else except that they do not have to go to the market square to do so

The growth of the World Wide Web has been phenomenal, and exponential growth rate curves are often associated with newly formed Internet companies and their business plans. The World Wide Web has been applied to many areas including:

- Travel industry (booking flights, train tickets and hotels)
- Online shopping (e.g. www.amazon.com)
- Online auction sites (e.g. eBay)
- Internet banking
- Online casinos (for gambling)
- Newspapers and news channels
- Portal sites (such as Yahoo)
- Recruitment services (such as www.jobserve.com)
- E-marketing
- Social media (Facebook and Twitter)

The prediction in the early days was that the new web-based economy would replace the traditional bricks-and-mortar companies. It was expected that most business would be conducted over the web, with traditional enterprises losing market share and going out of business. The size of the new web economy was estimated to be in trillions of US dollars, and exponential growth of the new-age companies was predicted.

New companies were formed to exploit the opportunities of the web, and existing companies developed e-business and e-commerce strategies in order to adapt to this brave new world. Companies providing full e-commerce solutions were concerned with the selling of products or services over the web to either businesses or consumers. These business models are referred to as *business to business* (B2B) or *business to consumer* (B2C). Later, business models included *consumer to consumer* (C2C) and *business to government* (B2G). E-commerce websites have the following characteristics (Table 3.1):

Table 3.1 Characteristics of e-commerce

Feature	Description
Catalogue of products	The catalogue of products details the products available for sale and their prices
Well designed and easy to use	This is essential as otherwise the website will not be used
Shopping carts	This is analogous to shopping carts in a supermarket
Security	Security of credit card information is a key concern for users of the web, as users need to have confidence that their credit card details will remain secure
Payments	Once the user has completed the selection of purchases, there is a checkout facility to arrange for the purchase of the goods
Order fulfilment/order enquiry	Following the confirmation of payment for the customer order, the ordered products must be delivered to the customer's home. The user should be able to determine the actual status of the order at any time from placement to delivery

Chapter 4
Amdahl Corporation

Amdahl Corporation was set up by Gene Amdahl (Fig. 4.1) in 1970 following his resignation from IBM. He had irreconcilable differences with IBM on his ideas for future computer development, and this led him to set up his own computer company, Amdahl Corporation, in California. Amdahl Corporation was later to become a major competitor to IBM in the mainframe market during the 1970s and 1980s.

Amdahl initially had difficulty in raising sufficient capital to start his business. However, he succeeded in obtaining funding from Fujitsu which was interested in a joint development program and also from Nixdorf which was interested in representing Amdahl in Europe. Amdahl computers were compatible with IBM computers and software, but delivered a superior performance at a lower cost. Customers could run S/360 and S/370 applications on Amdahl hardware without buying IBM hardware.

Gene Amdahl was born in South Dakota in 1922, and he served in the US Navy during the Second World War. He obtained a degree in engineering physics from South Dakota University in 1948 and earned a PhD in theoretical physics in 1952 from the University of Wisconsin–Madison. His PhD thesis detailed the design of his first computer, the *Wisconsin Integrally Sequential Computer* (WISC), and the machine was built during the period 1951–1954.

He joined IBM in 1952 and became the chief designer of the IBM 704 computer. Amdahl and Backus[1] designed this large computer, and it was used for scientific and commercial applications. The 704 was released in 1954, and over 140 of these machines were sold. The 704 computer was a commercial success for IBM.

Amdahl became the chief architect for the IBM System 360 family of mainframe computers (Fig. 4.2). This influential family of computers was introduced in 1964, and the IBM chairman, Thomas Watson, called the event the most important product announcement in the company's history. Fred Brooks was the System 360 project manager, and he later wrote the influential paper *The Mythical Man-Month* [Brk:75] based on his experience as project manager for the project. He later argued

---

[1] John Backus and Fred Brooks are discussed in [ORg:13].

© Springer International Publishing Switzerland 2015

G. O'Regan, *Pillars of Computing*, DOI 10.1007/978-3-319-21464-1_4

Fig. 4.1 Gene Amdahl
(Photo courtesy of Perry
Pkivolowitz)

Fig. 4.2 IBM 360 model 30 (Courtesy of IBM Archives)

in *Essences and Accidents in Software Engineering* [Brk:86] that software projects
are inherently complex and that there is no silver bullet as such that will lead to the
productivity improvements that have been achieved in the hardware field [ORg:13].

The IBM 360 was a family of small to large computers, and it offered a choice of
five processors and nineteen combinations of power, speed and memory. There
were fourteen models in the family. The concept of a *family of computers* was a
paradigm shift away from the traditional *one size fits all philosophy of the computer
industry*, as up until then, every computer model was designed independently.

The family of computers ranged from minicomputers with 24 KB of memory to supercomputers for US missile defense systems. However, all these computers employed the same user instruction set, and the main difference was that for the larger computers the more complex machine instructions were implemented with hardware, whereas the smaller machines used microcode. A customer could start with a small member of the S/360 family and upgrade over time into a larger computer in the family. This helped to make computers more affordable for businesses and stimulated growth in computer use.

The S/360 was used extensively in the Apollo mission to place man on the moon. The contribution by IBM computers and personnel were essential to the success of the project. IBM invested over $5 billion in the design and development of the S/360. However, the gamble paid off, and it was a very successful product line for the company.

Amdahl was appointed an IBM fellow in 1965 in recognition of his contribution to IBM, and he was appointed director of IBM's Advanced Computing Systems (ACS) Laboratory in California and given freedom to pursue his own research projects.

However, he resigned from IBM and set up Amdahl Corporation in 1970, and his goals were to develop a mainframe that would provide better performance than the existing IBM machines, and would do so at lower cost, and would be compatible with IBM hardware and software. Nixdorf and Fujitsu invested in the company. Amdahl had intended launching an IBM-compatible S/360 mainframe, but following IBM's introduction of its IBM 370, Amdahl revised his plans to launch an IBM-compatible S/370 mainframe.

Amdahl Corporation launched its first product, the Amdahl 470V/6, in 1975. This was an IBM-compatible S/370 mainframe that could run IBM software, and so it was an alternative to a full IBM proprietary solution. It meant that companies around the world now had the choice of continuing to run their software on IBM machines or purchasing the cheaper and more powerful IBM compatibles produced by Amdahl.

Amdahl's first customer was the NASA Goddard Institute for Space Studies, which was based in New York. The Institute needed a powerful computer to track data from its Nimbus weather satellite, and it had a choice between a well-established company such as IBM and an unknown company such as Amdahl. This meant that there was a degree of risk associated with Amdahl, and so it seemed likely that IBM would be the chosen supplier. However, the Institute was highly impressed with the performance of the Amdahl 470V/6, and its cost was significantly less than the IBM machine.

The Amdahl 470 competed directly against the IBM System 370 family of mainframes. It was compatible with IBM hardware and software but cheaper than the IBM product, i.e. the Amdahl machines provided better performance for less money. Further, the machine was much smaller than the IBM machine due to the use of large-scale integration (LSI) with many integrated circuits on each chip. This meant that the Amdahl 470 was one-third of the size of IBM's 370. It was over twice as fast and sold for about 10 % less than the IBM 370.

IBM's machines were water-cooled, while Amdahl's were air-cooled, which decreased installation costs significantly. Machine sales were slow initially due to concerns over Amdahl's long-term survival and the risks of dealing with a new player. Further, there was a tradition of purchasers ordering from IBM in light of its long established reputation as the leader in the computer field. The University of Michigan was Amdahl's second customer, and it used the 470 in its education centre. Texas A&M was Amdahl's third customer, and they used the 470 for educational and administrative purposes. Amdahl was well on its way to success, when by 1977 it had over 50 470V/6 machines installed at various customer sites.

Amdahl launched a successful initial public offering in 1976 which allowed it to convert its debt to equity, as well as creating substantial cash reserves. Its revenues grew from less than $14 million in 1975 to over $320 million in 1977, with net income of $48 million.

IBM launched a new product, the IBM 3033, in 1977 to compete with the Amdahl 470. However, Amdahl responded with a new machine, the 470V/7, which was one and a half times faster than the 3033 and only slightly more expensive. Customers voted with their feet and chose Amdahl as their supplier, and by late 1978 it had sold over a hundred of the 470V/7 machines.

Gene Amdahl resigned from the company in late 1979, and he formed a start-up company, Trilogy Systems, the following year. This company focused on developing very-large-scale integration (VLSI) technology. Amdahl worked closely with Fujitsu to improve circuit design, and Fujitsu's influence on the company increased following Gene Amdahl's departure. Fujitsu's stake in the company increased to 49 % by 1984.

IBM introduced a medium-sized computer, the 4300 series, in early 1979, and in late 1980 it announced plans for the 3081 processor which would have twice the performance of the existing 3033 on its completion in late 1981. In response, Amdahl announced the 580 series, which would have twice the performance of the existing 470 series. The 580 series (Fig. 4.3) was released in mid-1982, but their early processors had some reliability problems and lacked some of the features of the new IBM product.

Amdahl moved into large system multiprocessor design from the mid-1980s. It introduced its 5890 model in late 1985, and its superior performance allowed Amdahl to gain market share and increase its sales to approximately $1 billion in 1986. It now had over 1300 customers in around 20 countries around the world. It launched a new product line, the 5990 processor, in 1988, and this processor outperformed IBM by 50 %. Customers voted with their feet and chose Amdahl as their supplier, and it was clear that Amdahl was now a major threat to IBM in the high-end mainframe market. Amdahl had a 24 % market share and annual revenues of $2 billion at the end of 1988.

Amdahl Corporation was now posing a serious challenge to IBM in large-scale computer placements, and this led to a price war with IBM, with the latter offering discounts to its customers to protect its market share. Amdahl responded with its own discounts, and this led to a reduction in profitability for the company.

Fig. 4.3 Amdahl 5860 (Courtesy of Roger Broughton, University of Newcastle)

The IBM personal computer was introduced in the early 1980s, and by the early 1990s it was clear that the major threat to Amdahl was the declining mainframe market. Revenue and profitability fell, and Amdahl shut factory lines and cut staff numbers. By the late 1990s, Amdahl was making major losses, and there were concerns about the future viability of the company.

It was clear by 2001 that Amdahl could no longer effectively compete against IBM following IBM's introduction of its 64-bit zSeries architecture. Amdahl had invested a significant amount in research on a 64-bit architecture to compete against the zSeries, but the company estimated that it would take a further $1 billion and two more years to create an IBM-compatible 64-bit system. Further, it would be several years before they would gain any benefit from this investment as there were declining sales in the mainframe market due to the popularity of personal computers.

By late 2001 the sales of mainframes accounted for just 10 % of Amdahl's revenue, with the company gaining significant revenue from the sale of Sun servers. Amdahl became a wholly owned subsidiary of Fujitsu in 1997, and it exited the mainframe business in 2002. Today, it focuses on the server and storage side as well as on services and consulting.

Chapter 5
Apple Inc.

Apple Inc. is a well-known American corporation that was founded by Steve Wozniak and Steve Jobs (Fig. 5.1) at Cupertino, California, in 1976. It has made major contributions to the computing field, and it is renowned for its innovative products and services. It has designed and developed computer hardware and software such as the Apple and Macintosh computers, dazzling smartphones such as the iPhone and the iPad tablet computer. It is the largest music vendor in the world, as its online iTunes digital media store has over 35 million songs and 45,000 films. Its App Store allows users to download applications developed for Apple's iOS to their iPhone or iPad. It has annual revenues of over $180 billion and net income of over $39 billion.

Jobs and Wozniak were two college dropouts, and both attended the Homebrew Computer Club of computer enthusiasts in Silicon Valley during the mid-1970s. They formed Apple Computers in 1976, and Apple commenced operations in Job's family garage. Their goal was to develop a user-friendly alternative to the existing mainframe computers produced by IBM and Digital. Wozniak was responsible for product development and Jobs for marketing.

The Apple I computer was released in 1976, and it retailed for $666.66. It generated over $700,000 in revenue for the company, but it was mainly of interest to computer hobbyists and engineers. This was due to the fact that it was not a fully assembled personal computer as such, and it was essentially an assembled motherboard that lacked features such as a keyboard, monitor and case. It used a television as the display system, and it had a cassette interface to allow programs to be loaded and saved. It used the inexpensive MOS Technology 6502 microprocessor chip, which had been released earlier that year, and Wozniak had already written a BASIC interpreter for this chip.

The Apple II computer (Fig. 5.2) was released in 1977, and it was a significant advance on its predecessor. It was a personal computer with a monitor, keyboard and case, and it was one of the earliest computers to come preassembled. It was a popular 8-bit home computer, and it was one of the earliest computers to have a colour display with colour graphics.

© Springer International Publishing Switzerland 2015
G. O'Regan, *Pillars of Computing*, DOI 10.1007/978-3-319-21464-1_5

Fig. 5.1 Steve Jobs at
Macworld 2005 (Photo
Public Domain)

Fig. 5.2 Apple II
computer (Photo Public
Domain)

Fig. 5.3 Apple Macintosh
computer (Photo Public
Domain)

The BASIC programming language was built in, and it contained 4K of RAM (which could be expanded to 48K). The VisiCalc spreadsheet program was released on the Apple II, and this helped to transform the computer into a credible business machine. The Apple II retailed for $1299, and it was a major commercial success for Apple generating over $139 million in revenue for the company.

Apple became a public listed company in 1980 with a market value of over $1 billion. John Sculley[1] became CEO of Apple in 1983. Sculley was a former president of Pepsi Cola, and he had a strong background in marketing and branding. He served as CEO of Apple from 1983 to 1993, and sales at Apple increased from $800 million to over $8 billion under his direction. However, Sculley and Jobs clashed over management styles and priorities, and following an internal power struggle in the company, Jobs left the company in 1985.

The Apple Macintosh (Fig. 5.3) was announced during a famous television commercial aired during the third quarter of the Super Bowl in 1984. This was one of the most creative advertisements of all time, and it ran just once on television. It generated more excitement than any other advertisement up to then, and it immediately positioned Apple as a creative and innovative company while implying that its competition (i.e. IBM) was stale and robotic.

It presented Orwell's totalitarian world of 1984, with a lady runner wearing orange shorts and a white tee shirt with a picture of the Apple Macintosh running towards a big screen and hurling a hammer at the big brother character on the screen. The audience is stunned at the broken screen, and the voice-over

---

[1] Sculley was the president of Pepsi Cola from 1977 to 1983, and Jobs is reported to have asked him *Do you want to sell sugared water for the rest of your life? Or do you want to come with me and change the world?*

states *On January 24th Apple will introduce the Apple Macintosh and you will see why 1984 will not be like '1984'*. The short film was directed by Ridley Scott who has directed well-known films such as Alien, Blade Runner, Robin Hood and Gladiator.

The Macintosh project began in Apple in 1979 with the goal of creating an easy-to-use low-cost computer for the average consumer. It was initially led by Jef Raskin, and the project team included Bill Atkinson, Burrell Smith and others. It was influenced by the design of the Apple Lisa, and it employed the Motorola 68000 processor. Steve Jobs became involved in the project in 1981 and Raskin left the project. Jobs negotiated a deal with Xerox that allowed him and other Apple employees to visit the Xerox PARC research centre at Palo Alto in California to see their pioneering work on the Xerox Alto computer and their work on a graphical user interface. PARC's research work had a major influence on the design and development of the Macintosh, as Jobs was convinced that future computers would use a graphical user interface. The design of the Macintosh included a friendly and intuitive graphical user interface (GUI), and the release of the Macintosh was a major milestone in computing.

The Macintosh was s a much easier machine to use than the existing IBM PC. Its friendly and intuitive graphical user interface was a revolutionary change from the command-driven operating system of the IBM PC, which required the users to be familiar with its operating system commands. The introduction of the Mac GUI is an important milestone in the computing field, and it was 1990 before Microsoft introduced its Windows 3.0 GUI-driven operating system.

Apple intended that the Macintosh would be an inexpensive and user-friendly personal computer that would rival the IBM PC and compatibles. However, it was more expensive it retailed for $2495 which was significantly more expensive than the IBM PC. Further, initially it had a limited number of applications available, whereas the IBM PC had spreadsheets, word processors and database applications, and so it was more attractive to customers. The technically superior Apple Macintosh was unable to break the IBM dominance of the market. However, the machine became very popular in the desktop publishing market, due to its advanced graphics capabilities.

Apple went through financial difficulty in the mid-1980s, and Jobs resigned from Apple in 1985 following serious disagreements at board level on the direction for the company. Apple introduced its Macintosh Portable in 1989, and this was its first battery-powered portable Macintosh personal computer. It was an expensive machine at $6,500, and its sales were quite low. It was discontinued in 1991 when Apple introduced its successful PowerBook series of Macintosh laptop computers. Microsoft pressurised Sculley to license parts of the Macintosh graphical user interface to Microsoft for use in its Windows operating system by threatening to discontinue Microsoft Office for the Macintosh. This would later affect the outcome of the Apple vs. Microsoft lawsuit.

Apple released the Newton Message personal digital assistant (PDA) in 1993, and the phrase *personal digital assistant* was coined by Sculley. The Newton (Fig. 5.4) included various application software such as Notes which allowed the

Fig. 5.4 Apple Newton
(Photo Public Domain)

user to type small documents, Names which allowed the user to store contacts, Dates which included a calendar and allowed the user to enter meetings and events and calculators. However, this product was unsuccessful due mainly to reliability problems.

IBM, Apple and Motorola entered an alliance in 1994 aimed at challenging the dominance of the Windows and Intel architecture. This initiative involved IBM and Motorola designing and producing the Power CPUs for the new desktop computers and servers. The responsibilities of Apple were to port its Mac OS to the new architecture. Despite some success, this initiative eventually failed, and Apple began using Intel microprocessors from 2006.

Jobs formed a new software company called NeXT, Inc., and purchased an animation company the following year. This company became Pixar Animation Studios, and it went on to produce successful animation films such as Toy Story. The studio merged with Walt Disney in 2006. NeXT released a framework for web application development called WebObjects in 1996, and the object-oriented operating system on the NeXT computer (NeXTSTEP) was selected by Apple for its next operating system. The Macintosh OS X and *i*Phone operating system (*i*OS) were based on this operating system. NeXT was purchased by Apple in 1997, and Jobs returned to Apple as CEO. Under Job's leadership Apple became a highly innovative company and introduced products that dazzled and delighted its customers. These included products such as the *i*Mac, *i*Book, the *i*Pod, the *i*Phone and the *i*Pad.

Jobs developed an alliance between Apple and Microsoft on his return. The *i*Mac (a Macintosh desktop computer) was released in 1998, and it was a major commercial success for the company. The letter *i* stands for the *Internet* and also represents the fact that the product is a personal device designed for the *individual*. The *i*Mac originally employed the PowerPC chip designed and developed by IBM and Motorola, but these were replaced with Intel processors in 2006. The entire Macintosh line was transitioned to Intel processors later that year.

Fig. 5.5 Apple iPhone 4
(Photo Public Domain)

It released the *i*Book (a line of personal laptops) in 1999 and the *i*Pod in 2001, and these were major commercial successes for the company. The *i*Pod is a portable hard disc MP3 player with a capacity of 5 GB, and it could hold up to 1,000 MP3 songs. The *i*Pod prepared the way for *i*Tunes and the *i*Phone.

Apple entered the mobile phone market with the release of the *i*Phone (Fig. 5.5) in 2007. This is an Internet-based touchscreen multimedia smartphone, and it includes features such as a video camera, email, web browsing, text messaging and voice. It released the *i*Pad in 2010, which is a large-screen tablet-like device that uses a touchscreen operating system.

The *i*Tunes Music Store was launched in 2003, and it is the largest music vendor in the United States. It allows songs to be downloaded for a small fee, and individual songs are sold for the same price and without a subscription fee for access to the catalogue. There are over 35 million songs in the catalogue, and approximately 45,000 movies are also available for purchase.

Jobs was diagnosed with a rare form of pancreatic cancer in 2003. He initially tried alternative medicines such as herbal remedies, acupuncture and a vegan diet, and he delayed appropriate medical intervention and surgery for several months. He then received medical treatment and this appeared to remove the tumour. However, he took 6 months of medical leave from Apple in 2009 to focus on his health, and he underwent a successful liver transplant. His prognosis was described as excellent, and he returned to Apple as CEO. However, in early 2011 he went on medical leave again, and he resigned as CEO of Apple in August 2011. He died in October 2011.

Chapter 6
Atari, Inc.

Atari, Inc., is a name that is legendary in the world of video games, and the company also designed and manufactured home computers. It laid the foundation for the modern video game industry, and it developed video games such as Pong, Asteroids, Tempest, Centipede and Star Wars.

Atari, Inc., was founded by Nolan Bushnell (Fig. 6.1) and Ted Dabney in 1972. They had founded the engineering firm, Syzygy Engineering, in 1971, and the company designed and developed the first arcade video game, *Computer Space*, later that year. This computer game was functionally quite similar to an early computer game called Spacewar, and it was not entirely successful as it was perceived as being a little complicated to use. However, it still sold over 1500 units, and Syzygy Engineering was incorporated as Atari, Inc., in 1972. The name was taken from the ancient Chinese board game "Go" of which Bushnell was a fan. The name *atari* is used in Japanese when a prediction comes through or when someone wins the lottery. It comes from the Japanese verb *ataru* which means "to hit a target", and it is associated with good fortune.

Bushnell and Dabney met in California in the late 1960s when they were both working for a company called Ampex. Bushnell had developed a fascination for one of the earliest video games, *Spacewar*, while he was a student at the University of Utah. This computer game was developed on a Digital PDP-1 computer in the early 1960s by Steve Russell and others at MIT.

The field of computer graphics emerged with the development of computer graphics hardware, and Ivan Sutherland of MIT (and later the University of Utah) played an important role. He developed sketchpad software in the late 1950s that allowed a user to draw simple shapes on the computer screen, and he invented the first computer-controlled head-mounted display (HMD) in the mid-1960s. The University of Utah became the leading research centre in computer graphics in the late 1960s, and Bushnell had a solid foundation in the computer graphics field.

Bushnell had worked in an amusement arcade during his school holidays, and it occurred to him that a video game could potentially operate as a coin-operated machine. At the time arcades were dominated by coin-operated machines such as

© Springer International Publishing Switzerland 2015
G. O'Regan, *Pillars of Computing*, DOI 10.1007/978-3-319-21464-1_6

Fig. 6.1 Nolan Bushnell

Fig. 6.2 Original Atari
Pong video game console

pinball cabinets, slot machines and other trivial games of skill and chance. Bushnell's
vision was that of an arcade that would contain coin-operated video games that
would inspire and challenge teenagers, and the founding of Atari enabled his vision
to become a reality. Atari went on to become one of the leading players in this new
world of arcade video games.

Atari, Inc., hired Al Alcorn as their first design engineer, and he had previously
worked with Bushnell and Dabney at Ampex. Alcorn had no background in computer game development, and Computer Space was the first computer game that he
had actually seen. Nevertheless, he designed and developed Pong (Fig. 6.2), which

Fig. 6.3   Atari Video Computer System (VCS)

was an arcade version of an existing tennis game[1] for the Magnavox Odyssey home video game console. Bushnell had attended the demonstration of this first ever home video game console, and Alcorn made significant improvements to Magnavox's existing game. The new game was called "Pong", and it was a sports game that simulated table tennis. The player could compete against a computer or against another player. Alcorn's improvements included speeding up the ball the longer the game went on and also adding sound. Pong was an immediate success and digital table tennis became highly addictive.

Pong was a commercial success with a single unit earning approximately $40 per day, and Atari was soon receiving orders faster than it could deliver them. Over 8,000 machines were delivered to bars, amusement arcades and other places around the world by 1974. Pong showed that a coin-operated video game could be both popular and profitable. The home version of Pong was released in 1975, and it sold 200,000 units in its first year.

Atari did not have any patents protecting Pong, and soon other vendors were offering imitation products. Atari continued to innovate and released successful Atari cabinets including Space Race, Tank, Gotcha and Breakout in the mid- to late 1970s.

Atari had been looking for a way to bring all of its existing arcade game to the home market. It designed the Atari Video Computer System (VCS) in 1977, which was later marketed as the Atari 2600 (Fig. 6.3). This was a home game console which used the MOS 6052 microprocessor, and it provided an affordable way for high-quality video games to be played at home. There were significant financial

---

[1] Atari later settled a court case brought against it by Magnavox over alleged patent infringement of Pong's design on Magnavox Odyssey tennis game. Magnavox won millions in various patent disputes involving the Odyssey-related patents. Atari became a licensee of Magnavox.

costs associated with the development and manufacture of the VCS, and Bushnell made a strategic decision to sell Atari to Warner for $26 million in order to secure the required funding. The Atari VCS was introduced in 1977, and it was priced at $199. It would eventually become one of the most successful video game consoles, but its sales were quite low initially.

Bushnell left the company in 1978 and Ray Kassar took over. By 1979 over a million units of the Atari 2600 were sold, and over 10 million units were sold in 1982. Atari entered the home computer market in 1979 with its release of the Atari 400 and 800 8-bit home computers.

However, there were deep problems at Atari despite the success of the Atari 2600. Warner did not fundamentally understand a technology business, and its management alienated many of the creative software development staff. Several of Atari's key engineers left the company to form Activision, a new company that made third-party games for the VCS. Activision's games were better than Atari's, and third-party software developers were also creating games specifically for the Atari 2600. This helped sales of the Atari 2600 to soar, but the quality of the games being produced by Atari began to deteriorate.

Atari now had three areas of business: the arcade business, the home video game business and its home computer business. However, these three business areas were not working closely together, and Warner did not invest sufficiently in new technology and product development for future success. This was to prove fatal for the company.

The market reaction to Atari's release of Pac-Man and E. T., the Extra-Terrestrial, in 1982 was very negative, and Atari was left with a large quantity of unsold inventory that depressed prices. Atari's problems were compounded with the video game crash of 1983, and it lost over $300 million in the second quarter of that year. It was also facing major challenges in the home computing market with users moving from game machines to home computers. Arcades had become less important as video games were now being played at home, and Atari was failing to innovate with new products.

Warner sold the home computing portion of the Atari business to Jack Tramiel[2] in 1984, and Tramiel later renamed it to Atari Corporation. Atari Corporation developed and sold video game consoles, video games developed for home use as well as home and personal computers.

Warner held on to its arcade business until 1985 when it sold it to Namco. Atari's arcade business faded into obscurity, but Atari Corporation continued in business as a designer of home and personal computers until the early 1990s.

6.1   Atari Computers

Atari designed and produced four lines of home and personal computers from the late 1970s up to the early 1990s. These were the 8-bit Atari 400 and 800 line, the 16-bit ST line, the IBM PC compatible series and the 32-bit series.

---

[2] Jack Tramiel was the founder of Commodore Business Machines.

Fig. 6.4 Atari 1040 ST (Courtesy of Bill Bertram)

The Atari 8-bit series began as a next-generation follow-up to its successful Atari 2600 video game console. Atari's management noted the success of Apple in the early personal computer market, and they tasked their engineers to transform the hardware into a personal computer system. The net result was the Atari 400 and the Atari 800 home computers, which were introduced in 1979. The Atari 800 came with 8 KB of RAM, and it retailed for $1000, and the Atari 400 was a lower-specification version which retailed for $550. The Atari 800 and 400 made an impact on home computing in the early 1980s, and the Atari 600 XL with 16 KB of RAM and the Atari 800 XL with 64 KB of RAM were released in 1983.

Jack Tramiel (the founder and former CEO of Commodore) acquired Atari's home computing division in 1984, and he renamed the company to Atari Corporation. Atari designed the 16-bit GUI-based personal computer, the Atari ST, in 1985. This machine was priced at an affordable $799, and it included a 360 KB floppy disc drive, a mouse and a monochrome monitor. A colour monitor was provided for an extra $200, and the machine came with 512 KB of RAM. It used a colour graphical windowing system called GEM. The Atari ST included two Musical Instrument Digital Interface (MIDI) ports which made it very popular with musicians.

The Atari 1040 ST (Fig. 6.4) was introduced in 1986, and this 16-bit machine differed from the Atari ST in that it integrated the external power supply and floppy disc drive into one case. It contained 1 MB of RAM and retailed for $999. It came as a complete system with a base unit, a monochrome monitor and a mouse. Atari released advanced versions of these models, called the Atari 520 STE and the Atari 1040 STE, in 1989. The Atari ST line had an impressive life span starting in 1986 and ending with the Atari Mega STE, which was released in 1990.

Atari released its first personal computer, the Atari PC, in 1987. This IBM-compatible machine was an 8-MHz 8088 machine with 512 KB of RAM and a 360-KB 5.25-in. floppy disc drive in a metal case. It released the Atari PC2 and PC3 later that year, and the PC3 included an internal hard disc. The Atari PC4 included a faster 16-MHz 80286 CPU and 1 MB of RAM, and it was released the same year. The PC5 was released in 1988 and it had a 20-MHz 80386 CPU and 2 MB of RAM.

The Atari ABC (Atari Business Computer) was released in 1990. The 286 version shipped with a range of CPU and storage choices ranging from an 8-MHz to a 20-MHz CPU and a 30–60-MB hard disc. The Atari ABC 386 version included a 20-MHz or 40-MHz CPU and a 40-MB or 80-MB hard disc. The ABC 386 shipped with Microsoft Windows 3.0.

Atari shut down its home computer business in 1993 to focus on making its own console. It released the Atari Jaguar, the first 64-bit console, in 1993, and although this was a powerful consoler for its time, it had a poor controller and poor software support. It failed to succeed against its competitor products such as Super Nintendo and Sega Genesis.

Atari Corporation ceased trading in 1996, and its name and assets were sold to a hard disc drive manufacturer called JTS. JTS was later acquired by Hasbro. The history of Atari and Atari computers is described in more detail in [Edw:11, IGN:14].

Chapter 7
Bell Labs

Bell Labs (also known as Bell Laboratories, AT&T Bell Labs or Lucent Bell Labs) was founded by Western Electric Research Laboratories and the American Telephone and Telegraph company (AT&T) in 1925. Its goals were to explore fundamental areas of science likely to shape the telecoms industry.

It has a long and distinguished history of applied research, and its many inventions[1] include statistical process control which was developed by Walter Shewhart in the 1920s. Information theory and the field of cryptography were developed by Claude Shannon in the late 1940s. The invention of the transistor was a major milestone in the computing field, and it was developed by William Shockley and others in the late 1940s/early 1950s.

Error detecting and error correcting codes were developed by Richard Hamming in the late 1940s, and the UNIX operating system and the C programming language were developed by Dennis Ritchie and Kenneth Thompson in the early 1970s. The C++ programming language was developed by Bjarne Stroustroup in the early 1980s.

Eight Nobel Prizes have been awarded to Bell Labs researchers for their inventions, and the prestigious Turing Award has been won on two occasions by its researchers. Richard Hamming was awarded the Turing Prize in 1968 for his work on error detecting and error correcting codes, while Kenneth Thompson and Dennis Ritchie were awarded the Turing Prize for their work in the development of the UNIX operating system.

Bell Labs statisticians played an important role in the field of statistical process control, with Walter Shewhart developing a control chart to determine if process performance is under control and within the defined upper and lower control limits. Deming and Juran worked with Shewhart at Bell Labs in the 1920s, and these quality gurus developed important quality improvement programmes that later played an important role in transforming American and Japanese industry.

---

[1] It is not possible due to space limitations to discuss all of Bell Labs inventors and inventions, and the selection chosen inevitably reflects the bias of the author.

© Springer International Publishing Switzerland 2015
G. O'Regan, *Pillars of Computing*, DOI 10.1007/978-3-319-21464-1_7

Shannon's [Sha:48] developed a unified theory for communication as well as the mathematical foundations for the field. The key problem in communication theory is the reliable transmission of a message from a source point over a communications channel to a destination point. There may be noise in the channel that distorts the message, and the engineer wishes to ensure that the message received is that which has been sent. Shannon proposed two important theorems that establish the fundamental limits on communication. The first theorem deals with communication over a noiseless channel, and the second theorem deals with communication in a noisy environment.

Shannon is considered the father of modern cryptography with his influential 1949 paper [Sha:49] on secrecy systems. He established a theoretical basis for cryptography, and he defined the basic mathematical structures that underlie secrecy systems.

The transistor was invented by Bardeen, Brattan and Shockley in 1947, and they shared the 1956 Nobel Prize in Physics for this revolutionary invention. The transistor is a fundamental building block in electronics, and it acts as an electronic switch. It is used to implement Boolean functions in logic, and it consumes very little power and is much more reliable that the bulky vacuum tubes that preceded it.

Richard Hamming developed Hamming codes which are used for error detection and correction. Coding theory is a practical branch of mathematics that is concerned with the reliable transmission of information over communication channels. It allows errors to be detected and corrected, which is essential when messages are transmitted through a noisy communication channel. The channel could be a telephone line, radio link or satellite link. It is also applicable to storing information on storage systems such as the compact disc.

Researchers at Bell Labs have been active in the development of programming languages and operating systems. Kenneth Thompson and Denis Ritchie developed the UNIX operating system and C programming language, and Bjarne Stroustroup invented the C++ programming language. Bell Labs was also involved in the development of the first mobile phone system. There is more detailed information on Bell Labs in [Ger:13]. Next we discuss a selection of the Bell Labs inventors and their inventions.

7.1   Statistical Process Control

Walter Shewhart (Fig. 7.1) was a statistician at Bell Labs, and he is regarded as the founder of statistical process control (SPC). He developed the control chart (Fig. 7.2), which is a tool to monitor and control the process, with upper and lower limits for process performance specified. The process is under control if it is performing within these defined limits.

The Shewhart model (also known as the *PDCA Cycle*) is a systematic approach to problem solving and process control (Table 7.1). It consists of four steps (Fig. 7.3) which then repeat, and these steps are *plan, do, check* and *act*. Shwehart's ideas

Fig. 7.1 Walter Shewhart

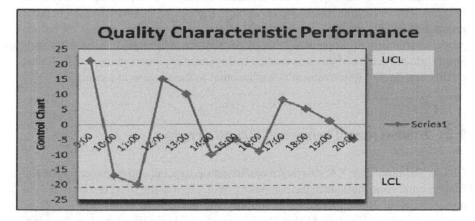

Fig. 7.2 Shewhart's control chart

Table 7.1 Shewhart cycle

Step	Description
Plan	This step identifies an improvement opportunity and outlines the problem or process improvement that will be addressed
	Select the problem to be addressed
	Describe current process
	Identify the possible causes of the problem
	Find the root cause of problems
	Develop an action plan to correct the root cause
Do	This step involves carrying out the improvements and it may involve a pilot of the proposed changes to the process
Check	This step involves checking the results obtained against the expected results to determine their effectiveness
Act	This step includes the analysis of the results to adjust process performance to achieve the desired results

Fig. 7.3 Shewhart's
PDCA cycle

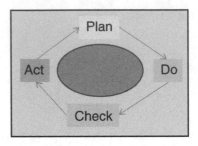

were later applied to the Capability Maturity Model (CMM) as a way to control key software processes. Statistical process control plays an important role in process improvement.

Shewhart argued that quality and productivity improve as process variability is reduced. His influential book, *The Economic control of quality of manufactured product* [Shw:31] outlines the methods of statistical process control to reduce process variability. It prophesized that productivity would improve as process variability was reduced, and this was verified by Japanese engineers in the 1950s. Today, quality and quality improvement is fundamental to the success of a company.

7.2   Information Theory and Cryptography

Claude Shannon (Fig. 7.4) was an American mathematician and engineer who made fundamental contributions to the computing field. He was the first person[2] to see the applicability of Boolean algebra to simplify the design of circuits and telephone routing switches. He showed that Boole's symbolic logic developed in the nineteenth century provided the perfect mathematical model for switching theory and for the subsequent design of digital circuits and computers.

His influential *Master's Thesis* [Sha:37] *is a key milestone in computing*, and it shows how to lay out circuits according to Boolean principles. It provides the theoretical foundation of switching circuits and *his insight of using the properties of electrical switches to do Boolean logic is the basic concept that underlies all electronic digital computers.*

Shannon realized that you could combine switches in circuits in such a manner as to carry out symbolic logic operations. This allowed binary arithmetic and more complex mathematical operations to be performed by relay circuits. He designed a circuit which could add binary numbers, and he later designed circuits which could make comparisons and thus is capable of performing a conditional statement. *This was the birth of digital logic and the digital computing age.*

---

[2]Victor Shestakov at Moscow State University also proposed a theory of electric switches based on Boolean algebra around the same time as Shannon. However, his results were published in Russian in 1941 whereas Shannon's were published in 1937.

Fig. 7.4 Claude Shannon

He moved to the Mathematics Department at Bell Labs in the 1940s and commenced work that would lead to the foundation of modern *Information Theory* and to the field of cryptography.

Shannon's work on Information theory was an immediate success with communications engineers. He established the theoretical basis for cryptography and defined the basic mathematical structures that underlie secrecy systems. He also made contributions to genetics and invented a chess-playing computer program in 1948.

7.2.1   *Information Theory*

The fundamental problem in information theory is to reproduce at a destination point, either exactly or approximately, the message that has been sent from a source point. The problem is that information may be distorted by noise, leading to differences between the received message, and the message that was originally sent. Shannon provided a mathematical definition and framework for information theory in *A Mathematical Theory of Communication* [Sha:48].

He proposed the idea of converting data (e.g., pictures, sounds or text) to binary digits: i.e., binary bits of information. The information is then transmitted over the communication medium. Errors or noise may be introduced during the transmission, and the objective is to reduce and correct them. The received binary information is then converted back to the appropriate medium.

There were several communication systems in use prior to Shannon's 1948 paper. These included the telegraph machine, the telephone, the AM radio and early television from the 1930s. These were all designed for different purposes and used various media. Each of these was a separate field with its own unique problems, tools and methodologies.

Shannon's classic 1948 paper [Sha:48] provided a unified theory for communication and a mathematical foundation for the field. The message may be in any

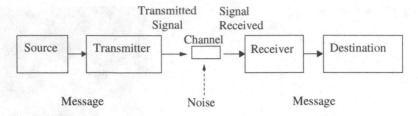

Fig. 7.5 Information theory

communications medium; e.g., television, radio and telephone. Information theory provides answers as to how rapidly or reliably a message may be sent from the source point to the destination point. Shannon identified five key parts of an information system (Fig. 7.5):

– Information Source
– Transmitter
– Channel
– Receiver
– Destination

He derived formulae for the information rate of a source and for the capacity of a channel including noiseless and noisy cases. These were measured in bits per second, and he showed that for any information rate R less than the channel capacity C,[3] it is possible (by a suitable encoding) to send information at rate R, with an error rate less than any pre-assigned positive ε, over that channel.

Shannon's theory of information is based on probability theory and statistics. One important concept is that of *entropy*[4] which measures the level of uncertainty in predicting the value of a random variable. For example, the toss of a fair coin has maximum entropy, as there is no way to predict what will come next. Another words, a single toss of a fair coin has an entropy of one bit.

Shannon proposed two important theorems that establish the fundamental limits on communication. The first theorem (*Shannon's source coding theorem*) essentially states that *the transmission speed of information is based on its entropy or randomness*. It is possible to code the information (based on the statistical characteristics of the information source) and to transmit it at the maximum rate that the channel allows. Shannon's proof showed that an encoding scheme exists, but did not show how to construct one. This result was revolutionary as communication engineers at the time thought that the maximum transmission speed across a channel was related to other factors and not on the concept of information.

Shannon's *noisy-channel coding theorem* states that reliable communication is possible over noisy channels provided that the rate of communication is below a

---

[3] The channel capacity C is the limiting information rate (i.e., the least upper bound) that can be achieved with an arbitrarily small error probability. It is measured in bits per second.

[4] The concept of entropy is borrowed from the field of Thermodynamics.

certain threshold called the *channel capacity*. This result was revolutionary as it showed that a *transmission speed arbitrarily close to the channel capacity could be achieved with an arbitrarily low error*. The assumption at the time was that the error rate could only be reduced by reducing the noise level in the channel. Shannon showed that the desired transmission speed could be achieved by using appropriate encoding and decoding systems.

Shannon's theory also showed how to design more efficient communication and storage systems.

7.2.2   Cryptography

Shannon is considered the father of modern cryptography with his influential 1949 paper *Communication Theory of Secrecy Systems* [Sha:49]. He established a theoretical basis for cryptography and defined the basic mathematical structures that underlie secrecy systems (Fig. 7.6).

A secrecy system is defined to be a transformation from the space of all messages to the space of all cryptograms. Each possible transformation corresponds to encryption with a particular key, and the transformations are reversible. The inverse transformation allows the original message to be obtained provided that the key is known. A basic secrecy system is described in Fig. 7.6.

The first step is to select the key and to send it securely to the intended recipient. The choice of key determines the particular transformation to be used, and the message is then converted into a cryptogram (i.e., the encrypted text). The cryptogram is then transmitted over a channel (that is not necessarily secured from an enemy cryptanalyst) to the receiver, and the recipient uses the key to apply the inverse transformation. This allows the original message to be deciphered from the cryptogram.

The enciphering of a message is a functional operation. Suppose M is a message, K the key and E is the encrypted message then:

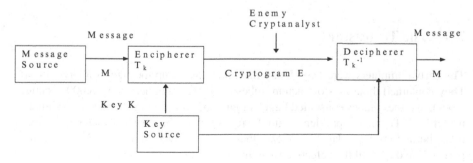

Fig. 7.6 Cryptography

$$E = f(M, K)$$

This is often written as a function of one variable $E = T_i M$ (where the index i corresponds to the particular key being used). It is assumed that there are a finite number of keys $K_1, \ldots, K_m$ and a corresponding set of transformations $T_1, T_2, \ldots, T_m$. Each key has a probability p_i of being chosen as the key. The encryption of a message M with key K_i is therefore given by:

$$E = T_i M$$

It is then possible to retrieve the original message from the received encrypted message by:

$$M = T_i^{-1} E$$

The channel may be intercepted by an enemy who will examine the cryptogram, and attempt to guess the key to decipher the message. For example, the cryptanalysts working at Bletchley Park in England during the Second World War regularly intercepted encrypted German naval messages being transmitted to their submarines in the Atlantic. They then used a machine that they had developed (called the "Bombe") to find the settings of the Enigma machine for that particular day. This allowed them to decipher the message and to protect Allied shipping in the Atlantic [ORg:11].

Shannon also showed that Vernam's cipher (also known as the *one time pad*) is a theoretically unbreakable cipher. Further, any unbreakable system must have essentially the same characteristics as the Vernam cipher. This cipler was invented by Gilbert Vernam at Bell Labs.

The Lorenz SZ 40/42 machine was used to encipher and decipher messages based on the Vernam cipher. These messages were sent by the German High Command in Berlin to Army Commands throughout occupied Europe. Tommy Flowers of the Post Office Research Station and the cryptanalysts at Bletchley Park developed the Colossus Mark I computer to crack the Lorenz codes, and this was work was invaluable around the time of the Normandy landings [ORg:12].

7.3   The Transistor

The early computers were large bulky machines taking up the size of a large room. They contained thousands of vacuum tubes (ENIAC contained over 18,000 vacuum tubes), and these tubes consumed large amounts of power and generated a vast quantity of heat. This led to problems with the reliability of the early computer, as several tubes burned out each day. This meant that machines were often non-functional for parts of the day, until the defective vacuum tube was identified and replaced.

There was therefore a need to find a better solution to vacuum tubes, and Shockley (Fig. 7.7) set up the solid physics research group at Bell Labs after the Second

Fig. 7.7 William Shockley
(Courtesy Chuck Painter,
Stanford News Service)

Fig. 7.8 Replica of
transistor (Courtesy of
Lucent Bell Labs)

World War. His goal was to find a solid-state alternative to the existing glass based vacuum tubes.

Shockley was born in England in 1910 to American parents, and he grew up at Palo Alto in California. He earned his PhD from Massachusetts Institute of Technology in 1936, and he joined Bell Labs shortly afterwards. The solid physics research team included John Bardeen and Walter Brattain, and they would later share the 1956 Nobel Prize in Physics with him for their invention of the transistor.

Their early research was unsuccessful, but by late 1947 Bardeen and Brattan succeeded in creating a point contact transistor independently of Shockley, who was working on a junction-based transistor. Shockley believed that the points contact transistor would not be commercially viable, and his junction point transistor was announced in mid-1951 with a patent granted later that year (Fig. 7.8). The junction point transistor soon eclipsed the point contact transistor and became dominant in the market place.

Shockley published a book on semiconductors in 1950 [Sho:50], and he resigned from Bell Labs in 1955. He formed Shockley Laboratory for Semiconductors (part of Beckman Instruments) at Mountain View in California. This company played an important role in the development of transistors and semiconductors, and several of its staff later formed semiconductor companies in the Silicon Valley area.

Shockley was the director of the company but his management style alienated several of his employees. This led to the resignation of eight key researchers in 1957 following his decision not to continue research into silicon-based semiconductors. This gang of eight went on to form Fairchild Semiconductors and other companies in the Silicon Valley area in the following years.

They included Gordon Moore and Robert Noyce, who founded Intel in 1968. National Semiconductors and Advanced Micro Devices were formed by other employees from Fairchild. Shockley Semiconductors and these new companies formed the nucleus of what became Silicon Valley.

7.4   Hamming Codes

Richard Hamming (Fig. 7.9) was born in Chicago in 1915 and he obtained his bachelor's degree in mathematics from the University of Chicago in 1937. He earned his PhD degree in mathematics from the University of Illinois in 1942. He worked on the Manhattan project at the Los Alamos Laboratory from 1945 to 1946, and he took a position at Bell Labs in 1946.

He became interested in the problem of the reliable transmission of information over a communication channel, and in particular in detecting whether an error has actually occurred in transmission, and algorithms for correcting such errors. He created a family of error correcting codes which are called *Hamming Codes*, and he introduced fundamental concepts such as *Hamming Distance*, *minimum Hamming Distance* and *Hamming Matrix*.

Fig. 7.9 Richard Hamming

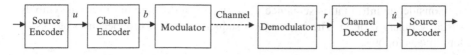

Fig. 7.10 Basic digital communication

Coding theory is a practical branch of mathematics that allows errors to be detected and corrected, and this is essential when messages are transmitted through a noisy communication channel. The channel could be a telephone line, radio link or satellite link, and coding theory is applicable to fixed line, mobile and satellite communications. It is also applicable to storing information on storage systems such as the compact disc.

Coding includes theory and practical algorithms for error detection and correction, and this is essential in modern communication systems that require reliable and efficient transmission of information.

An error correcting code encodes the data by *adding a certain amount of redundancy* to the message. This enables the original message to be recovered if a small number of errors have occurred. The extra symbols added are also subject to errors, as reliable transmission cannot be guaranteed in a noisy channel.

The basic structure of a digital communication system is shown in Fig. 7.10. It includes transmission tasks such as source encoding, channel encoding and modulation; and receiving tasks such as demodulation, channel decoding and source decoding.

The modulator generates the signal that is used to transmit the sequence of symbols b across the channel. The transmitted signal may be altered due to the fact that there is noise in the channel, and the signal received is demodulated to yield the sequence of received symbols r.

Therefore a channel code is employed to enable errors to be detected and corrected. The channel encoder introduces redundancy into the information sequence u, and the channel decoder uses the redundancy for error detection and correction. This enables the transmitted symbol sequence $\hat{u}$. to be estimated.

Coding theory is based on pure mathematics and it uses fundamental results from group theory, ring theory, vector spaces and finite field theory. There is a readable introduction to coding theory in Chap. 9 of [ORg:12].

7.4.1 Block Codes

A (n,k) block code is a code in which all codewords are of length n and all information words are of length k and $n > k$. The fundamental idea of the (n,k) block code is that the information word (i.e., a block of length k) is converted to a codeword (i.e., a block of length n).

Consider an information sequence $u_0, u_1, u_2, \ldots$ of discrete information symbols (usually binary 0 or 1). The information sequence is then grouped into blocks of length k as follows:

$$\underbrace{u_0 u_1 u_2 \ldots u_{k-1}} \quad \underbrace{u_k u_{k+1} u_{k+2} \ldots u_{2k-1}} \quad \underbrace{u_{2k} u_{2k+1} u_{2k+2} \ldots u_{3k-1}} \cdots$$

Each block is of length k (i.e., the information words are of length k), and each information word is then encoded separately into codewords of length n. For example, the information word $u_0 u_1 u_2 \ldots u_{k-1}$ is uniquely mapped to a code word $b_0 b_1 b_2 \ldots b_{n-1}$

$$\left(u_0 u_1 u_2 \ldots u_{k-1}\right) \quad \rightarrow \boxed{\text{Encoder}} \rightarrow \quad \left(b_0 b_1 b_2 \ldots b_{n-1}\right)$$

These code words are then transmitted across the communication channel and the received words are then decoded. The received word $r = (r_0 r_1 r_2 \ldots r_{n-1})$ is then decoded into the information word $\hat{u} = (\hat{u}_0 \hat{u}_1 \hat{u}_2 \ldots \hat{u}_{k-1})$.

$$\left(r_0 r_1 r_2 \ldots r_{n-1}\right) \quad \rightarrow \boxed{\text{Decoder}} \rightarrow \quad \left(\hat{u}_0 \hat{u}_1 \hat{u}_2 \ldots \hat{u}_{k-1}\right)$$

The decoding is done in two steps with the received n-block word r first decoded to an n-block codeword, which is then decoded into the k-block information word $\hat{u}$. The encoding, transmission and decoding of an (n,k) block is summarized in Fig. 7.11 below.

A generator matrix is typically employed to provide an efficient encoding and decoding mechanism [ORg:12].

7.4.2 Hamming Distance

The distance between two codewords $b = (b_0 b_1 b_2 \ldots b_{n-1})$ and $b' = (b_0' b_1' b_2' \ldots b_{n-1}')$ measures how close the codewords b and b' are to each other. It is given by the *Hamming distance*:

$$\text{dist}(b, b') = \left|\left\{i : b_i \neq b_i', 0 \leq i < n\right\}\right|$$

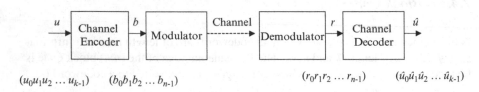

Fig. 7.11 Encoding and decoding of an (n,k) block

Fig. 7.12 Error correcting
capability sphere

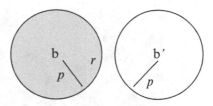

The *minimum Hamming distance* for a code **B** consisting of M codewords $b_1,\ldots, b_M$
is given by:

$$d = \min\left\{\text{dist}\left(b,b'\right): \text{where } b \neq b' \text{ and } b,b' \in \mathbf{B}\right\}$$

The minimum Hamming distance offers a way to assess the error detection and
correction capability of a channel code. Consider two codewords b and b' of an (n,k)
block code $\mathbf{B}(n,k,d)$.

Then, the distance between these two codewords is greater than or equal to the
minimum Hamming distance d, and so errors can be detected as long as the erro-
neously received word is not equal to a codeword different from the transmitted
code word.

That is, the *error detection capability* is guaranteed as long as the number of
errors is less than the minimum Hamming distance d, and so the number of detect-
able errors is $d-1$.

The distance between any two codewords is at least d, and so if the number of
errors is less than $d/2$ then the received word can be correctly decoded to the codeword b. That is, the *error correction capability* is given by:

$$E_{cor} = \frac{d-1}{2}$$

An error-correcting sphere (Fig. 7.12) is employed to illustrate the error correction of a received word to the correct codeword b. This may be done when all
received words are within the error-correcting sphere with radius p $(<^{d}/_{2})$.

If the received word r is different from b in less than $d/2$ positions, then it is
decoded to b (as it is more than $d/2$ positions from the next closest codeword b'). That
is, b is the closest codeword to the received word r (provided that the error- correcting radius is less than $d/2$).

7.5   UNIX and C

The UNIX operating system was developed by Ken Thompson, Dennis Ritchie and
others at Bell Labs in the early 1970s (Fig. 7.13). It is a multitasking and multiuser
operating system that is written almost entirely in C.

Fig. 7.13 Ken Thompson and Dennis Ritchie with President Clinton in 1999

Denis Ritchie was an American computer scientist who developed the C programming language at Bell Labs. He also co-developed the UNIX operating system with Ken Thompson. He was born in New York in 1941, and he earned a PhD in Physics and Applied Mathematics from Harvard University in 1967.

He joined Bell Labs in 1967 and designed and implemented the C programming language at Bell Labs in the early 1970s. The origin of this language is closely linked to the development of the UNIX operating system, and C was originally used for systems programming. It later became very popular for both systems and application programming, and it influenced later language development such as C++ and Java.

7.5.1   C Programming Language

Richie developed the C programming language at Bell Lab in 1972, and it became a popular programming language that is used widely in industry. It is a systems and applications programming language.

It was originally designed as the language to write the kernel for the UNIX operating system. It had been traditional up to then to write the operating system kernel in an assembly language, and the use of a high-level language such as C was a paradigm shift. This led to C's use as a systems programming language on several other operating systems (e.g., Windows and Linux), and C also influenced later language development. The C programming language is described in detail in [KeR:78].

The language provides high level and low-level capabilities, and a C program that is written in ANSI C is quite portable. It may be compiled for a wide variety of computer platforms and operating systems (with minimal changes to the source code). C is a procedural programming language, and it includes conditional statements such as the *if statement*; the *switch statement*; iterative statements such as the *while* statement and *do* statement; and the assignment statement which is specified by "=".

The language includes several pre-defined data types including integers and floating point numbers.

int   (integer)

long   (long integer)

float   (floating point real)

double   (double precision real)

It allows more complex data types to be created using the concept of a structure (*struct*). It allows the use of pointers to access memory locations, and this allows the memory locations to be directly referenced and modified.

C is a block structured language, and a program is structured into functions (or blocks). Each function block contains its own variables and functions. A functions may call itself (i.e., *recursion is allowed*).

One key criticism of C is that it is easy to make errors in C programs and to thereby produce undesirable results. For example, one of the easiest mistakes to make is to accidently write the assignment operator "=" for the equality operator "==". This totally changes the meaning of the original statement.

The philosophy of C to allow statements to be written as concisely as possible, and this is potentially dangerous.[5] The use of pointers potentially leads to problems as uninitialised pointers may point anywhere in memory, and the program may potentially overwrite anywhere in memory.

Therefore, the effective use of C requires experienced and disciplined programmers; well documented source code; and formal peer reviews of the source code by other team members to ensure that the code is readable and easy to maintain, as well as providing confidence in its correctness.

7.5.2   UNIX

The UNIX operating system was developed by Ken Thompson, Dennis Ritchie and others at Bell Labs in the early 1970s. It is a multitasking and multiuser operating system that is written almost entirely in C. UNIX arose out of work by Massachusetts Institute of Technology, General Electric and Bell Labs on the development of a general timesharing operating system called *Multics*.

---

[5] It is easy to write a one line C program that is incomprehensible. The maintenance of poorly written code is a challenge unless programmers follow good programming practice. This discipline needs to be enforced by formal reviews of the source code.

Bell Labs decided in 1969 to withdraw from the Multics project and to use General Electric's GECOS operating system. However, several of the Bell Lab researchers decided to continue the work on a smaller scale operating system using a Digital PDP-7 minicomputer. They later used a PDP-11 minicomputer, and the result of their work was UNIX. It became a popular and widely used operating system that was used initially by universities and the US government, but it later became popular in industry.

It is a powerful and flexible operating system and is used on a variety of machines from micros to supercomputers. It is designed to allow several users access the computer at the same time and to share its resources, and it offers powerful real time sharing of resources.

It includes features such as *multitasking* which allows the computer to do several things at once; *multiuser* capability which allows several users to use the computer at the same time; *portability* of the operating system which allows it to be used on several computer platforms with minimal changes to the code; and a collection of tools and applications.

There are three levels of the UNIX system: *kernel, shell,* and *tools and applications.* For more detailed information on UNIX see [Rob:05].

7.6   C++ Programming Language

The C++ programming language was developed by Bjarne Stroustroup (Fig. 7.14) at Bell Labs in the early 1980s. It was designed as an object-oriented language, and it provides a significant extension to the capabilities of the C programming language.

Fig. 7.14 Bjarne Stroustroup

Stroustroup was born in Aarhus, Denmark in 1950, and he earned his PhD degree in Computer Science from the University of Cambridge in 1979. His PhD was concerned with the design of distributed systems.

He moved to New Jersey in 1979 and joined the Computer Science research center at Bell Labs. He developed the C++ programming language at Bell Labs, and C++ is a widely used object-oriented language.

Stroustroup was the head of the Large Scale Programming Research Department from its creation until 2002, when he moved to the University of Texas. He developed the C++ programming language in 1983 as an object-oriented extension of the C programming language.

C++ was designed to use the power of object-oriented programming and to maintain the speed and portability of C. It provides a significant extension of C's capabilities, but it does not force the programmer to use the object-oriented features of the language.

A key difference between C++ and C is in the concept of a class. A *class* is an extension to the concept of a structure which is used in C. The main difference is that while a C data *structure* can hold only *data,* a C++ *class* may hold both *data* and *functions*.

An *object* is an instantiation of a class: i.e., the class is essentially the type, whereas an object is essentially a variable of that type. Classes are defined in C++ by using the keyword *class*.

The members of a class may be either data or function declarations, and an access specifier is used to specify the access rights for each member (e.g., *private, public* or *protected*).

Private members of a class are accessible only by other members of the same class; public members are accessible from anywhere where the object is visible; and protected members are accessible by other members of same class and also from members of their derived classes.

7.7   Advanced Mobile Phone System

Bell Labs played an important role (with Motorola) in the development of the analog mobile phone system in the United States. It developed a system in the mid-1940s that allowed mobile users to place and receive calls from automobiles, and Motorola developed mobile phones for automobiles. However, these phones were large and bulky and they consumed a lot of power. A user needed to keep the automobile's engine running in order to make or receive a call.

Bell Labs first proposed the idea of a cellular system back in the late 1940s, when they proposed hexagonal rings for mobile communication. Large geographical areas were divided into cells, where each cell had its own base station and channels. The available frequencies could be used in parallel in different cells without disturbing each other. Mobile telephone could now, in theory, handle a large number of subscribers. However, it was not until the late 1960s that Bell prepared a detailed plan for the cellular system.

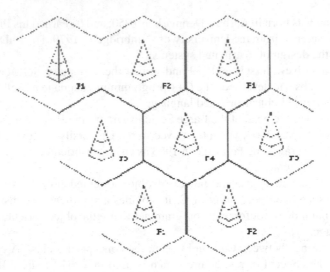

Fig. 7.15 Frequency reuse in cellular networks

The Advanced Mobile Phone System (AMPS) standard was developed by Bell Labs from 1968 to 1983 (Fig. 7.15), and it was introduced into the United States in 1983. Motorola and other telecommunication companies designed and built phones for this cellular system. AMPS uses separate frequencies (or channels) for each conversation and requires considerable bandwidth for a large number of users.

Motorola was the first company to develop a hand-held mobile phone. This was the DynaTAC (or *Brick*), and the Motorola team was led by Martin Cooper (Fig. 23.1). Cooper made the first mobile call to Joel Engels of Bell Labs. The phone weighed over a kilogram and it had a talk time of about 30 min. Further, it took over 10 h to recharge.

AMPS is the first generation of cellular technology, and so it has several weaknesses when compared to today's cellular systems. It was susceptible to static or noise, and there was no protection from eavesdropping with a scanner.

AMPS was later replaced by Global System for Mobile Communication (GSM) and Code Division Multiple Access (CDMA) technologies.

Chapter 8
Cisco Systems

Cisco Systems is a Silicon Valley success story, and it was one of the first companies to sell commercially successful routers supporting multiple network protocols. It is an American multinational with headquarters in San Jose, California, and it is a leading supplier of networking products, systems and services. It designs, manufactures and sells network equipment to customers around the world. It has revenue of approximately $47 billion and net income of $7.8 billion. The company has approximately 74,000 employees in various locations around the world.

Its products include routers, switches, remote access devices, Internet services devices, networking and network management software. These products link together geographically dispersed local area networks (LANs), wide area networks and the Internet itself.

Cisco was founded in late 1984 by a husband and wife team from Stanford University. Leonard Bosack (Fig. 8.1) and Sandy Lerner were the two main founders as well as Richard Troiano and others. The name of the company was chosen as *Cisco* which is a shortened form of "San Francisco". Bosack and Lerner were employed at Stanford University, with Bosack working as a manager at the computer science department's laboratory and Lerner working at the Graduate School of Business.

The company was established on a tight budget with Bosack and Lerner mortgaging their home, running up debt and deferring salary payments. Bosack adapted existing multiple protocol routing software originally written by a Stanford colleague, William Yeager, to create Cisco's first product. Bosack and Lerner resigned from Stanford University in 1986 to devote themselves fulltime to running the company.

There was some controversy with respect to the unapproved use of Stanford's intellectual property to create the Cisco Internetwork Operating System (IOS). This problem was later amicably resolved when Stanford licensed its router software and two computer boards to Cisco in 1987.

Cisco's earliest product was a router for the Transmission Control Protocol (TCP)/Internet Protocol (IP) protocol suite, and this was the first multi-protocol

© Springer International Publishing Switzerland 2015
G. O'Regan, *Pillars of Computing*, DOI 10.1007/978-3-319-21464-1_8

Fig. 8.1 Leonard Bosack

router. An internetworking router is a hardware device with software to automatically select the most effective route for data to flow between networks. Cisco's routers provided support for multiple protocols for data transmission, and they could link various types of networks together.

Cisco had just eight employees in 1987, and it initially marketed its routers to universities, research centres and the aerospace industry. It began to target corporations with geographically dispersed branches from 1988, and its routers supported a greater number of communication protocols than the competitor routers. The commercial market for internetworking and routers took off in the late 1980s, and Cisco was well placed with its reasonably priced high-performance routers.

Cisco ran short of cash in 1988, and Bosack and Lerner approached a venture capitalist, Donald Valentine, of Sequoia Capital, to take an equity stake in the company. Valentine became the chairman of Cisco and John Morgridge was hired as the CEO.

Cisco became a public company in 1990 with a market capitalisation of over $220 million. Lerner and Bosack left the company later that year, and they set up their own charity foundation which finances a range of animal welfare and science projects.

Morgridge built up a sales force to market Cisco's products to corporate clients. The company grew at a blistering pace as the market was expanding rapidly in the early 1990s, with companies of all sizes installing local area networks (LANs). There was a huge market in linking these networks together or linking them with existing minicomputers and mainframe computers. Cisco's sales and net income leaped, and it became one of the fastest growing companies in the United States during the 1990s.

The invention of the World Wide Web by Tim Berners-Lee led to exponential growth of the Internet, and the Internet Protocol (IP) became widely adopted with multiple network routing becoming less important. The phenomenal growth of the

Fig. 8.2 Front of Cisco
12006 router

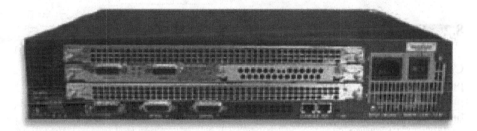

Fig. 8.3 Cisco AS 5200 universal access server

Internet led to changes to the telecom world, with Cisco's products such as the modem access shelves (AS 5200) (Fig. 8.3) and Gigabit Switch Routers (GSR) (Fig. 8.2) becoming essential to Internet service providers. Cisco had a de facto monopoly in this key market segment by the late 1990s, and it became one of the most valuable companies in the world during the dot-com frenzy of the late 1990s. Cisco remains a highly valuable company today.

Cisco had annual sales of over $1 billion for 1994, and Morgridge stepped down as CEO in 1995. John Chalmers became CEO the same year, and Cisco's phenomenal growth continues. By the late 1990s, Cisco was the undisputed leader of the networking world. Morgridge became the chairman of Cisco in 1995, and he served as chairman until his retirement in 2006.

8.1 Cisco Products

Cisco's earliest product was a router for the Transmission Control Protocol (TCP)/ Internet Protocol (IP) protocol suite. The Cisco IOS software is a multitasking operating system that is used on most Cisco routers and network switches. It includes functionality for routing, switching, internetworking and telecommunications.

Cisco has introduced many new products such as the Gigabit Switch Router (GSR) (which is also known as the Cisco 12000), and it also introduced the Cisco AS 5200 universal access server (Fig. 8.3). The GSR is a series of large network routers with a high-performance backbone that perform Internet routing and switching at gigabit speed. The GSR 12000 series of routers (Fig. 8.2) rapidly became essential to Internet service providers, and, by the late 1990s, Cisco dominated this market.

The Cisco AS 5200 universal access server is a data communication platform that provides the functions of an access server, a router, modems and terminal adapters. The access server is optimised for high-speed modem access and is suitable for dial-up application such as connecting to a host, electronic mail, file transfer and dial in access to a LAN. The system components include several ports including two serial WAN ports and an Ethernet LAN port.

8.2   Cisco Acquisitions

Cisco embarked on several acquisitions in the mid-1990s to enhance its product portfolio and to stay ahead of its competitors. These acquisitions also allowed it to provide one-stop networking shopping to its customers, and it also allowed it to break into emerging networking sectors.

It acquired Grand Junction in 1995, and this company had several Ethernet switching products. It acquired Granite Systems in 1996 for its high-speed Gigabit Ethernet switches.

It acquired StrataCom in 1996 as this company was a leading supplier of ATM and frame relay WAN switching equipment. This technology was quite important at the time as telecommunication companies needed to increase the capacity of their networks, and this helped Cisco to become a provider of telecommunications equipment.

It acquired NetSpeed in late 1998, and this company was a specialist in digital subscriber line (DSL) equipment. DSL provides homes and small offices with high-speed access to the Internet via existing telephone lines.

It acquired LightSpeed International and Selsius Systems in the late 1990s to gain a presence in the Internet telephony sector. Voice over IP (VOIP) technology allows the routing of telephone calls over the Internet.

It acquired several fibre-optic companies in the late 1990s to break into this market. Fibre-optic networks were being built by telecommunication companies, and these provide massive capacity for voice, video and data.

Chapter 9
Commodore Business Machines

Commodore Business Machines was a leading North American home computer and electronics manufacturing company. It played an important role in the development of the personal computer industry in the 1970s and 1980s, and it is especially famous for its development of the Commodore PET computer which was very popular in the education field. It also developed the VIC-20 and Commodore 64 home computers which were very popular machines with millions of units sold.

The company was founded in Canada by Jack Tramiel in 1955 (Fig. 9.1). Tramiel was a Polish immigrant who had survived the horrors of Auschwitz during the Second World War. He relocated to the United States after the war and worked for the US Army where he learned how to repair office equipment. He set up Commodore as a typewriter repair business in New York, and he signed a deal with a Czech company to assemble and sell their typewriters in the United States. He set up an office in Canada so that he could deal directly with the Czech company, as there were restrictions at the time in the United States in dealing with Warsaw Pact countries.

Commodore initially manufactured typewriters for the North American market, and it diversified into the manufacture of mechanical calculators for bookkeeping operations (adding machines) from the early 1960s. It became a public company in the early 1960s, but it began to face intense competition from Japanese manufacturers of typewriters, and it started to lose money. It exited the typewriter business and began to manufacture adding machines. However, it began to face major Japanese competition as well in this line of business from the late 1960s, and it made a strategic decision to exit this business and to move into the manufacturing of electronic calculators.

Commodore introduced both consumer and scientific calculators in the late 1960s, and by the early 1970s it was one of the most popular brands for calculators. The calculators used Texas Instruments chips, but when Texas Instruments entered the calculator market in the mid-1970s, Commodore was unable to compete with the prices offered by Texas.

© Springer International Publishing Switzerland 2015
G. O'Regan, *Pillars of Computing*, DOI 10.1007/978-3-319-21464-1_9

Fig. 9.1 Jack Tramiel
(Courtesy of Alex Handy)

Commodore purchased the semiconductor company, MOS Technology, with the intention of using MOS chips in its calculators. However, Chuck Peddle, one of MOS's employees convinced Tramiel that the future was in computers and not calculators. Commodore used one of MOS's Technology chips, the 8-bit 6502, to enter the home computer market in 1977 with the launch of its Commodore Personal Electronic Transactor (PET) computer. This popular computer was mainly used in schools, and one of its models was called the *Teacher's PET*. The first Commodore printers were introduced in 1979.

Commodore introduced the 8-bit VIC-20 home computer in 1981, and this low-cost machine had 5 Kb of memory and a colour display. It enabled users to learn about programming and to play video games. Its successor, the Commodore 64, was introduced the following year. This popular machine had good sound and graphics, a colour display, 64 Kb of RAM and Microsoft BASIC.

Tramiel resigned from Commodore in 1984 following internal disagreements within the company. Tramiel's military background may have led to his philosophy that business is a form of warfare, and he had poor relations with dealers and customers. He purchased Atari's computer division which later became a major competitor to Commodore.

Commodore purchased a start-up company called Amiga in 1984, and it introduced the 32-bit Amiga 1000 computer in 1985. This machine had advanced graphics and sound, and it used the Motorola 68000 microprocessor, and it had 250 Kb of RAM. New and more powerful Amiga models were introduced up to the mid-1990s. There was intense rivalry between the Amiga and Atari families of personal computers. However, ultimately it was the IBM PC and its clones and the Apple Macintosh that would dominate the personal computer market, and this led to the demise of Commodore in the mid-1990s.

Commodore introduced an IBM-compatible PC in the early 1990s, but it failed to make a major impact. The company began to experience major financial difficulties from the early 1990s, and the company was liquidated in 1994.

9.1 Commodore PET

Commodore introduced its first computer, the Commodore Personal Electronic Transactor (PET) home computer, in 1977 (Fig. 9.2). This successful home computer was very popular in the education market. It used the MOS 8-bit 6502 microprocessor which was designed by Check Peddle and others at MOS Technology. The 6502 controlled the screen, keyboard, the cassette recorder and any peripherals connected to the expansion ports. The machine used the Commodore BASIC operating system. There were several models of the Commodore PET introduced during its lifetime including the PET 2001 series, the PET 4000 series and the SuperPET 8000 series.

The first model introduced was the PET 2001, which had either 4 Kb or 8 Kb of RAM. It had a built-in monochrome monitor with 40×25 character graphics enclosed in a metal case. It included a magnetic data storage device known as a datasette (data+cassette) in the front of the machine as well as a small keyboard. There were complaints with respect to the small keyboard which soon led to the appearance of external replacement keyboards.

The PET 4000 series was launched in 1980, and the 4032 model was very successful at schools as its all-metal construction and all in one design made it ideal for the challenges in the classroom. The 4000 series used a larger 12-in monitor and an

Fig. 9.2 Commodore PET 2001 home computer

enhanced BASIC 4.0 operating system. Commodore manufactured a successful variant called the *Teacher's* PET.

Commodore introduced the 8000 series and the last in the series was the SuperPET or SP9000. It used the Motorola 6809 microprocessor, and it provided support for several programming languages such as BASIC, Pascal, COBOL and FORTRAN.

9.2   Commodore 64

The Commodore 64 (C64) was a very successful 8-bit home computer introduced by Commodore in 1982 (Fig. 9.3). Its main competitors at the time were the Atari 400 and 800 and the Apple II computer. The cost of the C64 machine was $595 which was significantly less than its rivals, and Commodore cleverly exploited the price difference to rapidly gain market share. Approximately 15 million of the Commodore 64 machines were sold.

The C64 used the MOS 6501 microprocessor and it came with 64 kilobytes of RAM. It had 320×200 colour graphics with 16 colours using the VIC-II graphics chip, and the MOS Sound Interface Device (SID) chip. The SID chip was one of the first sound chips to be included in a home computer. The C64 dominated the low-end home computer market for most of the 1980s.

It came with the Commodore BASIC, but support for other languages such as Pascal and FORTRAN was also available. Programmers also wrote programs in assembly language to maximise speed and memory use. The Commodore 64's graphics and sound capabilities were quite advanced for the time, and the C64 was very popular for computer games.

Commodore published detailed technical documentation to assist programmers and enthusiastic users to design and develop applications for the Commodore 64. This led to the development of over 10,000 commercial software applications such as development tools, games and office productivity applications for the machine. Atari was Commodore's main competitor, but it kept its technical information a secret.

The C64 included a ROM-based version of the BASIC 2.0 programming language. There was no operating system as such, and instead the kernel was accessed

Fig. 9.3 Commodore 64
home computer

via BASIC commands. BASIC did not allow commands for sound or graphics manipulation, and instead the user had to use the "POKE" command to access these chips directly.

The Commodore 64 remained highly popular throughout the 1980s, and it was still being sold up to the early 1990s.

9.3 Amiga

Commodore bought a small start-up company called the Amiga Corporation in August 1984, and it became a subsidiary called Commodore–Amiga, Inc. This acquisition was made shortly after Jack Tramiel left the company,[1] as a result of major disagreements at board level following the 1983 home computer price war with Atari, Texas Instruments and other computer vendors. Commodore brought its first Amiga computer to the market in 1985.

The Amiga was a family of personal computers sold by Commodore in the 1980s and 1990s. The first model, the Amiga 1000 (or A1000), was released in 1985, and it became popular for its graphical, audio and multitasking capabilities. The A1000 had a powerful CPU and advanced graphics and sound hardware. It was based on the Motorola 68000 series of microprocessor, and it had 256 kilobytes of RAM, which could be upgraded with a further 256 Kb of RAM. It retailed for $1295.

The Amiga 500 (Fig. 9.4) was the best-selling model in the Amiga family, and it was released in 1987. It was a highly popular home computer with over 6 million

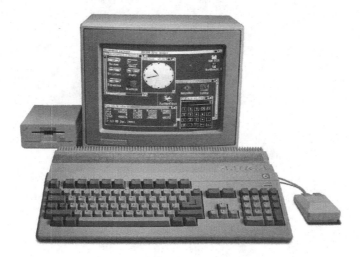

Fig. 9.4 Amiga 500 home computer (1987) (Courtesy of Bill Bertram)

---

[1] Tramiel later bought the consumer side of Atari, Inc., from Warner Communications.

machines sold. Several other models of the Amiga machines were introduced including the A3000, the A500+ and A600 and the A1200 and A4000 machines.

The August 1994 edition of the *Byte* magazine [By:94] spoke highly of the early Amiga machines. It called the A1000 machine the first multimedia computer, as it was so far ahead of its time with advanced graphics and sound.

9.4   The Demise of Commodore

By the late 1980s the personal computer market was dominated by the IBM personal computer and the Apple Macintosh. The performance of the IBM PC and compatibles was catching up with the Amiga by the early 1990s, and the Amiga failed to make an impact on the business market where high-performance graphics and sound were irrelevant.

Commodore introduced its own PC compatibles in the early 1990s, but these were not very successful. It released further computers such as the A4000 and A1200 in 1992, but these were not very successful. The company began to become unprofitable with only a small number of international operations making a profit.

Commodore filed for bankruptcy in 1994, and Amiga, Inc., became a separate company. Commodore computers are still produced today by an unrelated Florida company called Commodore USA which purchased the brands. For further information on Commodore, see [Bag:12].

Chapter 10
Dell, Inc.

Dell is a private American multinational computer company, and it is one of the largest technology companies in the world. It manufactures and sells computers, servers, data storage devices, software, cameras and printers.

Dell Computer Corporation was founded by Michael Dell (Fig. 10.1) in 1984, and it did business initially as PC's Ltd. Michael Dell was a student at the University of Texas in Austin, and he initially set up a computer assembly business from his campus accommodation, where he built IBM-compatible computers from PC components. He decided to drop out of university to focus his attention on developing the business.

The company developed the first computer of its own design in 1985. This was the *Turbo PC* and it sold for $795. The machine contained an Intel 8088-compatible microprocessor running at a speed of 8 MHz. Dell sold its computers directly to its customers, and each machine was custom-built for each client depending on the options chosen when the order was placed. It focused on businesses rather than consumers in the early years, and it advertised its products on the existing national computer magazines. The company had revenues in excess of $73 million in its first year of business.

The company dropped its "PC's Ltd." name to become just the "Dell Computer Corporation" in 1987, and the company expanded into international markets. The company developed close links with Microsoft and Intel, and Dell personal computers used one of Microsoft's operating systems and one of Intel's microprocessors. It became a public company in mid-1988.

Dell employs lean manufacturing which provides it with a flexible approach to adapt rapidly to a changing market and allows it to customise individual orders, rather than mass-producing a standard product.

The company expanded its product range to include servers from the mid-1990s. Its servers were based on Microsoft NT running on Intel chips, and they were cheaper than the existing competitor products in the server market, such as products from IBM, HP and Compaq. By the late 1990s, Dell was the main provider of Intel-based servers with over 30 % market share.

© Springer International Publishing Switzerland 2015
G. O'Regan, *Pillars of Computing*, DOI 10.1007/978-3-319-21464-1_10

Fig. 10.1 Michael Dell

The rise of the Internet gave Dell the opportunity to expand its direct sales model from mainly business sales to both business and consumers. The consumer market had been plagued with high costs and low profit margins, but the effective use of the Internet helped to change this. The company's Internet site became operational in 1996, and it included a product line designed for individual users. Customers could now buy directly from Dell, and they could customise their order to meet their specific requirements (e.g. processing power, storage, memory, etc.) Dell's computers were highly rated for their reliability, and the company had a good reputation for its customer service and support.

Dell gained market share from its competitors throughout the late 1990s with customers liking its direct sales model and the facility to customise their order to meet their specific needs. Customers voted with their feet, and Dell soon overtook rivals such as Gateway, Packard Bell and Compaq to become the largest maker of personal computers in the world in 1999.

Dell has been very effective in devising supply chain efficiencies to sell established technologies at competitive prices, rather than being an innovator in technology. Its spending on R&D was quite low compared to its competitors, which prevented it from breaking into other lucrative markets such as MP3 players and mobile devices. It expanded its product line to include printers and televisions from 2002, but in 2005 approximately 66 % of Dell's sales remained in the mature personal computer market. Other computer manufacturers such as HP had improved their supply chains and were now as efficient as Dell, and so Dell's profit margins declined.

Dell traditionally had a good reputation for customer service, but this changed for the worse as it moved its call centres offshore. Dell embarked on a series of changes and cost-cutting from 2007, which resulted in plant closures and transfers of work to overseas contractors. The shift in technology from personal computers and laptops to tablets impacted Dell, as it needs to develop effective products to compete in this market. It expanded into the enterprise market with servers, networking software and services as it is now facing intense competition in the personal computer market from Asian rivals such as Lenovo, which has lower production costs and is willing to accept lower profit margins.

Its revenue and share price decline has continued, and in 2013 Michael Dell and a number of partners bought Dell's public shares in a $24 billion buyout. Dell is now a private company. For more information on Dell, see [DeF:10].

10.1 Dell and Lean Manufacturing

Dell employs lean manufacturing as a tool to respond to changing market conditions and to allow it to provide customised rather than mass-produced products. Lean manufacturing is designed to identify defects earlier and to reduce waste, with staff empowered to use their initiative on the shop floor.

Each customer is viewed as unique and having specific requirements that need to be explicitly stated, rather than Dell predicting what the customer actually wants. Lean manufacturing allows the company to eliminate or maintain very low inventory levels, and it enables the company to respond better and faster to changes in market conditions.

Lean manufacturing employs *just-in-time* (JIT) delivery with components ordered only when they are needed. They are delivered fast enough to be classified as just-in-time. The great advantage of JIT is that the waste associated with maintaining a large warehouse of inventory that may go out of date quickly is avoided.

The only disadvantage is that the cost savings associated with bulk buying is not achieved, but this is more than offset by the savings made in eliminating waste. Table 10.1 describes the Dell lean manufacturing process.

10.2 Dell Acquisitions

Dell has acquired several companies over the years to enhance its product portfolio, as well as improving the efficiency of its manufacturing process. It has spent billions of dollars in acquisitions, and these have included companies such as Perot Systems and Quest Software.

Perot Systems is an information technology company that was founded by Ross Perot and others in 1988. It is a leading provider of information technology services to clients in several sectors, including healthcare, government and other commercial segments. Perot Systems was acquired by Dell for $3.9 billion in 2009.

The acquisition allowed Dell to provide a broader range of IT services and solutions, as well as optimising how they are delivered. It enabled Dell to expand its

Table 10.1 Dell lean manufacturing

Step	Description
1.	The customer places an order
	The order is sent to the manufacturing centre closest to the customer's address (within 2 h)
	The order is transferred into the manufacturing schedule at the production centre
	The orders for components are sent out regularly (typically every 2 h)
	Dell does not have a warehouse and so frequent deliveries are made (stock levels are kept low)
	There is no inventory waste (as components are ordered only when a customer requirement has been established)
2.	The components are sent down the line for the next stage
	They are fitted with unique identifiers (which are used throughout the lifetime of the product)
	This allows the customer to quote the component number to Dell (for customer service/ support)
	It allows Dell to monitor the quality of the components
	The service tag of the customer requirements to build the PC is scanned
	Each part is scanned to connect components to the service tag
3.	The machine is assembled and tested
	The customer requested software is installed onto the machine
	Once all items are installed, the machine is tested again
	The PC is sent to the boxing area
4.	The service tag is scanned on arrival and the machine is placed in the shipping box
	It is sent to the shipping or accumulation area

enterprise solutions capabilities, as well as gaining efficiencies from combining both companies. Dell Perot Systems was ranked as the number one vendor in a survey of healthcare providers in 2010.

Quest Software is a Californian company that offers products for application management, database management, Microsoft Windows management and virtualisation management. It was acquired by Dell for $2.4 billion in 2012.

Chapter 11
Digital Equipment Corporation

Digital Equipment Corporation (DEC) was founded in 1957 by Ken Olsen (Fig. 11.1) and Harlan Anderson with venture capital from American Research and Development Corporation. It was a forward-thinking innovative company, and it became the second largest computer company in the world in the late 1980s, with revenues of over $14 billion and over 100,000 employees. It dominated the mini-computer era from the 1960s to 1980s, with its PDP and VAX series of computers, which were very popular in the engineering and scientific communities.

Olsen and Anderson were engineers who had worked on early machines at the Massachusetts Institute of Technology. Olsen had served in the US Navy between 1944 and 1946, and he was involved in a project to build a flight simulator at the Office of Naval Research. He studied electrical engineering at the Massachusetts Institute of Technology after the war, and he received a bachelor's degree in 1950 and a master's degree in 1952. He worked at MIT's Lincoln computer laboratory after graduation, and he was part of the team that was working on the SAGE air defence system. He was involved in building a transistorised research computer, and he also worked on ways to improve the magnetic core memory developed by his MIT colleague, Jay Forrester.

DEC's first computer, the *Programmed Data Processor* (PDP-1), was released in 1961 (Fig. 11.2). It was a relatively inexpensive computer for the time and costs $110,000. The existing IBM mainframes cost over $2 million, and so DEC's mini-computers were relatively affordable to businesses. It was a simple and reasonably easy-to-use computer with 4,000 words of memory.

The PDP-1 was an 18-bit machine, and *Spacewar*, one of the earliest computer games, was developed for this machine. The PDP series of minicomputers were elegant and reasonably priced and dominated the new minicomputer market segment. They were an alternative to the multimillion-dollar mainframe computers offered by IBM to large corporate customers. Research laboratories, engineering companies and other organisations with large computing needs all used DEC's minicomputers.

© Springer International Publishing Switzerland 2015
G. O'Regan, *Pillars of Computing*, DOI 10.1007/978-3-319-21464-1_11

Fig. 11.1 Ken Olsen

Fig. 11.2 PDP-1 computer

Olsen and Anderson were engineers rather than managers, and DEC's culture was that of an engineering company. The company was divided into competing product groups, with line managers given complete authority to get their jobs done. The only control was budgetary, and the groups were given complete freedom in product development. There was a certain lack of central direction, but it meant that each group was, in effect, in charge of its own destiny. If things were not working effectively, then the budget would dry up, and staff would be reassigned to other product groups.

The PDP series of minicomputers became popular in the 1960s. The PDP-8 minicomputer was released in 1965, and it was a 12-bit machine with a small instruction set. It was a major commercial success for DEC with many sold to

Fig. 11.3 Gordon Bell
(Courtesy of Queensland
University of Technology)

schools and universities. The PDP-11 was a highly successful series of 16-bit minicomputer, and it remained a popular product for over 20 years from the 1970s to the 1990s.

Gordon Bell (Fig. 11.3) knew Olsen and Anderson from his time at MIT, and he joined DEC in 1960, becoming one of the earliest employees of the company. He played an important role in the development of the PDP family of minicomputers. He designed the multiplier/divider unit and the interrupt system for the PDP-1 computer, which built upon work done at the MIT Lincoln laboratory.

He later became vice president of research and development at DEC, and he was the architect of several PDP computers. He later led the development of the 32-bit VAX series of computers, and he was involved in the design of around 30 microprocessors.

The VAX series of minicomputers were derived from the best-selling PDP-11, and the VAX was the first widely used 32-bit minicomputer (Fig. 11.4). The VAX-11/780 was released in 1978, and it was a major success for the company. The VAX product line was a competitor to the IBM System 370 series of mainframe computers. The VAX minicomputers used the operating system known as Virtual Memory System (VMS).

The rise of the microprocessor and microcomputer led to the availability of low-cost personal computers, and this later challenged DEC's product line. DEC was slow in recognising the importance of these developments, and Olsen's statement from the mid-1970s *There is no need for any individual to have a computer in his home* suggests that DEC was totally unprepared for the revolution in personal computing and its threat to DEC's business.

DEC responded with its own personal computer after the launch of the IBM PC. The DEC machine easily outperformed the PC, but it was more expensive, and it was incompatible with the IBM PC hardware and software. DEC's microcomputer efforts were a failure, but its PDP and VAX products were continuing to sell. By the late 1980s DEC was threatening IBM's number one spot in the industry. However, the increasing power of the newer generations of microprocessors began to challenge DEC's minicomputer product range.

Fig. 11.4 VAX-11/780

Ultimately, Olsen and the company were too late in responding to the paradigm shift in the industry, and this proved to be fatal for the company. Digital was a strong engineering company, and it seemed to believe that the engineering excellence of its computer products would drive the market and be sufficient for its financial success.

It seemed to believe that it knew better than its customers on what was needed for the industry, and these views bordered on technological arrogance. Olsen was sceptical of personal computers and thought of them as merely toys for playing video games, rather than as serious machines in their own right. He seemed to believe that a customer would only be interested in a computer for serious scientific work, such as the elegant machines developed by DEC.

He failed to recognise the importance of the release of the Apple computer and its successors and the IBM personal computer. The company failed to adapt in time to the personal computer market, and its sales declined from the early 1990s. Further, indecision and infighting inside the company delayed an appropriate response to the challenges.

Olsen retired in 1992 and Robert Palmer became the new CEO. He was given the responsibility of returning the company to profitability, and he attempted to change the business culture and to sell off noncore businesses. This led to massive layoffs, and, eventually, Compaq acquired Digital in 1998 for $9.8 billion. Compaq later merged with HP. For more detailed information on DEC, see [Sch:04].

Fig. 11.5 PDP-11

11.1 PDP-11

The Programmed Data Processor-11 (PDP-11) (Fig. 11.5) is one of the most famous computers in history. It is a family of 16-bit minicomputers produced by Digital from 1970 up to the early 1990s, and its members include models such as the PDP-11/45, PDP-11/70, PDP-11/34, PDP-11/60, PDP-11/44, PDP-11/24, PDP-11/83, PDP-11/93 and PDP-11/94. It was designed by Harold McFarland who had been working on several computer architectures at Carnegie Mellon University prior to joining DEC. The prototype was ready in 1969, and the PDP-11 was released in 1970.

It was one of DEC's most successful computers, with over 600,000 machines sold. It was the only 16-bit computer made by the company, as its successor was the 32-bit VAX-11 series. It started its life as a minicomputer and ended its life as micro/super-microcomputer. The release price of the PDP-11 in 1970 was a very affordable $20,000, which was very competitive at that time.

Its central processing unit had eight 16-bit registers, six general-purpose registers, the stack pointer and a program counter. It included software such as an editor, debugger and utilities. The size of its memory was 128 Kb.

The PDP-11 was very useful for multiuser and multitask applications, and the first version of the UNIX operating system ran on a PDP-11/20 in 1970. The VAX line at Digital began as an enhancement to the PDP-11architecture.

11.2   VAX-11/780

The Virtual Address eXtension (VAX) was a family of minicomputers produced by Digital from the mid-1970s up to the late 1980s. This family used processors implementing the VAX instruction set architecture, and its members included minicomputers such as the VAX-11/780, VAX-11/782,VAX-11 /784, VAX-11/785, VAX-11/787, VAX-11/788, VAX-11/750, VAX-11/725 and VAX-11/730. The VAX product line was a competitor to the IBM System 370 series of computers.

The VAX series was derived from the PDP-11 minicomputer, and the VAX-11/780 (Fig. 11.4) was the first member of the family. It was the first widely used 32-bit minicomputer, and it was released in 1978. It was the first one MIPS (Million Instructions per Second) machine, and it was a major success for the company.

Several programming languages including Fortran-77, BASIC, COBOL and Pascal were available for the machine. The VAX-11/780 used the Digital VMS operating system, which was a multiuser, multitasking and virtual memory operating system. The VAX-11/780 remained the base system that every computer benchmarked its speed against for many years.

It supported 128 kB to 8 MB of memory through one or two memory controllers, and the memory was protected with error-correcting codes. Each memory controller could support 128 kB to 4 MB of memory.

Chapter 12
Digital Research Inc.

Digital Research Inc. (DRI) was a Californian company founded by Gary Kildall and his wife Dorothy in the mid-1970s (Fig. 12.1). It was initially called Galactic Digital Research Inc., and it was set up to develop, market and sell the CP/M operating system. The significance of Digital Research is that it developed the first microprocessor disc operating system and the first programming language and compiler for a microprocessor. The CP/M disc operating system was the basis for the operating system used on the IBM personal computer, and if things had turned out differently at the time, Digital Research Inc. could well have been the *Microsoft* of the PC revolution.

Kildall was one of the early people to recognise the potential of the microprocessor as a computer in its own right, and he began writing experimental programs for the Intel 4004 microprocessor in the early 1970s. The Intel 4004 was the first commercially available microprocessor, and Kildall worked as a consultant with Intel on the 8008 and 8080 microprocessors.

He developed the first high-level programming language for a microprocessor (PL/M) in 1973, and he developed the CP/M operating system (Control Program for Microcomputers) in the same year. This operating system allowed the 8080 to control a floppy drive, and CP/M combined all of the essential components of a computer at the microprocessor level.

Kildall was born in Seattle, Washington, in 1942, and he obtained a bachelor's degree in mathematics from the University of Washington in 1967. He became interested in computing, and he pursued a postgraduate degree in computer science at the university. His master's degree was awarded in 1968, and he then embarked on a PhD degree. He became an assistant professor at the Naval Postgraduate School at Monterey in California, and he became interested in the developments in the computing field at nearby Silicon Valley. His PhD degree was awarded in 1972.

Kildall became aware of early work taking place at Intel on microprocessors, and he travelled to Silicon Valley on his days off from the Naval Postgraduate School to work as a consultant with Intel. He soon recognised the potential of the microprocessor as a computer in its own right, and he began writing experimental programs

© Springer International Publishing Switzerland 2015
G. O'Regan, *Pillars of Computing*, DOI 10.1007/978-3-319-21464-1_12

Fig. 12.1 Gary Kildall
(Courtesy of Wikipedia)

for the newly released Intel 4004. He also worked with Intel on the 8008 and 8080 microprocessors, and he developed the first high-level programming language for a microprocessor (PL/M) in 1973. PLM enabled programmers to write applications for microprocessors.

He developed CP/M as the first disc operating system for a microcomputer in 1973, and the Control Program for Microcomputers (CP/M) allowed the Intel 8080 microprocessor to control a floppy disc drive allowing files to be read and written to and from an eight-inch floppy disc. The development of CP/M made it possible for computer hobbyists and companies to build the first home computers.

Kildall made CP/M hardware independent by creating a separate module called the BIOS (Basic Input/Output System). He added several utilities such as an editor, debugger and assembler, and by 1977 several manufactures were including CP/M with their systems. He set up Digital Research Inc. (DRI) in 1976 to develop, market and sell the CP/M operating system.

IBM approached DRI in 1980 with a view to licencing the CP/M operating system for its new IBM personal computer. IBM decided to use the Intel 8088 microprocessor, and Digital Research was working at the time on CP/M-86 for the Intel 16-bit 8086 microprocessor. However, IBM and Digital Research failed to reach an agreement on the licencing of CP/M for the personal computer. Bill Gates had been negotiating a Microsoft BASIC licence agreement with IBM, and he saw an opportunity for Microsoft, and he offered to provide a DOS/BASIC package to IBM on favourable terms. IBM made a deal with Microsoft, and the rest, as they say, is history.

Microsoft hired Tim Patterson to modify an existing quick and dirty version of CP/M (called QDOS) for the 8086 microprocessor for the 8088 microprocessor. DRI released CP/M-86 shortly after IBM released DOS 1.0, and it quickly became apparent to Digital Research that DOS 1.0 copied all of the CP/M system calls. DRI considered suing Microsoft and IBM but eventually decided against legal action due to its limited resources. Digital Research was purchased by Novell in 1991.

12.1   Licencing CP/M to IBM

Digital Research lost out on the opportunity of a lifetime to supply the operating for the IBM personal computer to IBM (Fig. 19.11), and instead it was Microsoft that supplied the DOS operating system and reaped the benefits. Microsoft would later become a technology giant and a dominant force in the computer industry.

Bloomberg Businessweek published an article in 2004 describing the background to the development of the operating system for the IBM PC and the failed negotiations between Digital Research and IBM on the licencing of the CP/M operating system. The article was titled "The Man who could have been Bill Gates" [Blo:04].

Don Estridge led the IBM team that was developing the IBM personal computer. The project was subject to an aggressive delivery schedule, and while traditionally IBM developed a full proprietary solution, it decided instead to outsource the development of the microprocessor to a small company called Intel and to outsource the development of the operating system. The IBM team initially asked Bill Gates and Microsoft in Seattle to supply them with an operating system. Microsoft had already signed a contract with IBM to supply a BASIC interpreter for the IBM PC, but they lacked the expertise to develop the operating system. Gates referred IBM to Gary Kildall at DRI, and the IBM team approached Digital Research with a view to licencing its CP/M operating system.

Digital Research was working on CP/M-86 for the Intel 16-bit 8086 microprocessor that had been introduced by Intel in 1978. IBM decided to use the Intel 8088 for its new personal computer product, and the 8088 processor, which was introduced in 1979, was a lower cost and slower version of the 8086.

IBM and Digital Research failed to reach an agreement on the licencing of CP/M for the IBM PC. The precise reasons for failure are unclear, but some immediate problems arose with respect to the signing of an IBM nondisclosure agreement during the visit. It is unclear whether Kildall actually met with IBM and whether there was an informal handshake agreement between both parties. However, there was certainly no documented legal agreement between IBM and DRI.

There may also have been difficulties in relation to the amount of royalty payment being demanded by Digital Research, as well as practical difficulties in achieving the required IBM delivery schedule (due to Digital Research's existing commitments to Intel). Kildall was superb at technical innovation, but he may have lacked the appropriate business acumen to secure a good deal, or he may have oversold his hand.

Gates had been negotiating a Microsoft BASIC licence agreement with IBM, and he now saw a business opportunity for Microsoft. He offered to provide an operating system (later called PC/DOS) and BASIC to IBM on favourable terms. The offer was accepted by IBM, and Microsoft reaped the benefits.

Gates was aware of the work done by Tim Patterson on a simple quick and dirty version of CP/M (called QDOS) for the 8086 microprocessor for Seattle Computer Products (SCP). Gates licenced QDOS for $50,000, and he hired Patterson to modify it to run on the IBM PC for the 8088 microprocessor. Gates then licenced the operating system to IBM for a low per-copy royalty fee.

IBM called the new operating system PC/DOS, and Gates retained the rights to MS/DOS which were used on IBM-compatible computers produced by other hardware manufacturers. In time, MS/DOS would become the dominant operating system (eclipsing PC/DOS due to the open architecture of the IBM PC and the rapid growth of clones) leading to the growth of Microsoft into a major corporation.

DRI released CP/M-86 shortly after IBM released PC DOS. Kildall examined PC/DOS, and it was clear to him that it had been derived from CP/M. He was furious and met separately with IBM and Microsoft, but nothing was resolved. Digital Research considered suing Microsoft for copying all of the CP/M system calls in DOS 1.0, as it was evident to Kildall that Patterson's QDOS was a copy of CP/M.

He considered his legal options but his legal advice suggested that as intellectual copyright law had only been recently introduced in the United States, it was not clear what constituted infringement of copyright. There was no guarantee of success in any legal action against IBM, and considerable expense would be involved. Kildall threatened IBM with legal action, and IBM agreed to offer both CP/M-86 and PC/DOS. However, as CP/M was priced at $240 and DOS at $60, few personal computer owners were willing to pay the extra cost. CP/M was to fade into obscurity.

Perhaps, if Kildall had played his hand differently, he could have been in the position that Bill Gates is in today, and Digital Research could well have been, the *Microsoft* of the PC industry. Kildall's delay in developing the 16-bit operating system gave Patterson the opportunity to create his own version. IBM was under serious time pressures with the development of the IBM PC, and Kildall may have been unable to meet the IBM deadline. This may have resulted in IBM dealing with Gates instead of DRI.

Further, the size of the royalty fee demanded by Kildall for CP/M was not very sensible, as the excessively high royalty fee demanded resulted in very low sales for the DRI product, whereas if a more realistic price had been proposed, then DRI may have made some reasonable revenue.

Nevertheless, Kildall could justly feel hard done by, and he may have viewed Microsoft's actions as the theft of his intellectual ideas and technical inventions. It shows that technical excellence and innovation is not in itself sufficient for business success, and that a certain business acumen or entrepreneurial flair is also required.

Kildall became embittered as a result of the IBM/Microsoft experience, and in later life he had problems with alcohol addiction. He died in tragic circumstances in 1994 at the young age of 52. He received a posthumous award from the Software Publishers Association, and the University of Washington awards the Gary Kildall Endowment Scholarship annually to outstanding undergraduate computer science students.

Chapter 13
eBay Inc.

eBay is an American corporation and e-commerce company that manages the online auction and shopping site *ebay.com*. It offers a virtual market place for the sales of goods and services between individuals, and it enables *business-to-consumer* and *consumer-to-consumer* sales over the Internet.

Its e-commerce site allows virtually anything to be auctioned on the site,[1] as long as it is not illegal and does not violate eBay's policies. It creates a virtual market place that allows buyers and sellers to come together and to do negotiate over the prices with the goal of to making a deal. The sellers may be businesses or individuals, and the market participants may bid for a particular item. The seller may decide to accept or reject the offer made.

The company was founded in 1995 by Pierre Omidyar who is a French–American entrepreneur (Fig. 13.1). Omidyar was born in Paris to Iranian immigrants, and he immigrated with his family to the United States when he was a child. He graduated from Tufts University in 1988 with a bachelor's degree in computer science, and he worked for Claris (a spin-off from Apple) for a couple of years. He founded a computer start-up in the early 1990s.

He began working on the development of an individual-to-individual auction site for collectibles in the mid-1990s, and he launched his *Auction Web* site in late 1995. The company was founded in the living room of his home in San Jose, and it would eventually become the auction site *eBay.com*. Auction Web became extremely popular with individuals registering an extraordinary variety of goods and paying a small fee for each sale made. The site had hosted over 250,000 auctions by the end of 1996, and in the first month of 1997, it hosted two million auctions. By mid-1997 it was hosting 800,000 auctions a day.

Omidyar changed the name of the company to eBay in late 1997, and he recognised that he needed a good senior management team to enable the company to

---

[1] There have been a number of bizarre auctions on eBay. For example, an Australian placed the home of Lord of the Rings, New Zealand, for sale in 2006. The bidding had reached $300 before it was withdrawn due to violation of eBay's policies.

© Springer International Publishing Switzerland 2015
G. O'Regan, *Pillars of Computing*, DOI 10.1007/978-3-319-21464-1_13

Fig. 13.1 Pierre Omidyar
at Las Vegas in 2007

Fig. 13.2 Meg Whitman
at the Tech Museum,
San Jose, in 2009

grow and achieve its potential. Jeffrey Skoll, a Canadian, became the first president
of eBay in 1996, and he formulated a business plan for the company to transform it
from a start-up to a successful company. Skoll brought in Meg Whitman[2] who was
a branding expert, and she helped to formulate the mission of the company *as a
business that connects people rather than a company that sells things* (Fig. 13.2).

Whitman became president of eBay after Skoll's departure in 1998, and she
brought in an experienced management team to enable the company to achieve its
mission. The company has created a person-to-person marketplace on the web that
allows users to list items for sales, and interested buyers may then bid for them.
The company has pioneered and internationalised automated person-to-person

---

[2] Whitman later became the CEO of HP in 2011.

auctioning, and previously such business was done at garage sales, classified advertisements and so on.

The company went public during the dot-com boom in 1998, and its share price almost tripled on the first day of trading. The IPO valued the company at around $2 billion, and today it has a market capitalisation of over $60 billion. The company has annual revenues of over $16 billion, and its profits are approximately $3 billion.

The initial market of the company was in collectibles, but it quickly expanded into other markets such as automobiles, business and industrial equipment and consumer electronics. This helped to increase the average sales price (ASP) for each sale and thereby helped to increase eBay's revenue which is a percentage of each sale. The eBay site is organised by categories such as collectibles, electronics, fashion, motors, entertainment, sporting goods, toys, books and so on.

The site is well organised and it is easy for a seller to list items, and it is easy for a buyer to browse through the listed items. There are no fees charged for browsing or bidding during an auction, but sellers are charged two or more fees. The first fee is a non-refundable *placement fee* for the insertion of the item on the eBay site, and the second fee is a *commission fee* that is charged when the auction is complete. Additional fees may be applied depending on how the item has been listed and marketed on the site.

Once the auction is finished, eBay notifies the buyer and seller by email if the bid exceeds the seller's minimum price, and the buyer and seller complete the transaction independently of eBay which collects its final commission fee. Another words the *final contract is between the buyer and seller only*, and *eBay's role is to act as the intermediary that brings the buyer and seller together*. More detailed information on eBay is in [Coh:03].

eBay purchased Paypal, a young company specialising in payments and money transfer services over the Internet, in 2002. Today, most of eBay auctions accept Paypal payments, and Paypal is the payment method of choice used by the majority of eBay users. Initially, most of Paypal users came from the eBay auction site, but it now has over 150 million domestic and international users, and it transferred over $180 billion across 190 countries in 2013.

Paypal today is one of the largest Internet payment companies in the world, and it performs online processing for online vendors, auction sites and so on. eBay plans to spin off Paypal into an independent company in 2015.

13.1 eBay Business Model

eBay has an elegant and simple business model, and its mission is to be the intermediary that brings buyers and sellers together. The fact that it is an intermediary, and not a manufacturer or seller, means that it does not need to maintain costly inventory or maintain products in stock or maintain warehouses. It earns revenue from acting as an intermediary in bringing buyers and sellers together in the marketplace.

The first fee that eBay charges the seller is a non-refundable *placement fee*, for the insertion of the item on its site, and this fee is based on the sellers opening bid on the item. The placement fee generally ranges between $0.10 and $2. The second fee applied is a *commission fee* which is charged when the auction is complete, and it typically ranges from 0.75 to 10 % of the final sale price (which includes the price of the item plus shipping fees).

Other optional fees may be charged depending on how the item is marketed and displayed.

13.2   Paypal

Paypal is one of the world's largest Internet payment companies, and it allows payments and money transfers to be made over the Internet. It performs payment processing for online vendors, auction sites and other commercial users, and it earns its revenue by charging a fee for these services.

The company was founded as Confinity in the United States in late 1988, and it initially developed software for handheld devices. Confinity developed and launched Paypal as an online payment method in 1999, and the company was renamed to Paypal in 2001. The company launched its successful IPO in 2002, and it was acquired by eBay for $1.5 billion the same year. The company headquarters are in San Jose, California.

Paypal is the payment method used by the majority of eBay users, and Paypal continues to enhance its payments solutions. It developed and launched the Paypal secure card in partnership with Mastercard in 2007, and this software allows payments to be made on websites that do not accept Paypal directly.[3] It acquired Fraud Sciences, an Israeli start-up, in 2009 to enhance its fraud management capabilities.

Paypal has over 150 million users around the world, and it is highly profitable. eBay has announced plans to spin off its Paypal subsidiary into an independent company in 2015.

---

[3] A single-use MasterCard number is generated for each transaction.

Chapter 14
EMCC, Sperry and Unisys

The Eckert–Mauchly Computer Corporation (EMCC) was founded by Presper Eckert and John Mauchly in 1947 (Fig. 14.1). It was one of the earliest computer companies in the world, and it pioneered a number of fundamental computer concepts such as the *stored program*, *subroutines*, *programming languages* and *compilers*.

Mauchly was an American physicist and engineer who worked with Eckert and others on the design and development of the ENIAC and EDVAC computers at the Moore School of Electrical Engineering at the University of Pennsylvania. These were among the earliest digital computers, and Mauchly and Eckert recognised the future potential of computers and decided to set up their own company.

EMCC was awarded a contract from the US Census Bureau in 1948 to develop the *Universal Automatic Computer* (UNIVAC) for the 1950 census. This was one of the first commercially available computers when it was delivered in 1951 (too late for the 1950 census), and it was designed for business and administrative use, rather than for complex scientific calculations. The UNIVAC machine was later used to accurately predict the result of the 1952 presidential election in the United States from a sample of 1 % of the population.

The UNIVAC I was initially priced at $159,000 and the price gradually increased over the years to reach between $1.2 and $1.5 million. Over 46 of these computers were built and delivered. It employed magnetic tape for high-speed storage and it used 5200 vacuum tubes. It consumed 125 kW of electricity and could carry out 1905 operations per second. It took up 400 square foot of space, and its main memory consisted of 1000 words of 12 characters.

EMCC developed the BINAC computer for the Northrop Corporation, and this machine was delivered in 1949. There were issues with its performance, and this may have been due to the fact that the machine was assembled by Northrop, rather than by EMCC's skilled engineers. The machine was assembled by a newly hired Northrop engineer who lacked the required knowledge and experience.

EMCC experienced cash flow and financial difficulties early in its existence, and it was taken over by Remington Rand in 1950. Remington had a background in the

© Springer International Publishing Switzerland 2015
G. O'Regan, *Pillars of Computing*, DOI 10.1007/978-3-319-21464-1_14

Fig. 14.1 John Mauchly

production of typewriters, and *the Remington Typewriter was the first to use the* QWERTY *keyboard*. Remington was also a major pistol manufacturer, and its acquisition of EMCC allowed it to enter the electronics market. EMCC became the UNIVAC division of Remington Rand, and when Remington Rand was taken over by Sperry in 1955, it became known as Sperry Rand (and later just Sperry).

Sperry's background was in the military sector, and its acquisition of Remington Rand allowed it to enter the electronics sector. It continued the development of the UNIVAC computer series, and it signed an important cross-licencing deal with IBM.

Mauchly became embroiled in a legal dispute in the 1973 *Honeywell vs. Sperry Rand* patent court case in the United States. This controversy arose from a patent dispute between Sperry and Honeywell, and John Atanasoff was called as an expert witness in the case.

Atanasoff's ABC computer [ORg:13] was ruled by the court to be the first electronic digital computer, and the legal judgement confirmed that the ABC existed as *prior art* at the time of Mauchly and Eckert's patent application. It is fundamental in patent law that the invention is novel and that there is no existing prior art. This meant that Mauchly and Eckert's patent application was invalid, and John Atanasoff was named by the US court as the inventor of the first digital computer. The court ruled that Mauchly derived his invention of ENIAC from Atanasoff. Sperry merged with Burroughs to become Unisys in 1986.

14.1 ENIAC

The Electronic Numerical Integrator and Computer (ENIAC) was one of the first large general-purpose electronic digital computers (Fig. 14.2). It was used to integrate ballistic equations and to calculate the trajectories of naval shells. It was completed in 1946 and remained in use until 1955. The original cost of the machine was approximately $500,000.

Fig. 14.2 Setting the switches on ENIAC's function tables (US Army photo)

It was designed by John Mauchly who was a lecturer at the Moore School of Electrical Engineering at the University of Pennsylvania and Presper Eckert who was an engineering student at the Moore School of Electrical Engineering. Mauchly made a proposal to build an electronic computer using vacuum tubes that would be faster and more accurate than the existing differential analyzer used in the school. The US Army agreed to provide funding to build the machine in 1943.

The machine had to be physically rewired in order to perform different tasks, and it was clear that there was a need for an architecture that would allow a more efficient way of performing different tasks. This led to the concept of the *stored program*, which was implemented in EDVAC (the successor to ENIAC). The idea is that the program is stored in memory, and when there is a need to change the task that is to be computed, then all that is required is to place a new program in memory rather than rewiring the machine.

ENIAC was a large bulky machine over 100-ft long, 10-ft high and 3-ft deep and it weighed about 30 tons. It was built for the US Army's Ballistics Research Laboratory. There were over 18,000 vacuum tubes in the machine, and the computer generated a vast quantity of heat, as each vacuum tube generated heat like a light bulb. The ENIAC used 150 kW of power and air conditioning was employed to cool the machine.

The ENIAC employed decimal numerals and it could add 5000 numbers and perform over three hundred and fifty 10-digit multiplications or thirty-five 10-digit divisions in 1 s. It could be programmed to perform complex sequences of operations, and this included loops, branches and subroutines. However, the task of taking a problem and mapping it onto the machine was complex, and it usually took weeks to perform. The first step was to determine what the program was to do on paper; the second step was the process of manipulating the switches and cables to enter the program into ENIAC, and this usually took several days. The final step was verification and debugging, and this often involved single-step execution of the machine.

Fig. 14.3 Replacing a valve on ENIAC (US Army photo)

There were problems with the reliability of ENIAC as several vacuum tubes burned out most days (Fig. 14.3). This meant that the machine was often nonfunctional as high-reliability tubes were not available until the late 1940s. However, most of these problems occurred during the warm-up and cool-down periods, and therefore it was decided not to turn the machine off. This led to improvements in its reliability to the acceptable level of one tube every 2 days. The longest continuous period of operation without a failure was 5 days.

The very first program run on ENIAC took just 20 s, and the answer was manually verified to be correct after 40 h of work with a mechanical calculator. One of the earliest problems solved was related to the feasibility of the hydrogen bomb, and the program ran for 6 weeks and gave an affirmative reply. ENIAC was a major milestone in the history of computing, and it was preceded in development by the Atanasoff Berry Computer (ABC), the Colossus computer in the United Kingdom, and the Z3 in Germany.

14.2   EDVAC

The EDVAC (Electronic Discrete Variable Automatic Computer) was the successor to the ENIAC, and this stored-program computer was proposed by Eckert and Mauchly in 1944 to address the limitations of ENIAC.

It cost $500,000 and it was delivered to the Ballistics Research Laboratory in 1949. It employed 6000 vacuum tubes and its power consumption was 56,000 watts. It had 5.5 Kb of memory. It commenced operations in 1951 and it remained in use until 1961.

The EDVAC was one of the earliest stored-program computers, and the program instructions were placed in memory. There was no need to rewire the machine each time, and instead a new program was loaded into memory. EDVAC implemented the concept of a stored program in 1949, just after its implementation on the Manchester baby prototype machine at the University of Manchester in England [ORg:11].

von Neumann became involved in some of the engineering discussions during the development of EDVAC, and he produced a draft report describing the proposed computer. The concept of a stored-program and von Neumann architecture is detailed in von Neumann's report on EDVAC [VN:45].

This report was intended to be internal, but circumstances changed due to legal issues which arose with respect to intellectual property and patents. This led to the resignation of Mauchly and Eckert from the Moore School of Electrical Engineering, as they wished to protect their patents on ENIAC and EDVAC. They set up their own computer company (EMCC) to exploit the new computer technology.

The Moore School of Electrical Engineering then removed the names of Mauchly and Eckert from von Neumann's report and circulated the report to the wider community. The report mentioned the fundamental computer architecture that is known today as the *von Neumann architecture*, and Mauchly and Eckert received no acknowledgement for their contributions.

14.3   UNIVAC and Early Computing

UNIVAC is the name of a series of digital computers produced by EMCC and its successors (i.e. Remington Rand, Sperry and Uniysys). The original model was the UNIVAC I (Universal Automatic Computer I), and this machine had 1000 words of memory with each word consisting of 12 alphanumeric characters. The successor models in the original UNIVAC series included the UNIVAC II which was released in 1958 and the UNIVAC III which was released by Sperry Rand in 1962.

Sperry introduced the 36-bit UNIVAC 1100/2000 series in the early 1960s, and the first model was the UNIVAC 1107 which was released in 1962. The UNIVAC 1108 was introduced in 1964, the 1106 in 1969, the 1110 in 1972, and a new series including the UNIVAC 1100/10, 1110/20 and so on from the mid-1970s. The name "UNIVAC" was discontinued from 1983 and replaced with the "SPERRY" series, and this included models such as the SPERRY 2200/100 which was introduced in 1985.

EMCC set up a department to develop software applications for the UNIVAC computer, and it hired Grace Murray Hopper in 1949 as one of its first programmers (Fig. 14.4). Hopper played an important role in the development of programming languages, and she made important contributions to the early development of compilers, programming language constructs, data processing and the COBOL programming language.

Hopper joined the US Navy when the United States entered the Second World War, and she was based at Cuft Laboratories at Harvard. She became familiar with the Harvard Mark 1 computer [ORg:13], and she worked on the Mark II and Mark III

Fig. 14.4 Grace Murray
Hopper and UNIVAC

computers. She coined the term *computer bug* when she traced an error in the
Mark II computer to a moth stuck in one of its relays. The bug was carefully removed
and taped to a daily logbook, and the term "bug" is now ubiquitous.

She developed the concept of a compiler, as it was very evident that programming in binary machine code is tedious and error prone. Machine code consists of
writing a string of 0s and 1s, and so it is easy to make mistakes and time consuming
to identify and correct them. She believed that the development of a user-friendly
language would encourage wider use of computers, and she recognised that libraries
of code would also help to reduce errors and duplication of effort.

This led to her idea for a compiler that would act as an intermediate program that
would translate the program instructions into machine code that could then be
understood by the computer. This would allow programmers to employ the friendly
and intuitive notation of a high-level programming language, rather than writing
tedious and lengthy instructions in binary code.

Her first compiler, the A-O, appeared in 1949, and it used symbolic mathematical
code to represent binary code combinations. She followed this with the B-0 or
Flow-Matic compiler in 1952, and this is considered the first data processing compiler. She contributed to standardising compilers and compiler verification.

She recognised the need for a user-friendly programming language that would be
easy for business users, and she was the technical adviser to the CODASYL com-
mittee that defined the specification of the COBOL language. This was the first
business-oriented programming language, and the Flow-Matic compiler was
employed to assist in its development.

COBOL was introduced in 1959, and she participated in public demonstrations of
the first COBOL compiler and designed manuals and tools for the language. It provided a degree of machine independence, as the source code was written once and
then compiled into the machine language of the targeted machine.

Chapter 15
Ericsson

L.M. Ericsson is a Swedish multinational provider of telecommunications technology and services, and it employs over 100,000 people around the world. Its headquarters are in Stockholm, and it has plants in Europe, Asia and North America. It is a world leader in communications technology and in the mobile network infrastructure market, and it has customers in over 180 countries. It has a long and distinguished history in fixed-network and mobile network communication, and it is a highly innovative company with a large intellectual property portfolio.

The company was founded in Stockholm by Lars Magnus Ericsson (Fig. 15.1) in 1876, and it initially made telegraph equipment for the state railway. The first telephone was introduced into Sweden in 1877, and Ericsson began receiving telephones to repair. This motivated L.M. Ericsson to design his first telephone, and it was based on the American Bell Company's prototype. He began to manufacture and sell telephones and telephone switches from 1878, and these became popular and his business expanded. Sweden's first telephone network was introduced in 1880, and Sweden had the greatest telephone penetration in the world in 1895.

The oldest telephones had large and bulky components that had to be arranged in an appropriate manner. They evolved into wall-mounted functional wooden boxes, and Ericsson differentiated itself from other manufacturers by employing skilled cabinet makers to design aesthetically pleasing wall boxes. It introduced its wall telephone set (Fig. 15.2) in 1882, and it introduced an aesthetically pleasing desk telephone (Fig. 15.3) in 1893.

The invention of the telephone was a paradigm shift from face-to-face communication, where people met to exchange ideas and share information or where individuals wrote letters to each other to exchange information. The telephone which was a new medium that provided direct and instantaneous communication between two people. It allowed two individuals to establish and maintain two-way communication irrespective of being at two different physical locations.

Initially the telephone was used by the business community and the affluent members of society, but this changed rapidly in the years that followed its introduction.

© Springer International Publishing Switzerland 2015
G. O'Regan, *Pillars of Computing*, DOI 10.1007/978-3-319-21464-1_15

Fig. 15.1 Lars Magnus
Ericsson

Fig. 15.2 Ericsson 1882
wall telephone

L.M. Ericsson was incorporated as a limited company in 1896, with Lars Magnus Ericsson holding 90 % of the shares and becoming president of the company and chairman of the board. It became a major telephone manufacturing company, and it expanded into international markets from the 1890s. It set up plants in Britain and Russia to meet the demand, and these plants were highly profitable. By 1901, the

Fig. 15.3 Ericsson 1893
desk telephone

Fig. 15.4 Ericsson's St. Petersburg Plant, 1905

year when Lars Magnus Ericsson stepped down from office, Ericsson was a major multinational company with over 95 % of its sales coming from outside of Sweden.

It set up a plant in Buffalo, New York, in 1907, but this plant proved to be unsuccessful, and it was to be the early 1980s before Ericsson began to achieve success in the United States. Its plants in Britain and Russia were profitable, and it also had a presence in several other European countries including France, Austria and Hungary. However, the Russian plant (Fig. 15.4) was nationalised by the Russian government during the October 1917 revolution, and Ericsson received no compensation for its assets in Russia.

Ericsson merged with the Swedish telephone operator Stockholms Allmänna Telefonaktiebolag (SAT) in 1918. The newly merged Ericsson received large contributions from the Swedish government for the telephone operations of a SAT subsidiary, and this helped it to deal with the losses that it incurred in Russia. The newly merged Ericsson was a company that manufactured telecommunications equipment, and it was active as a telephone operator outside of Sweden.

Ericsson went through financial difficulties in the 1930s following the worldwide depression after the Wall Street Crash in 1929. These difficulties were compounded by Ivar Kreuger, a rogue investor, who had purchased Ericsson stock and who went on to control Ericsson in 1930. His actions almost bankrupt the company, as he embezzled millions of dollars, and he almost delivered Ericsson into the hands of ITT, its American competitor.

There was a major fall in demand for telephones and switches in the 1930s, and the value of Ericsson's exports fell by 60 %. Swedish banks became involved in rescuing the company, and the Wallenberg family took a controlling stake in the company. The Wallenberg family had a background in banking, and today it still retains large stakes in several Swedish multinationals including Ericsson.

Ericsson diversified into other sectors in the 1930s including electricity meters, cash registers, electronic tubes as well as its core telephone equipment, and its focus was on the domestic market during the Second World War with exports just accounting for 15 % of its revenue in 1944. Its contributions during the war years included the manufacture of field telephones, telephone equipment for warships, ammunition and heavy machine guns.

After the war, Ericsson's focus remained on the manufacturing and sale of telephones and telephony switching equipment, and it expanded into markets in Latin America and Australia. It introduced the world's first automatic mobile telephony system version A (MTA) in 1956. The system allowed the subscriber to make a phone call directly from a vehicle without any assistance from a switchboard operator. However, the system was expensive and it had only a small number of subscribers.

Ericsson became a leader in fixed-line phone technology in the late 1970s, and it became a leader in mobile technology from the late 1980s. It jointly developed (with Televerket) and manufactured the AXE digital telephone exchanges from the late 1970s, and this system has been deployed in many telephone exchanges in over 130 countries.

Bell Labs had developed the first cellular network standard called Advanced Mobile Phone System (AMPS) in the United States (discussed in Chap. 7), and it became operational in the late 1980s. The Total Access Communication (TACS) and Extended TACS (ETACS) system were variants of AMPS and were employed in the United Kingdom and Europe. These analog standards employed separate frequencies or channels for each conversation using frequency division multiple access (FDMA). However, the analog system suffered from static and noise, and there was no protection from eavesdropping using a scanner.

Ericsson soon became a leader in the first generation of mobile with Motorola, and over time mobile technology evolved from the AMPS analog standard to the second-generation digital GSM standard, to GPRS, to third-generation mobile including 3G and WCDMA and to fourth-generation mobile (4G). The extent of

Ericsson's leadership was clear when its proposed design for digital mobile radio transmission was selected as the US standard for cellular communications over entries from Motorola and AT&T in 1989.

Ericsson also became a leading manufacturer of mobile phones and maintained this position with Nokia and Motorola until the late 1990s. It began to lose market share of the mobile handset market in the late 1990s due to major competition from Finland's Nokia as well as from other telecom vendors. Its market share in the mobile handset market fell to around 10 % and it began to experience financial difficulties.

The dot-com crash in early 20,000 made things even worse and Ericsson embarked on a major restructuring programme with the aim of returning the company to profitability. It decided to outsource the manufacture of mobile phones to Flextronics, and it launched a joint venture with Sony that would include the mobile phone businesses of both companies.

Sony Ericsson Mobile Communications was launched in 2001. However, this joint venture was unsuccessful, and Sony bought out Ericsson's share in the venture in 2012. Ericsson maintains its leadership position in network infrastructure and remains a highly innovative company. For further information on L.M. Ericsson, see [McJ:01].

15.1   AXE System

The AXE (Automatic Exchange Electric) switching system was the first fully automated digital switching system, when it was introduced by Ericsson in 1977 (Fig. 15.5). It converted speech into digital (i.e. the binary language used by computers), while Ericsson's competitors were still using the slower and less reliable analog systems.

The analog system uses an electric current to convey the vibrations of the human voice, whereas a digital system uses a stream of binary digits to represent sound. The AXE system was an immediate success with telecom companies, and it has been sold in many countries around the world. AXE was originally a digital exchange for landline telephony, but it has been extended for use with mobile telephony systems.

The AXE system was developed by Ellemtel, which was a joint venture between Televerket (Sweden's state-owned PTT) and Ericsson. Ellemtel was established in 1970 as a pure research and development company, with production done by its parent companies. Its primary task was to develop an electronic and automated switching system for telephone stations that would become the AXE system.

Ericsson had been working to develop a commercial electronic switching system called AKE, while Televerket was working on its own electronic switch. Ericsson realised that its AKE system was not suitable for large switching stations and that it needed to develop a new generation of switching systems. It decided to combine its resources with Televerket and jointly develop an electronic telephone switching

Fig. 15.5 AXE system
(Courtesy of Ericsson)

system. Ericsson decided to discontinue its development of the AKE system and to focus its efforts on developing the AXE system.

The project manager for the AXE project was Bengt-Gunnar Magnusson, and the AXE system had a modular system design which made the system flexible. New functionality could be added and existing modules updated or replaced. The modular design also enabled the system to be easily adapted to different markets.

The development of AXE also involved the development of hardware and software such as programs and processors to control the AXE stations. The first prototype AXE system was installed at a Televerket station in 1976, and Ellemtel's task of developing the AXE system was complete in 1978.

The AXE system was then commercialised and many of Ellemtel's employees moved to Ericsson. AXE was an immediate success and Ericsson soon had customers in Sweden, Finland, France, Australia and Saudi Arabia. The Saudi order was the largest that Ericsson had ever received, and it involved increasing the capacity of the Saudi network by 200 % and installing the AXE system.

The introduction of AXE meant that by the early 1980s Ericsson had the market's most advanced and flexible switching system, and this made it ideally placed for the transition to mobile telephony. It meant that Ericsson had moved from being a minor player in the telecom business to a major league player.

Today, AXE has been installed in over 130 countries, and it laid the foundation for Ericsson's future success in mobile telephony. Ellemtel was integrated with Ericsson in the late 1990s.

15.2   Mobile Phone Systems

The AXE system provided the foundation for Ericsson's growth in mobile telephony. The flexible modular design of AXE allowed new functionality to be added, and by changing a module AXE could be reconfigured to handle mobile telephone calls. This allowed Ericsson to design the first mobile telephone exchange (MTX) by replacing the subsystem for fixed subscribers with a new subsystem for mobile subscribers. The MTX switch was developed in the late 1970s/early 1980s and was a key part of the Nordic Mobile Telephone system (NMT) which would be used in all Nordic countries.

Ericsson was awarded a large Saudi contract to deliver a fixed-line and mobile system, and it was agreed that the NMT standard would be used and that Ericsson would supply the entire system. The Saudi mobile phone network became operational from 1981, and Ericsson provided base stations, radio towers and switches. Ericsson had now acquired cell planning experience, and it was awarded the contract to develop the entire mobile telephone network in the Netherlands. Ericsson was now a total systems supplier in mobile telephony, and it provided the entire infrastructure such as switches and base stations. Today, its base stations range from small picocells to large macrocells.

Ericsson has successfully adapted to the different mobile standards such as the analog Advanced Mobile Phone System (AMPS) standard, the Total Access Communication System (TACS) standard, the Time Division Multiple Access (TDMA) standard which was a second-generation digital standard, the Personal Digital Cellular (PDC) standard which was used in Japan, the Global System for Mobile Communication (GSM) which is a second-generation mobile standard used throughout the world, the General Packet Radio Services (GPRS), 3G, and 4G.

Ericsson participated in the development of standards through its own research and development, and it also influenced the development of standards. It began to manufacture mobile phones, and the sales of phones was a major change from its usual one country, one customer (i.e. the sale of network infrastructure equipment to the network operator of the country) to sales of mobile phones to individual consumers in each country.

Ericsson became a leading player in the development of mobile phones and in the late 1990s the market for mobile phones was dominated by Nokia, Ericsson and Motorola.

However, while Ericsson remains a leader in network infrastructure, its mobile phone sales have experienced a serious decline. It formed a joint venture with Sony (Sony Ericsson) to manufacture and sell mobile phones, but this joint venture was unsuccessful. Sony purchased Ericsson's share of the venture in 2012, and Ericsson is focused on its network infrastructure business.

Chapter 16
Facebook

Facebook is the leading social networking site (SNS) in the world, and its mission is to make the world more open and connected. It helps users to keep in touch with friends and family, and it allows them to share their opinions on what is happening around the world. Users may upload photos and videos, express opinions and ideas and exchange messages. Facebook is very popular with advertisers as it allows them to easily reach a large target audience.

The company was founded by Mark Zuckerberg (Fig. 16.1) in 2004 while he was a student studying psychology at Harvard University. Zuckerberg was interested in programming, and he had already developed several social networking websites for his fellow students including *Facemash* which could be used to rate the attractiveness of a person and *Coursematch* which allowed students to view people taking their degree.

Zuckerberg launched *The Facebook* (thefacebook.com) at Harvard in February 2004, and over a thousand Harvard students had registered on the site within the first 24 h. Over half of the Harvard student population had a profile on Facebook within the first month. The membership of the site was initially restricted to students at Harvard, then to students at the other universities in Boston and then to students at the other universities in the United States. Its membership was extended to international universities from 2005.

The use of Facebook was extended beyond universities to anyone with an email address from 2006, and the number of registered users began to increase exponentially. The number of registered users reached 100 million in 2008 and 500 million in 2010, and it exceeded 1 billion in 2012. It is now one of the most popular websites in the world.

Advertisements are a key source of revenue for Facebook. Advertisers may target users based on the information shared by each user, such as age, gender, location, education, work history and interests. Facebook offers development tools and application program interfaces (APIs) to enable developers to create applications that will easily integrate with Facebook. Millions of mobile apps and websites have been integrated with Facebook.

© Springer International Publishing Switzerland 2015
G. O'Regan, *Pillars of Computing*, DOI 10.1007/978-3-319-21464-1_16

Fig. 16.1 Mark
Zuckerberg

Facebook offers an online payment service to enable developers to receive payment from the users, and payment revenue is an important source of Facebook's revenue.

Facebook has acquired more than 50 companies since its inception, and these include *WhatsApp* and *Instagram*. The acquisition of WhatsApp cost $19 billion and the acquisition of Instagram cost $1 billion.

16.1   The Facebook Business Model

Facebook's business model is quite distinct from that of a traditional business in that it does not manufacture or sell any products. Instead it earns its revenue mainly from advertisements, and its business model is based on advertisement revenue, with advertisements targeted to its over 1.3 billion users based on their specific interests.

Facebook has a powerful advertisement engine to generate revenue, and in contrast to a traditional company that sells products, Facebook is essentially selling its users to advertisers. The Facebook service is free to its users (as the users are essentially the product that is being offered to its customers, i.e. the advertisers). The users really do all the work, and Facebook collects data about them and classifies and categorises them, so that it is in a position to target advertisements that will potentially be of interest to them, so the advertisements are targeting the right audience.

It earns revenue from each advertisement, and its business model has been highly successful. The company has annual revenue of over $7.5 billion and net income of roughly $1.5 billion.

The success of Facebook in creating a vast consumer company is impressive, especially, given that it has been achieved without any manufacturing, distribution or person-to-person sales.

16.2   Facebook Acquisitions

Facebook has acquired over 50 companies since its inception, and these acquisitions have allowed it to grow in other areas of social networking and to develop other revenue streams apart from its core advertising model. Its acquisitions include well-known companies such as Instagram and WhatsApp, and many of these companies have grown rapidly since becoming part of the Facebook family.

Instagram is an online mobile photo-sharing, video-sharing and social networking site. It allows its users to take pictures or videos and to upload them to the Instagram site and to share them on a variety of social media platforms such as Facebook and Twitter.

Instagram photos are confined to a square share and the maximum length of an Instagram video is 15 s. Instagram was acquired by Facebook for $1 billion in 2012, and it has over 300 million active users.

Instagram became embroiled in controversy in early 2013, when it upgraded its terms and conditions to give it the right to sell user's photos and videos without notification and compensation. Instagram later issued a statement retracting the controversial terms.

Instagram's business model was initially quite weak, but it has adopted an advertisement-based business model, where it will start showing advertisements in its news feed. Video advertisements are also supported in its Instagram feeds.

WhatsApp is one of the largest and fastest growing mobile messaging platforms in the world. It allows instant messaging for smartphones and operates under a subscription model, where hundreds of millions of users pay to use its service.

The subscription fee charged is quite small, and as there are hundreds of millions of users, the annual revenue is quite large. The WhatsApp may send text messages, pictures, videos and audio media messages. It is one of the most popular messaging apps with over 600 million users around the world. It was acquired by Facebook for $19 billion in 2014.

16.3   The Facebook Revolution

Social media (especially Facebook and Twitter) have become important communication channels for educated young people to discuss their aspirations for the future, as well as their grievances with society and the state. The effectiveness of Facebook as a tool for protests and revolution is evident in the relatively short protests that culminated in the resignation of President Hosni Mubarak of Egypt in 2011.

Egypt was granted limited independence from Britain in 1922, and full independence was granted in 1936. British forces were allowed to remain in the Suez Canal zone until 1956.

Egypt has a young population with roughly 60 % of the population under the age of 30, and the country has faced many challenges since independence in improving education and literacy for its young population, as well as finding jobs for its citizens.

Facebook provided a platform for Egyptian youth to discuss issues such as unemployment, low wages, police brutality and corruption. Young Egyptians set up groups on Facebook to discuss specific issues (e.g. a group that aimed to provide solidarity with striking workers was set up). Further momentum for revolution followed the beating and killing of Khalid Mohammed Said, as photos of his disfigured body were posted over the Internet and went viral. An influential Facebook group called *We are All Khalid Said* was set up, and the killing provided a tangible focus for solidarity among young Egyptians.

The protests lasted for 18 days and it led to hundreds of thousands of young Egyptians taking to the streets and gathering in Tahrir Square in Cairo. They demanded an end to police brutality as well as the end of the 30 year reign of President Hosni Mubarak. The authorities reacted swiftly in closing down the Internet in Egypt, but this act of censorship failed to stop the protests against Mobarak, and social media played an important role in influencing the outcome of the revolution.

The protesters found other means of communication with the outside world, and especially with members of the Egyptian diaspora who were watching the news on Al Jazeera's news channel. The diaspora were active in communicating the latest developments to their friends and family in Egypt.

Chapter 17
Google

Google is an American multinational company which specialises in Internet-based services and products. Its products and services include *Google Search* which is the world's largest search engine, and which has transformed the notion of search. It offers many other products such as *Gmail* for email, a cloud storage service (*Google Drive*), an office suite (*Google Docs*), a social networking site (*Google+*), a video-sharing site (*Youtube*), a web mapping application (*Google Maps*) that offers satellite images and street views and the *Android* operating system software for mobile phones.

Google is the most widely visited web site in the world, and it is the most widely used web-based search engine. Most of the company's revenue is derived from online advertising from AdWords or AdSense. Google is one of the largest companies in the world with a market capitalisation of over $400 billion. It has annual revenues of approximately $60 billion and net income of approximately $13 billion. Its headquarters are at Mountain View in California.

The company was founded by Larry Page and Sergey Brin who were PhD students at Stanford University in the United States (Fig. 17.1). It started off initially as a research project involving Page and Brin at the university. Page was studying the abstract mathematical structure of the Web viewed as a vast graph, and he was interested in the problem of determining which web pages link to a given page, as well as determining the relative importance of individual web pages. Page and Brin developed the *PageRank algorithm* to rank the importance of a particular page, and they recognised that a search engine based on PageRank would give superior results to the existing techniques.

The domain *google.com* was registered in 1997, and Google was incorporated as a company in late 1998. The name *Google* was chosen as it is a common spelling of *googol* which refers to the number represented by 1 followed by a hundred zeroes (i.e. 10^{100}). The chosen name was appropriate for the search engine, as the company aspired to building a very large-scale engine that would be superior to any of its rivals.

© Springer International Publishing Switzerland 2015
G. O'Regan, *Pillars of Computing*, DOI 10.1007/978-3-319-21464-1_17

Fig. 17.1 Larry Page at
the European Parliament in
2009

Google had an index of 60 million pages in 1998, and today its index is over 30 trillion pages. The ranking procedure includes many factors such as the quality of the website, the age of the domain, the user location, prior searches and so on. The search results are then delivered to the computer, tablet or smartphone in a fraction of a second. The verb *to google* has entered the English language, and it means to perform a web search.

Google initially earned its revenue from keyword advertisements, and this involved associating a simple text advertisement with a search keyword. It launched its initial public offering (IPO) in August 2004, and the company was valued at $23 billion. Its stock market performance since then has been spectacular, and it has averaged a 30 % compounded annual return.

Google's *AdWords* is an online advertisement service that enables a business to be found by users who are searching for things that the company is offering. The advertisement appears alongside or above the search results, and it is a pay-per-click (PPC) service where the business is only charged if the user actually clicks on the link to visit the company's website. AdWords is Google's main source of revenue.

Google offers various products and services for the Internet apart from its core search engine. These include its popular Google Mail (*Gmail*) product which is the most widely used web-based email service. It provides free email to over 400 million users around the world. Google acquired Youtube in 2006, and this video-sharing site is used by millions around the world. Its Android operating system is a mobile operating system (OS) that is designed for touchscreen mobile devices and tablets. It is based on the Linux kernel, and it is the most widely used mobile operating system. It has also been used in other electronic devices such as game consoles, digital cameras and even personal computers.

It acquired Motorola Mobility in 2012 as a defensive move against patent litigation. Motorola Mobility had a large portfolio of intellectual property with thousands of patents in mobile telecommunications. This provided Google with the ability to defend itself in any patent litigation taken by its competitors in the mobile phone market. Google later sold Motorola Mobility (excluding its intellectual property) to Lenovo, a Chinese computer manufacturing company that manufactures and sells computers, tablets and mobile phones. For more detailed information about Google see [Lev:11].

17.1 Google Search Engine

The Google search engine is the most widely used search engine in the world with about a 66 % market share. It handles over 3 billion search requests per day (over 1.2 trillion per year). The order of the presentation of the search results is dependent on the importance of each web page, and this is determined by the Google PageRank algorithm which ranks each web page. Google's main competitors in the search engine market are Microsoft's Bing; Baidu, which is a popular Chinese search engine and Yahoo. Google's search engine allows the user to search for text in publicly accessible documents on web servers around the world.

The search engine takes the user's text and breaks it into a sequence of search terms which are usually words that are to appear in the results. The search engine also provides options for customised searches using Boolean operators and wildcards. Google has also launched its *Google Voice Search* that allows searching for a spoken rather than a written word.

The PageRank algorithm determines the order of presentation of the search results, and so webmasters will seek to influence and optimise their website ranking. Search engine optimisation is concerned with methodologies to improve a website's ranking and to draw more searchers to the particular website.

A Google search may leave traces on both the computer used to make the search and in records kept by Google. This has raised privacy concerns as such information may be obtained by a forensic examination of the computer or records obtained from Google or Internet service providers (ISP).

17.2 Gmail

Google Mail is the most widely use web-based email service with over 400 million users around the world. Google provides over 15 GB of free storage between Gmail, Google drive and Google+, and users can purchase additional storage as required up to a maximum of 300 TB. Gmail is available on personal computers as well as tablets and mobile devices. The Gmail interface supports over 50 languages.

Gmail includes a search bar for searching emails, and it also allows web searches to be performed. It automatically scans all incoming and outgoing mail for viruses in email attachments. It will prevent the message from being sent if a virus is found in an outgoing attachment, and it will attempt to remove a virus found in an incoming email attachment.

Gmail automatically scans the contents of emails to add context sensitive advertisements to them and to filter spam. This has raised privacy concerns as it means that all emails sent or received are scanned and read by some computer, and Google has stated in court filings that no *reasonable expectation exists among Gmail users with respect to the confidentiality of their emails*.

Further, Google argues that the automated scanning of emails is done for the benefits of the user, as it allows Google to provide customised search results, tailored advertisements and the prevention of spam and viruses.

17.3   Google Maps

Google Maps is a desktop and mobile web mapping service offered by Google, and it provides satellite imagery, street maps and street views. It also provides functionality for route planning, and up to four modes of transportation are supported (depending on the area). These include driving, cycling, walking and public transportation.

Google Maps provides high-resolution aerial views or satellite images of most urban areas of the world, and its Street View provides a 360 ° panoramic view of various locations. There is also an Underwater Street View which includes a 360 ° view of the 2,300 km Great Barrier Reef in Australia.

Google Maps for mobile is the most popular application for smartphones, with over 50 % of smartphone users typically using it at least once per month. The Google Maps application programming interface (API) allows developers to integrate Google Maps into their websites.

17.4   Google Docs

Google Docs, Sheets and Slides are a free web-based word processor, a spreadsheet program and a presentation program that are all offered by Google as part of its office suite on its Google Drive service. The software suite is compatible with Microsoft's Office, and it allows the user to create or edit documents online.

The documents may be saved to a user's local computer in a variety of formats (e.g. PDF and HTML). Google Docs is free for individuals but businesses are charged a monthly fee.

17.5   Google+

Goggle+ (or Google Plus) is a social networking site that has over 300 million active users. Circles are a key feature of the Google+ platform and it enables users to organise people into groups for sharing across Google products and services. A Google+ user can share specific private data to only that circle.

Hangouts enable free video conferencing calls to be made to other Google+ users, and users may also share documents or their screens inside the hangout. It also enables landline of mobile calls to be made if the user has credit to make the call.

17.6   Android

Android is a Linux-based operating system for mobile devices such as tablets and smartphones. It is the most widely used mobile operating system, and there are over 1 billion active Android users around the world. Although it has been primarily designed for touchscreen input, it has also been used for game consoles and digital cameras.

The Android software development kit includes a comprehensive set of development tools to develop applications (*apps*) to extend the functionality of the device. The Google Play Store has over a million Android apps, and there has been over 50 billion apps downloaded from the store.

Android has been released on an open source project under the Apache 2.0 licence. It is popular with technology companies as it provides a ready-made low-cost and customisable operating system for mobile devices. There is an active open source community that develops and distributes their own modified versions of the operating system.

17.7   Youtube

Youtube is a video-sharing website with headquarters in California. It was set up by three former Paypal employees in 2005, and the website was launched in late 2005. The site grew rapidly with thousands of videos being uploaded every day and hundreds of millions of video views per day. Today, billions of videos are viewed daily around the world and there are hundreds of millions of users. The videos may be viewed on a personal computer, smartphone or tablet. Youtube was acquired by Google for $1.6 billion in 2006.

The vast majority of the videos on Youtube are free to view, but it has launched a pilot programme that allows some content providers the facility to charge $0.99 per month to view certain channels.

Chapter 18
HP

Hewlett-Packard (HP) is an American computer corporation with headquarters at Palo Alto in California. It is one of the world's leading technology companies, and it is a major manufacturer of personal computers and printers. It provides hardware, software, consulting and services to businesses and consumers around the world. HP has been a highly innovative company since its foundation, and today it has annual revenues of over $110 billion and over 300,000 employees.

The company was founded by Bill Hewlett and Dave Packard (Fig. 18.1) in 1939. Hewlett and Packard knew each other from Stanford University, and they both graduated in 1934. Packard then took a position with General Electric in New York but returned to Stanford to earn a master's degree in engineering in 1938. Hewlett earned a Master of Science degree in electrical engineering at MIT in 1936, and he earned the degree of an electrical engineer from Stanford University in 1939.

They started their new two-person company with an initial investment of $538 in a Palo Alto garage (Fig. 18.2) on 367 Addison Street in 1938. The surrounding area was covered by fruit orchards, as Silicon Valley as known today did not exist. This 12 x 18-ft garage is now a historical landmark, and it has been officially declared the *birthplace of Silicon Valley*. HP purchased the property in 2000 to preserve it for future generations.

Dave Packard was the first CEO and chairman of the board and Bill Hewlett was its first president. Hewlett and Packard initially produced several prototype products including a medical device that they sold to a Palo Alto clinic. They produced a device to help astronomers to set a telescope properly, and this was used by the nearby Lick Observatory. Other inventions included a harmonica tuner and an electric eye for automatic toilet flushing.

Their goal was to create products that would make a difference to their customers, and their first real successful product was an audio oscillator (the HP200A) used by sound engineers. This was a device for testing and synchronising sound equipment, and this product line continued in use until the 1970s. Walt Disney Studios was one of HP's early customers, and they purchased eight model 200B

© Springer International Publishing Switzerland 2015
G. O'Regan, *Pillars of Computing*, DOI 10.1007/978-3-319-21464-1_18

Fig. 18.1 Bill Hewlett and Dave Packard (Courtesy of HP)

Fig. 18.2 HP Palo Alto garage. Birthplace of Silicon Valley (Courtesy of HP)

oscillators (a variant of the model 200A). This enabled Walt Disney to monitor its sound equipment and to prepare movie theatres for its new movie Fantasia which was released in 1940.

HP began to grow during the early 1940s with orders from the US government. It entered the microwave field during the Second World War, and it later became a leader in this technology. It invented the fast frequency counter (the 524A) in 1951, and this product reduced the time required to measure frequencies. It was a highly successful product line for the company. It invented its first oscilloscopes in 1956, and these became an important part of HP's test and measurement product line. HP became a public quoted company in 1957, and employees with over 6 months of service were granted stock in the company and became eligible for participation in the stock option programme.

It became involved in the printing business in 1958 following its acquisition of F.L. Moseley Co. It became a global company in 1959 when it set up a manufacturing plant in Germany and a marketing organisation in Switzerland.

It entered the medical device field through the acquisition of Sanborn Company in 1961, and this field became an important source of revenue for HP. It invented the HP atomic clock (HP 5060A) in 1964, and this set a new standard for international time. It introduced the cesium-beam atomic clock in 1967, and this clock coordinated international time to within a millionth of a second. This clock was used in time-critical applications.

It introduced its first spectrum analyser, the HP 8551, in 1964, and this product was indispensable on RF or microwave workbenches. HP's research laboratory (HP Labs) was established in 1966, and it became a leading commercial research centre that focused on exploring new ideas. HP's first computer, the HP 2116A, was introduced in 1966. It was designed as an instrument controller and allowed customers to computerise their instrument systems. Its first customer was an oceanographic centre, and it was used on board a research vessel for over 10 years.

It introduced the world's first programmable scientific desktop calculator, the HP 9100A (Fig. 18.3), in 1968. This was like a personal computer in that programs could be stored on a magnetic card, and science and engineering problems solved faster than many existing machines. It could handle trigonometric and logarithmic functions.

It introduced a laser interferometer in 1971 which was capable of taking infinitesimal measurements. It became a popular tool in microchip manufacturing. HP entered the business computing market in 1972 with the HP 3000.

Fig. 18.3 HP 9100A
(Courtesy of HP)

Fig. 18.4 HP-35 handheld
scientific calculator
(Courtesy of HP)

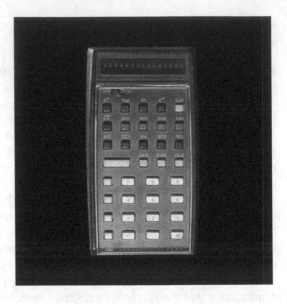

The company introduced the world's first handheld scientific calculator, the HP-35 (Fig. 18.4), in 1972, and this invention made the slide rule obsolete. The HP-35 contained both integrated circuits and LEDs (light-emitting diodes). More than 300,000 of the HP-35 calculators were sold.

HP introduced the first programmable handheld calculator, the HP-65, in 1974. This was the world's programmable pocket calculator, and it could fit inside a shirt pocket. Its computational power was greater than that of the large bulky early computers such as the ENIAC. It was the first programmable handheld calculator to be used in space as part of the 1975 Apollo Soyuz Test Project. HP introduced the HP-12C business calculator in 1982, and this became the world's standard financial calculator.

HP introduced its first personal computer, the HP 85, in 1980, and the machine had input and output modules that allowed it to control instruments. It introduced its first desktop mainframe, the HP 9000 technical computer in 1982, and this machine was as powerful as mainframes from the 1960s. It introduced a touchscreen personal computer in 1983, the HP-150, which allowed users to activate features by touching the screen. It introduced its first laptop, the HP 110, in 1984.

HP introduced thermal inkjet printing in 1984, and the HP LaserJet was introduced the same year. It became the world's most popular personal desktop laser printer, and HP introduced its first personal inkjet printer, the HP Deskjet, in 1988.

It created the Precision Architecture reduced instruction set computer (PA-RISC) architecture in 1986, which allowed computer instructions to be executed faster than existing chips. The PA-RISC architecture was first used on the HP 3000 Series, Model 930, and the HP 9000 Series, Model 840. This resulted in faster and less expensive computers. HP introduced its first generation of graphic workstations, the HP SRX, the same year.

It introduced its first x86 server in 1989. Its introduction in 1991 of the HP Deskjet 500C was a revolution in colour printing, and it led to major reductions in the cost of colour printing. It introduced the HP Office Jet personal printer–fax–copier in 1994.

It entered the home computer market in 1995 with the HP Pavilion PC. HP merged with Compaq in 2002 and the new company is known as HP. It has revenues of over $100 billion, employs over 300,000 people and has more than 1 billion customers in over 160 countries. It is a market leader in business infrastructure—including servers, storage, software, imaging and printing, personal computers and personal access devices. It is a leading consumer technology company offering a range of technology tools from digital cameras to PCs to handheld devices. HP acquired Electronic Data Systems Corporation (EDS) in 2006.

The rise of HP and insight into its business practices, culture and management style is described in a well-known book *The HP Way* by David Packard [Pac:95]. HP announced plans in late 2014 to split the PC and printer business from its enterprise products and services business. This will result in two publicly quoted companies: Hewlett-Packard Enterprise and HP, Inc., and this will be effective from late 2015.

18.1   HP Way

Hewlett and Packard created a management style for the company that became known as the HP way. This included a strong commitment by the company to its employees and a strong belief in the basic goodness of people and in their desire to do a good job. They believed that if employees are given the proper tools to do their job then they would do a good job. It was a core value that each employee had the right to be treated with respect and dignity. The HP way was highly effective, and its corporate culture was later copied by several technology companies.

The HP management technique is known as *management by walking around*, and this is characterised by the personal involvement of management. This includes good listening skills by the manager and the recognition that everyone in a company wants to do a good job. Hewlett and Packard regularly dropped by employee workspaces, to encourage dialogue and innovation.

The HP way involves management by objectives, i.e. senior managers communicate the overall objectives clearly to their employees. Employees are then given the flexibility to work towards those goals in ways that are best for their own area of responsibility. The HP Way was refined further in the late 1950s, and the company objectives included seven areas. These included profit, customers, growth, people, management and citizenship. The principles in the HP Way helped to distinguish HP from the top-down management style of most companies.

HP also established an open-door policy to create an atmosphere of trust and mutual understanding. The open-door policy encouraged employees to discuss problems with a manager without fear of reprisals or adverse consequences. HP addressed employees by their first name and provided good benefits such as free medical insurance and the provision of regular parties for employees. HP was the first company to introduce flexitime in the early 1970s. The concept was based on trust and it allowed employees to arrive early or late for work as long as they worked a standard number of hours. Flexitime was designed to enable employees have more time for family, leisure or personal matters.

Chapter 19
IBM

International Business Machines (IBM) is an American corporation with headquarters at Armonk, New York. This company is a household name and it has a long and distinguished history. It is has made important contributions to the computing field and in developing the computers that we are familiar with today. It is renowned for its excellence and innovation, with more patents granted annually than any other organisation. Its engineers and scientists have won major awards such as Nobel Prizes, Turing Award, National Medals of Technology and National Medals of Science. This remarkable company develops computer hardware and software for its customers around the world.

The origins of IBM go back to the processing of the 1880 census of the population of the United States. The processing of the 1880 census was done manually and it took 7 years to complete. It was predicted that the 1890 census would take in excess of 10 years to process, and the US Census Bureau recognised that its current methodology was no longer fit for purpose. It held a contest among its employees to find a more efficient approach to tabulate the census data, and the winner was Hermann Hollerith (Fig. 19.1) who was the son of a German immigrant.

His punched card tabulating machine (Fig. 19.2) used an electric current to sense holes in punched cards, and it kept a running total of the data. The new methodology enabled the results of the 1890 census to be available in 6 weeks, and the population was recorded to be over 62 million.

Hollerith founded the Tabulating Machine Company in Washington, D.C., in 1896, and this was the first electric tabulating machine company. It later merged with the International Time Recording Company to form the Computing Tabulating Recording Company (CTR) in 1911. The company focused on providing tailored tabulating solutions for its customers, and it changed its name to International Business Machines in 1924.

Thomas Watson Senior (Fig. 19.3) became president of CTR in 1914, and he transformed the company into an international company that sold punched card tabulating machines with operations in Europe and Australia. Its tabulating equipment allowed organisations and governments to process very large volumes of data.

© Springer International Publishing Switzerland 2015
G. O'Regan, *Pillars of Computing*, DOI 10.1007/978-3-319-21464-1_19

Fig. 19.1 Hermann
Hollerith (Courtesy of
IBM Archives)

Fig. 19.2 Hollerith's tabulator (1890) (Courtesy of IBM Archives)

It became a customer-focused and professional sales-driven company. Watson introduced the famous "THINK" signs that have been associated with IBM for many years.

Watson considered the motivation of the sales force to be an essential part of his job, and he introduced sales incentives to reward and motivate staff. The sales people were required to attend an IBM sing-along, with the verses in the songs were in

Fig. 19.3 Thomas
Watson, Sr (Courtesy of
IBM Archives)

praise of IBM and its founder Thomas Watson, Sr. The songs may seem a little strange today, but the purpose seems to have been to develop a loyal and motivated workforce that would provide excellent international service for the good of IBM and wider society.

These songs were published as a book *Songs of the IBM* in 1931 and included *Ever Onward, March on with IBM* and *Hail to the IBM*. Watson renamed CTR to International Business Machines (IBM) in 1924. It employed over three thousand people and had revenues of $11 million and a net income of $2 million. It had manufacturing plants in the United States and Europe. By 2013, IBM had revenues of over $99 billion and net income of $16 billion and it employed over four hundred thousand people.

IBM has successfully adapted its business to a changing world for over 100 years. Its early products were designed to process, store and retrieve information from tabulators and time-recording clocks. Today, the company is an industry leader that produces powerful computers and global networks and provides professional services to its customers around the world.

It developed the popular IBM punched card in the late 1920s which provided almost double the capacity of existing cards. The company introduced a mechanism by which staff could make improvement suggestions in the 1920s.

The great depression of the 1930s affected many Americans. Its impact on IBM was minimal, and IBM's policy was to take care of its employees. It was one of the first corporations to provide life insurance and paid vacations for its employees. Watson kept his workers busy during the depression by producing new machines even while demand was slack. IBM also won a major government contract to maintain employment records for over 26 million people.

Watson recognised the importance of research and development, and he created a division in the early 1930s to lead the engineering, research and development

Fig. 19.4 Harvard Mark 1 (IBM ASCC) (Photo Public Domain)

efforts for the entire IBM product line. IBM recognised the importance of education and the development of its employees to the success of its business. It launched an employee and customer magazine called *Think* in the 1930s, and this magazine included topics such as education and science.

IBM placed all of its plants at the disposal of the US government during the Second World War, and it expanded its product line to include military equipment. It commenced work on computers during the war years with the introduction of the Harvard Mark I (also known as the *IBM Automatic Sequence Controlled Calculator (ASCC)*). This machine was completed in 1944 and presented to Harvard University. It was essentially an electromechanical calculator that could perform large computations automatically.

The Harvard Mark I (Fig. 19.4) was designed by Howard Aiken of Harvard University to assist in the numerical computation of differential equations. It was funded and built by IBM, and it was 50-ft long and 8-ft high and weighed 5 tons. It performed additions in less than a second, multiplications in 6 s and division in about 12 s. It used electromechanical relays to perform the calculations.

The ASCC could execute long computations automatically. It used 500 miles of wiring and over 700,000 components. It was the industry's largest electromechanical calculator and had 60 sets of 24 switches for manual data entry. It could store 72 numbers, each 23 decimal digits long.

The announcement of the Harvard Mark 1 led to tension between Aiken and IBM, as Aiken announced himself as the sole inventor without acknowledging the important role played by IBM.

19.1 Early IBM Computers

IBM developed the Vacuum Tube Multiplier in 1943 which was an important move from electromechanical to electronic machines. It was one of the first complete machines to perform arithmetic electronically by substituting vacuum tubes for electric relays. The key advantages of the vacuum tubes was that they were faster, smaller and easier to replace than the electromechanical switches used in the Harvard Mark I. This allowed engineers to process information thousands of times faster.

IBM introduced its first large computer based on vacuum tubes in 1952. The machine was called the IBM 701, and it executed 17,000 instructions per second (Fig. 19.5). It was used mainly for government work and for business applications. Thomas Watson, Sr., retired in 1952 and his son, Thomas Watson, Jr., became chief executive officer the same year. IBM's revenue was $897 million and it employed over 72,000 people when Thomas Watson, Sr., died in 1956.

Thomas Watson, Jr. (Fig. 19.6), believed that the future of IBM was in computers rather than in tabulators. He recognised the future role that computers would play in business, and he realised that IBM needed to change to adapt to the computer technology. He played a key role in the transformation of IBM to a company that would become the world leader in the computer industry.

IBM introduced the IBM 650 (Magnetic Drum Calculator) in 1954. This was an intermediate-sized electronic computer designed to handle accounting and scientific computations. It was one of the first mass-produced computers, and it was used by

Fig. 19.5 IBM 701 (Courtesy of IBM Archives)

Fig. 19.6 Thomas
Watson, Jr (Courtesy of
IBM Archives)

universities and businesses from the 1950s to the early 1960s. It was a very successful product for IBM, with over 2000 machines built and sold between its product
launch in 1954 and its retirement in 1962. The machine included a central processing unit, a power unit and a card reader.

The IBM 704 data processing system was a large computer introduced in 1954.
It included core memory and floating-point arithmetic, and it was used for scientific
and commercial applications. It included high-speed memory which was faster and
much more reliable than the cathode-ray-tube memory storage mechanism used in
earlier machines. It also had a magnetic drum storage unit which could store parts
of the program and intermediate results.

The interaction with the system was either by magnetic tape or punched cards
entered through the card reader. The program instructions or data were initially
produced on punched cards. They were then either converted to magnetic tape or
read directly into the system, and the data processing was then performed. The output from the data processing was then sent to a line printer, magnetic tape or punched
cards. Multiplication and division was performed in 240 μs.

The designers of the IBM 704 included John Backus and Gene Amdahl. Backus
was one of the key designers of the FORTRAN programming language which was
introduced by IBM in 1957. This was the first scientific programming language, and
it is still popular with engineers and scientists. Gene Amdahl was discussed in Chap.
4, and he founded Amdahl Corporation in 1970 after his resignation from IBM, and
Amdahl Corporation later became a rival to IBM in the mainframe market.

The IBM 608 was the first IBM product to use transistor circuits instead of vacuum tubes. This transistorised calculator was introduced in late 1957, and it contained 3000 germanium transistors. It was similar to the operation of the older
vacuum tube IBM 604.

The IBM 7090 was one of the earliest commercial computers with transistor logic, and it was introduced in 1958. It was designed for large-scale scientific applications, and it was over thirteen times faster than the older vacuum tube IBM 701. It used 36-bit words, had an address space of 32,768 words and could perform 229,000 calculations per second. It was used by the US Air Force to provide an early warning system for missiles and also by NASA to control space flights. It cost approximately $3 million but it could be rented for over $60K per month.

IBM introduced the first computer disc storage system in 1957. This medium was called the Random Access Method of Accounting and Control (RAMAC), and it became the basic storage medium for transaction processing. The RAMAC's random access arm could retrieve data stored on any of the 50 spinning discs.

The IBM 1401 data processing system and the IBM 1403 printer were launched in 1959. The 1401 was an all-transistorised data processing system and it was aimed at small businesses. This computer replaced punched card-based tabulating equipment, and it included high-speed card punching and reading, magnetic tape input and output and high-speed printing. The 1403 printer was four times faster than any competitor printer.

IBM introduced a programme termed *Speak Up* to enhance staff communication in 1959. It opened its research division headquarters at Yorktown Heights, New York, in 1961.

19.2 IBM and SAGE

The Semi-Automated Ground Environment (SAGE) was an automated system for tracking and intercepting enemy aircraft in North America. It was used by the North American Aerospace Defence Command (NORAD) which is located in Colorado in the United States. The SAGE system was used from the late 1950s until the 1980s.

The interception of enemy aircraft was extremely difficult prior to the invention of radar during the Second World War. Its introduction allowed fighter aircraft to be scrambled just in time to meet the enemy threat. The radar stations were ground based, and they therefore needed to communicate with and send interception instructions to the fighter aircraft to deal with the hostile aircraft.

However, after the war the speed of aircraft increased considerably thereby reducing the time available to scramble fighter aircraft. This necessitated a more efficient and automatic way to transmit interception instructions, and there was a need for a new approach to solve this problem and to provide security for the United States. The SAGE system (Fig. 19.7) was designed to solve the problem, and it analysed the information that it received from the various radar stations around the country in real time, and it then automated the transmission of interception messages to fighter aircraft.

IBM and MIT played an important role in the design and development of SAGE. Some initial work on real-time computer systems had been done at Massachusetts Institute of Technology on a project for the US Navy. This project

Fig. 19.7 SAGE photo (Courtesy of Steve Jurvetson)

was concerned with building an aircraft flight simulator computer for training bombing crews, and it led to the development of the Whirlwind digital computer. This computer was originally intended to be an analog machine, but instead it became the Whirlwind digital computer, and it was used for experimental development of military combat information systems.

Whirlwind was the first real-time computer, and George Valley and Jay Forrester wrote a proposal to employ Whirlwind for air defence. This led to the Cape Cod system, which demonstrated the feasibility of an air defence system covering New England. Following its successful deployment in 1953, work on the design and development of SAGE (Fig. 19.8) commenced.

IBM was responsible for the design and manufacture of the AN/FSQ-7 vacuum tube computer used in SAGE. Its design was based on the Whirlwind II computer, which was intended to be the successor to Whirlwind. However, the Whirlwind II was never built, and the AN/FSQ-7 computer weighed 275 tons and included 500,000 lines of assembly code.

The AN/FSQ holds the current world record for the largest computer ever built. It employed 55,000 vacuum tubes, covered an area over 18,000 square feet and used about three megawatts of power.

There were 24 SAGE Direction Centres and three SAGE Combat Centres located in the United Sates. Each SAGE site included two computers for redundancy, and each centre was linked by long-distance telephone lines. Burroughs provided the communications equipment to enable the centres to communicate with one another, and this was one of the earliest computer networks.

Fig. 19.8 SAGE sector
control room (Photo Public
Domain)

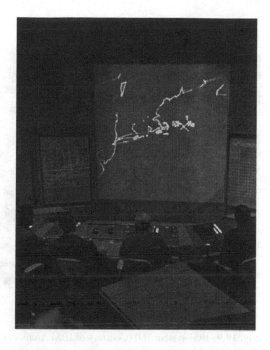

Each site was connected to multiple radar stations with tracking data transmitted by modem over a standard telephone wire. The SAGE computers then collected the tracking data for display on a cathode ray tube (CRT). The console operators at the centre could select any of the targets on the display to obtain information on the tracking data. This enabled aircraft to be tracked and identified, and the electronic information was presented to operators on a display device.

The engineering effort in the SAGE project was immense and the total cost is believed to have been several billion US dollars. It was a massive construction project which involved erecting buildings and building power lines and communication links between the various centres and radar stations.

SAGE influenced the design and development of the Federal Aviation Authority (FAA) automated air traffic control system.

19.3   The IBM System 360

Thomas Watson announced the new System 360 to the world at a press conference in 1964 and said:

> The System/360 represents a sharp departure from concepts of the past in designing and building computers. It is the product of an international effort in IBM's laboratories and plants and is the first time IBM has redesigned the basic internal architecture of its computers in a decade. The result will be more computer productivity at lower cost than ever before. This is the beginning of a new generation – not only of computers – but of their application in business, science and government.

Fig. 19.9   IBM system 360 (Courtesy of IBM Archives)

The IBM 360 (Fig. 19.9) was a family of small to large computers, and the concept of a *family of computers* was a paradigm shift away from the traditional *one size fits all* philosophy of the computer industry. The family ranged from minicomputers with 24 KB of memory to supercomputers for US missile defence systems. However, all of these computers had the same user instruction set, and the main difference was that the larger computers implemented the more complex machine instructions with hardware, whereas the smaller machines used microcode.

Its architecture potentially allowed customers to commence with a lower-cost computer model and to then upgrade over time to a larger system to meet their evolving needs. The fact that the same instruction set was employed meant that the time and expense of rewriting software was avoided. The System 360 was a very successful product line for IBM.

The S/360 was used extensively in the Apollo project to place man on the moon. The contribution by IBM computers and personnel were essential to the success of the mission.

19.4   The 1970s

IBM introduced the Customer Information Control System (CICS) in 1969. This transaction processing system was designed for online and batch processing. It was originally developed at IBM's Palo Alto laboratory, but development moved to IBM's laboratory at Hursley, England, from the mid-1970s.

It is used by banks and insurance companies in the financial sector for their core business functions. It can support several thousand transactions per second and up to 300 billion transactions flow through CICS every day. It is available on large mainframes and on several operating systems, including Z/OS, AIX, Windows and Linux. CICS applications have been written in COBOL, PL/1, C and Java.

The IBM System 370 was introduced in 1970. It was backward compatible with the older 360 system (i.e. programs that ran on the 360 could still run on the 370). This made it easier for customers to upgrade from their System 360 to the System 370. The S/370 employed virtual memory.[1]

The floppy disc was introduced in 1971, and it became the standard for storing personal computer data. The IBM 3340 Winchester disc drive was introduced in 1973. It doubled the information density on the disc surfaces, and it included a small light read/write head that was designed to ride on an air film that was 18×10^{-6}-in. thick. Winchester technology was employed up to the early 1990s.

IBM introduced the Systems Network Architecture (SNA) networking protocol in 1974, and this protocol provided a set of rules and procedures for communication between computers. It remained an important standard until the open architecture standards appeared in the 1990s.

It introduced the IBM 5100 portable computer in 1975 which cost under $20,000. This was a desktop machine used by engineers and scientists. IBM's Federal Systems Division built the flight computers and special hardware for the space-shuttle program.

IBM developed the Data Encryption Standard (DES) in the mid-1970s. DES provides a high degree of security during the transmission of data over communication channels. It specifies an algorithm that enciphers and deciphers a message, and the effect of enciphering a message is to make the message meaningless to unauthorised viewing. It is a major challenge to break the DES encryption algorithm.

19.5   The IBM Personal Computer Revolution

IBM introduced the IBM personal computer (PC) in 1981 as a machine to be used by small businesses and users in the home. The IBM goal at the time was to get quickly into the home computer market which was then dominated by Commodore, Atari and Apple.

IBM assembled a small team of 12 people led by Don Estridge (Fig. 19.10), and their objective was to get the personal computer to the market as quickly as possible. They designed and developed the IBM PC within 1 year, and as time to market was the key driver, they built the machine with *off-the-shelf* parts from a number of equipment manufacturers. The normal IBM approach to the design and development of a computer was to develop a full proprietary solution.

---

[1] Virtual memory was developed for the Atlas Computer at Manchester University in England in the early 1960s. It allowed the actual memory space of a computer to appear much larger by using the space available on the hard drive. The Atlas Computer was a joint venture between the Manchester University, Ferranti and Plessey.

Fig. 19.10 Don Estridge
(Courtesy of IBM
Archives)

The team had intended using the IBM 801 processor which was developed at the IBM Research Centre in Yorktown Heights. However, they decided instead to use the Intel 8088 microprocessor which was inferior to the IBM 801. They chose the PC/DOS operating system from Microsoft rather than developing their own operating system.

The unique IBM elements in the personal computer were limited to the system unit and keyboard. The team decided on an open architecture so that other manufacturers could produce and sell peripheral components and software without purchasing a licence. They published the *IBM PC Technical Reference Manual* which included the complete circuit schematics, the IBM ROM BIOS source code and other engineering and programming information.

The IBM PC (Fig. 19.11) was the cheapest IBM computer produced up to then, and it was priced at an affordable $1565. It offered 16 kilobytes of memory (expandable to 256 kilobytes), a floppy disc, a keyboard and a monitor. The IBM personal computer became an immediate success, and it became the industry standard.

The open architecture led to a new industry of *IBM-compatible* computers, which had all of the essential features of the IBM PC, except that they were cheaper. The terms of the licencing of PC/DOS operating system gave Microsoft the rights to the MS/DOS operating system on the IBM compatibles, and this led inexorably to the rise of the Microsoft Corporation. The IBM personal computer XT was introduced in 1983. This model had more memory, a dual-sided diskette drive and a high-performance fixed-disc drive. It was followed by the personal computer/AT introduced in 1984.

The development of the IBM PC meant that computers were now affordable to ordinary users, and this led to a huge consumer market for personal computers and software. It led to the development of business software such as spreadsheets and accountancy packages, banking packages, programmer developer tools such as compilers for various programming languages, specialised editors and computer games.

Fig. 19.11 IBM personal computer (Courtesy of IBM Archives)

The Apple Macintosh (see Chap. 5) was announced in a famous television commercial aired during the Super Bowl in 1984. It was quite different from the IBM PC in that it included a friendly and intuitive graphical user interface, and the machine was much easier to use than the standard IBM PC. The latter was a command-driven operating system that required its users to be familiar with the PC/DOS commands. The introduction of the user-friendly Mac GUI was an important milestone in the computing field.

However, the Apple Macintosh was more expensive than the IBM PC, and cost proved to be a decisive factor for consumers when purchasing a personal computer. The IBM PC and the various IBM-compatible computers remained dominant.

The introduction of the personal computer represented a paradigm shift in computing, and it led to a fundamental change in the way in which people worked. It placed computing power directly in the hands of millions of people. The previous paradigm was that an individual user had limited control over a computer, and the access privileges of the individual users were strictly controlled by the system administrators. The introduction of the client–server architecture led to the linking of the personal computers (clients) to larger computers (servers). These servers contained large amounts of data that could be shared with the individual client computers.

The IBM strategy in developing the IBM personal computer was deeply flawed, and it cost the company dearly. IBM had traditionally produced all of the components for its machines, but with its open architecture model, any manufacturer could now produce an IBM-compatible machine. IBM had outsourced the development of the microprocessor chip to Intel,[2] and Intel (see Chap. 20) later became the dominant player in the microprocessor industry. The development of the operating system, PC/DOS (PC disc operating system) was outsourced to a small company called Microsoft.[3] This proved to be a major mistake by IBM, as the terms of the deal with Microsoft (see Chap. 22) were favourable to the latter, and it allowed Microsoft to sell its own version of the operating system (i.e. MS/DOS) to other manufactures as the operating system for the many IBM compatibles. Intel and Microsoft would later become technology giants.

19.6   The 1980s and 1990s

The IBM token-ring local area network is essentially a computer network, in which all of the computers are arranged in a circle (or ring). It was introduced in 1985, and it enabled the users of personal computer to share printers, files and information within a building.

There is a special data frame termed a *token*, and it moves from a computer to the next computer until it arrives at a computer that needs to transmit data. This computer then converts the token frame into a data frame for transmission. That is, the computer that wishes to transmit catches the token, attaches a message to it and then sends it around the network. The token-ring network later became the IEEE 802.5 standard.

The Ethernet local area network was developed by Robert Metcalfe at Xerox PARC (see Chap. 35), and its performance was superior to the IBM token-ring network. Ethernet was first published as a standard in 1980, and it was later published as the IEEE 802.2 standard. Metcalfe formed the technology company 3Com to exploit the Ethernet technology.

IBM introduced the Advanced Peer-To-Peer Networking architecture (APPN) in 1984. This was widely used for communication by mid-range systems, and it allowed individual computers to talk to one another without the need for a central server.

John Cocke and others at IBM Research developed the reduced instruction set computer (RISC) architecture in the early 1980s. This technology boosts computer speed by using simplified machine instructions for frequently used functions. It reduces the time to execute commands and it was used on many workstations. This led to the design of the RS/6000 and the subsequent development of the PowerPC architecture. The RISC System 6000 was introduced in 1990. It is a family of workstations that were among the fastest and most powerful in the industry.

IBM introduced the next generation of personal computers termed the Personal System 2 (PS/2) in 1987. This personal computer used a new operating system

---

[2] Intel was founded by Bob Noyce and Gordon Moore in 1968.

[3] Microsoft was founded by Bill Gates and Paul Allen in 1975.

called Operating System 2 (OS/2), which gave the users access to multiple applications, very large programs and data, and it allowed concurrent communication with other systems. It was the first offering in IBM's Systems Application Architecture (SAA), which was designed to make application programs look and work in the same manner across different systems such as personal computers, midrange systems and larger systems.

A research group at IBM developed a suite of antivirus tools to protect personal computers from attacks from malicious software. This led to the establishment of the High-Integrity Computing Laboratory (HICL) at IBM, which went on to pioneer the science of computer viruses.

IBM researchers introduced very fast computer memory chips in 1988. These chips could retrieve a single bit of information in 2×10^{-8} of a second. IBM introduced the IBM Application System 400 (AS/400) in 1988. This was a new family of easy-to-use computers designed for small- and intermediate-sized companies. It became one of the world's most popular business computing systems.

A team of IBM researchers succeeded in storing a billion bits of information (i.e. a gigabit) on a single square inch of disc space in 1989. IBM introduced a laptop computer in 1991 to give customers computing capabilities on the road or in the air.

IBM, Apple and Motorola entered an agreement in 1991 to link Apple computers to IBM networks and to develop a new reduced instruction set microprocessors for personal computers. IBM and Motorola completed development and fabrication of the PowerPC 620 microprocessor in 1994. The new open-systems environment allowed both IBM AIX and Macintosh software programs to run on RISC-based systems from both companies.

IBM created the world's fastest and most powerful general-purpose computer in 1994. This was a massively parallel computer capable of performing 136 billion calculations per second. The increase in computational power of computers was becoming phenomenal.

The Deep Blue computer-programmed chess program defeated Garry Kasparov in 1997. Kasparov was then the existing world champion in chess, and the IBM victory showed that the computational power of computers could match or exceed that of a human. It was also the first time that a computer had defeated a top-ranked chess player in tournament play. Deep Blue had phenomenal calculating power, and it could calculate 200 million chess moves per second.

IBM and the US Energy Department introduced Blue Pacific which was the world's fastest computer in 1998. It was capable of performing 3.9 trillion[4] calculations per second, and it had over 2.6 trillion bytes of memory. An indication of its computability is given by the fact that the amount of calculations that this machine could perform in 1 s would take a person using a calculator over 63,000 years.

---

[4]We are using the US system with a trillion defined as 10^{12} and a billion defined as 10^9.

19.7 Challenges for IBM

IBM had traditionally provided a complete business solution to its clients with generally one key business executive making the decision to purchase the IBM computer system for the company. The personal computer market and the client–server architecture had now fragmented IBM's traditional market, as departments and individuals could now make their own purchasing decisions. The traditional customer relationship that IBM had with its clients was fundamentally altered. Further, IBM's decision to outsource the development of the microprocessor and the operating system for the IBM personal computer proved to be major blunders that cost the company dearly.

It took IBM some time to adjust to this changing world, and it incurred huge losses of over $8 billion in 1993. The company embarked on cost-cutting measures which involved reducing its workforce and rebuilding its product line. IBM's strength in providing integrated business solutions proved to be an asset in adapting to the brave new world.

IBM faced further challenges to adapt to the rise of the Internet and to network computing. The Internet was another dramatic shift in the computing industry, but IBM was better prepared this time after its painful adjustment in the client–server market. IBM's leadership helped to create the e-business revolution, and IBM actually coined the term *e-business*. IBM outlined to its customers and employees how the Internet had the ability to challenge older business models and that it would transform the nature of transactions between businesses and individuals.

IBM is a highly innovative company and is awarded more patents[5] in the United States than any other company. It earned over 3000 patents in 2004. The company is a household name and it has a long and distinguished history. The history of computing is, in many ways, closely related to the history of IBM, as the company has played a key role in the development of the computers that we are familiar with today. More detailed information on IBM is in [Pug:09].

---

[5] A patent is legal protection that is given to an inventor and allows the inventor to exploit the invention for a fixed period of time (typically 20 years).

Chapter 20
Intel

Intel is an American semiconductor giant with headquarters at Santa Clara in California. It is one of the largest semiconductor manufacturers in the world, with plants in the United States, Europe and Asia. It has played an important role in shaping the computing field with its invention of the microprocessor in 1971. It is the inventor of the x86 series of microprocessors that are used in most personal computers, and the company is renowned for its leadership in the microprocessor industry and for its excellence and innovation in microprocessor design and manufacturing.

The company was founded in 1968 by Robert Noyce and Gordon Moore as Integrated Electronics (Intel for short). Moore was a chemist who had worked at Shockley Semiconductor Laboratory. Shockley was one of the inventors of the transistor at Bell Labs, but he was not an easy person to work with. Following internal disagreements at the company, eight key employees (including Moore and Noyce) left to set up Fairchild Semiconductors. Noyce was one of the coinventors of integrated circuits while at Fairchild.[1]

Moore (Fig. 20.1) served initially as the executive vice president of the company. He was chief executive officer (CEO) of Intel from 1975 to 1987. He has made important contributions to the semiconductor field, and he is famous for his articulation of *Moore's law* in 1965. His initial formulation of the law predicted that the number of transistors that could be placed on a computer chip (i.e. the transistor density) would double every year. He revised his law in 1975 to state that the transistor density will double roughly every 2 years. His law has proved to be quite accurate, as the semiconductor industry has developed more and more powerful chips at lower costs.

The initial focus of Intel was on semiconductor memory products and to make semiconductor memory practical. Its goal was to create large-scale integrated (LSI) semiconductor memory. They introduced a number of products including the Intel 1103, which was a 1-kilobit (KB) dynamic random-access memory (DRAM) memory integrated circuit.

---

[1] Jack Kirby of Texas Instruments succeeded in building an integrated circuit made of germanium containing several transistors in 1958. Noyce built an integrated circuit on a single wafer of silicon in 1960.

© Springer International Publishing Switzerland 2015
G. O'Regan, *Pillars of Computing*, DOI 10.1007/978-3-319-21464-1_20

Fig. 20.1 Gordon Moore
(Courtesy of Steve
Jurvetson)

The company made a major impact on the computer industry with its introduction of the Intel 4004 microprocessor in 1971. This was the world's first microprocessor, and although it was initially developed as an enhancement to allow users to add more memory to their units, it soon became clear that the microprocessor had great potential for everything from calculators to cash registers and traffic lights.

20.1 Development of the Microprocessor

The invention of the microprocessor (initially called microcomputer) was a revolution in computing, and the world of computing was transformed with the power of a computer now available on a tiny microprocessor chip.

The microprocessor is essentially a computer on a chip, and its invention made handheld calculators and personal computers (PCs) possible. Intel's microprocessors are used on the majority of personal computers and laptops around the world.

Computers in the 1960s were expensive and bulky, and they filled an entire room. They were available only to a small number of individuals and government laboratories.

Noyce and others had shown how electronic circuits (ICs) could be miniaturised onto a silicon chip in the mid-1960s. However, large-scale integration of transistors onto silicon chips was still at the early stages.

The invention of the microprocessor happened by serendipity rather than actual design. Intel was requested by Busicom, a Japanese company, to design a set of integrated circuits for its new family of high-performance programmable calculators. At that time it was standard practice to custom design all logic chips for calculation or program execution for each customer's product. This clearly limited the applicability of a logic chip to a specialised domain.

The design proposed by Busicom required 12 integrated circuits. Tedd Hoff, an Intel engineer, studied Busicom's design and rejected it as unwieldy. He proposed a more elegant solution requiring just 4 integrated circuits, and his design included a chip that was a general-purpose logic device that derived its application instructions

Fig. 20.2 Intel 4004
microprocessor

from the semiconductor memory. His proposed design was accepted by Busicom, and it was then implemented by Intel engineers.

Hoff's 4004 microprocessor design included a central processing unit (CPU) on one chip. It contained 2300 transistors on a one-eighth- by one-sixth-inch chip surrounded by three ICs containing ROM, shift registers, input/output ports and RAM.

Busicom had exclusive rights to the design and components, but following discussion and negotiations, Busicom agreed to give up its exclusive rights to the chips. Intel shortly afterwards announced the availability of the first microprocessor, the Intel 4004 (Fig. 20.2).

This small microprocessor chip was launched in late 1971, and it could execute 60,000 operations per second. This tiny chip had an equivalent computing power as the large ENIAC computer which used 18,000 vacuum tubes and took up the space of an entire room [ORg:11].

The Intel 4004 sold for $200 and for the first time affordable computing power was available to designers of all types of products. The introduction of the microprocessor revolutionised everything from traffic lights to cash registers and to medical instruments and led to the development of home and personal computers.

20.2   Intel and the IBM PC

Intel has developed more and more powerful microprocessors since its introduction of the Intel 4004. It launched the 8-bit Intel 8080 microprocessor in 1974 and this was the first general-purpose microprocessor. It was sold for $360, i.e. a whole computer on one chip was sold for $360, while conventional computers sold for thousands of dollars. The Intel 8080 soon became the industry standard, and Intel became the industry leader in the 8-bit market.

The 16-bit Intel 8086 was introduced in 1978, but it soon faced competition from the 16/32-bit 68000 microprocessor, which was introduced by Motorola in 1979.

The Intel 8088 is an 8-bit variant of the 8086, and it was introduced in 1979. IBM considered several microprocessors for the IBM PC including the IBM 801 processor, the Motorola 68000 microprocessor and the Intel 8088 microprocessor. However, IBM chose the Intel 8088 chip for its personal computer, and it took a 20 % stake in Intel leading to strong ties between both companies.

Today Intel's microprocessors are used on a majority of personal computers around the world, and the award of the IBM contract to supply the Intel 8088 microprocessor was a major turning point for Intel. The company had been focused more on the sale of dynamic random-access memory chips, with sales of microprocessors in thousands or in tens of thousands. However, sales of microprocessors rocketed following the introduction of the IBM PC, and soon sales were in tens of millions of units.

The introduction of the IBM PC was a revolution in computing, and there are hundreds of millions of computers in use around the world today. It placed computing power in the hands of ordinary users, and today's personal computers are more powerful than the mainframes that were used to send man to the moon. The cost of computing processing power has fallen exponentially since the introduction of the first microprocessor, and Intel has played a key role in squeezing more and more transistors onto a chip leading to more and more powerful microprocessors and personal computers.

Intel is the dominant player in the microprocessor market, and it continues to innovate and introduce more and more powerful microprocessors.

20.3   Intel and Continuous Innovation

Intel has launched more and more powerful microprocessors since its introduction of the Intel 4004. It introduced the 16-bit 286 processor in 1982, and this had 134,000 transistors and it provided about three times the performance of other 16-bit processors.

It introduced the 32-bit Intel 386 which had 275,000 transistors in 1985, and this microprocessor could perform 5 million instructions per second (5 MIPS). It introduced the Intel 486 microprocessor in 1989, and this microprocessor was described by *Businessweek* as *a verifiable mainframe on a chip*. It had over a million transistors, and it had the first built-in math coprocessor.

It introduced the Pentium generation of microprocessor in 1993, and the Pentium processor used over three million transistors with speeds of 90 MIPS. The Pentium Pro was introduced in 1995, and this microprocessor had 5.5 million transistors and speeds of up to 300 MIPS. The Pentium II was introduced in 1997 and had 7.5 million transistors; the Pentium III was released in 1999 and the Pentium IV in 2000.

The manufacturing processes were initially quite primitive, but today Intel has sophisticated Fab plants around the world. The silicon transistors have shrank, and workers wear special suits with face masks, safety glasses, gloves and shoe coverings in a clean room environment that minimises contamination.

Intel dominates the microprocessor market and has a broad product line including motherboards, flash memory, switches, and routers. It has made a major contribution to the computing field. For more detailed information on Intel, see [Mal:14].

20.4 Moore's Law

Gordon Moore observed that over a period of time (from 1958 up to 1965) that the number of transistors on an integrated circuit doubled approximately every year. This led him to formulate what became known as *Moore's Law* in 1965 [Mor:65], which predicted that this trend would continue for at least another 10 years. He refined the law in 1975 and predicted that a doubling in transistor density would occur every 2 years for the following 10 years.

His prediction of *exponential growth* in transistor density has proved to be accurate over the last 50 years, and the capabilities of many digital electronic devices are linked to Moore's Law.

The exponential growth in the capability of processor speed, memory capacity and so on is all related to this law. It is likely that the growth in transistor density will slow to a doubling of density every 3 years by 2015.

The phenomenal growth in productivity is due to continuous innovation and improvement in manufacturing processes. It has led to more and more powerful microprocessors and computers running more and more sophisticated applications.

Chapter 21
LEO Computers Ltd.

Lyons Electronic Office (LEO) Computers was one of the earliest British computer companies when it was founded by J. Lyons and Co. in 1954. The company designed and manufactured the LEO I, LEO II and LEO III business computers, which were mainly used for business applications such as valuation, payroll and inventory. LEO later became part of English Electric LEO Marconi (EELM), and this company later became part of International Computers Ltd. (ICL) in 1968.

J. Lyons and Co. was a well-known British conglomerate that was founded in the late nineteenth century. It was one of the largest catering and food manufacturing companies in the world, and it owned and operated a chain of restaurants and hotels. It was also a major food manufacturer, and the company operated a chain of Lyons teashops which provided similar food and beverages at an identical price. The company gained a reputation for good quality at an affordable price, and it was also renowned for its good customer service and for its thorough investigation of any customer complaints.

The company diversified into other businesses such as operating hotels, laundries and tea estates, producing meat pies, ice cream, soft drinks and confectionary. Their contributions during the Second World War included preparing rations for allied troops around the world.

J. Lyons and Co. was an innovative and forward-thinking company, and it was committed to finding ways to continuously improve to serve its customers better. It sent two of its executives to the United States shortly after the Second World War to evaluate new methods to improve business processes. These two executives came across the early computers that had been developed in the United States, including the ENIAC computer that had been developed by John Mauchly and others. They recognised the potential of these early machines for business data processing.

They also became aware during their visit to the United States that Maurice Wilkes and others at Cambridge University in England were working on the design of a computer based on the ideas detailed in von Neumann's report. On their return to England, they visited Wilkes at Cambridge University, who was working on the design of the EDSAC computer (Fig. 21.1). They were impressed by his ideas and

© Springer International Publishing Switzerland 2015
G. O'Regan, *Pillars of Computing*, DOI 10.1007/978-3-319-21464-1_21

Fig. 21.1 EDSAC computer (Courtesy of the Computer Laboratory, University of Cambridge)

technical knowledge and the potential of the planned EDSAC computer. They prepared a report for Lyon's board recommending that a computer designed for data processing should be the next step in improving business processes and that Lyons should develop or acquire a computer to meet its business needs.

Lyons and Cambridge entered a collaboration arrangement where Lyons agreed to help fund the completion of EDSAC, and Cambridge agreed to help Lyons to develop their own computer which was called the Lyons Electronic Office or LEO Computer (Fig. 21.2). This machine was based on EDSAC but adapted to business data processing.

The Electronic Delay Storage Automatic Calculator (EDSAC) was completed and ran its first program in 1949, and the LEO I computer was completed and ran its first program in late 1951. Lyons developed several applications for the LEO computer, and soon the LEO computer was used to process business applications (e.g. payroll) for other companies. Lyons recognised that more and more companies would require computing power, and they saw a business opportunity. They decided to set up a subsidiary company to focus on computers for commercial applications.

Leo Computers Ltd. was set up in 1954 and it was based in London. It designed and developed a new computer, the LEO II, which was purchased by several British companies. The LEO III was released in 1961, and it was sold to customers in the United Kingdom and overseas.

LEO Computers Ltd. merged with English Electric in 1963 to become English Electric LEO. This later became English Electric LEO Marconi (EELM), and this

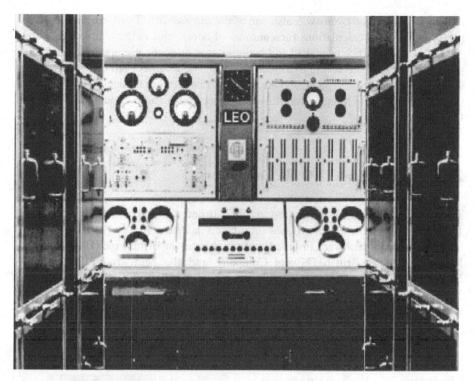

Fig. 21.2 LEO I computer (Courtesy of LEO Computer Society)

company became part of ICL in 1968. More detailed information on Lyons teashops and LEO is in [Fer:03].

21.1 LEO I Computer

The LEO I computer was one of the earliest business computers, and it was modelled on the Cambridge EDSAC computer designed by Wilkes and others. Lyons partially funded the development of EDSAC, and EDSAC ran its first program in 1949. Lyons set up a project team led by John Pinkerton to develop its own computer that would be suitable for business applications. Wilkes provided training for Lyon's engineers, and the LEO computer ran its first program in late 1951.

LEO's clock speed was 500 kHz with most instructions taking 1.5 milliseconds to complete. The machine was linked to fast paper tape readers and fast punched card readers and punches. It had 8.75 Kb of memory holding 2048 35-bit words.

The LEO I was initially used for valuation jobs but this was later extended to payroll, inventory and other applications. One of the early applications developed by Lyons was an early version of an integrated management information system to manage its business. Lyons was also one of the pioneers of IT outsourcing in that it performed payroll calculations for a number of companies in the United Kingdom.

The UK Met Office used the LEO I computer in an early attempt at using a computer for weather forecasting in the early 1950s. The weather prediction model was solved on the LEO I computer, and the first predictions were made in 1954. The Met Office later used the Manchester Mark I and more powerful computers for weather forecasting.

21.2   LEO II and LEO III Computers

The LEO II computer was released in 1957. It had 4.875 Kb of memory holding 1024 39-bit words. The LEO III was introduced in 1961.

LEO II computers were installed in many offices in Britain including the Ford Motor Company, British Oxygen Company and the Ministry of Pensions in Newcastle.

The LEO III (Fig. 21.3) was installed in Customs and Excise, Inland Revenue and the Post Office. It was also sold in Australia, South Africa and Czechoslovakia.

Fig. 21.3   LEO III computer (Courtesy of LEO Computer Society)

Chapter 22
Microsoft

Microsoft is an American corporation that is based in Redmond, Washington. It has dominated the personal computer operating system market since the 1980s,[1] and its best known products today are its Microsoft Windows suite of operating systems, its Microsoft Office suite of products and its Internet Explorer. It also produces hardware such as the Xbox game console, as well as tablets and mobile phones as a result of its acquisition of Nokia's mobile phone business.

Microsoft was founded by Bill Gates (Fig. 22.1) and Paul Allen in 1975, and its initial focus was on the development of BASIC interpreters for the Atari 8800 computer. Steve Ballmer joined the company in 1980, and Microsoft's first real success was with the Microsoft Disc Operating System (MS/DOS) for personal computers.

IBM had originally intended awarding the contract for the operating system to Digital Research (see Chap. 12) for a version of their CP/M operating system. However, negotiations between IBM and Digital Research failed in 1980, and IBM awarded the contract to Microsoft to produce a version of the CP/M operating system for its personal computers.

Microsoft purchased a CP/M clone called QDOS and enhanced it for the IBM personal computer. IBM renamed the new operating system to PC/DOS, and Microsoft created its own version called MS/DOS. The terms of the contract with IBM allowed Microsoft to have control of its own QDOS derivative. This proved to be a major mistake by IBM, as MS/DOS became popular in Europe, Japan and South America. The flood of PC clones on the market allowed Microsoft to gain major market share with effective marketing of its operating system to the various manufacturers of the cloned PCs. This led to Microsoft becoming a major player in the personal computer operating system market.

The company released its first version of Microsoft Word in 1983, and this would later become the world's most popular word-processing package. It released its first version of Microsoft Windows in 1985, and this product was a graphical extension

---

[1] Today, the Android operating system is the dominant operating system if all computer platforms such as tablets and mobile phones are considered.

© Springer International Publishing Switzerland 2015
G. O'Regan, *Pillars of Computing*, DOI 10.1007/978-3-319-21464-1_22

Fig. 22.1 Bill Gates
(Photo Public Domain)

of its MS/DOS operating system. Microsoft and IBM commenced work in 1985 on a new operating system called Operating System 2 (OS/2) for the IBM PS/2 personal computer.

The Microsoft Office suite of products was introduced in 1989, and these include Microsoft Word, Microsoft Excel and Microsoft PowerPoint. It introduced Windows 3.0, in 1990, and this operating system included a friendly graphical user interface.

Windows (and its successors) became the most popular and widely used GUI-driven operating systems. Microsoft's office suite gradually became the dominant office suite with a far greater market share than its competitors such as WordPerfect and Lotus 1-2-3.

Microsoft released its Windows 3.1 operating system and its Access database software in 1992. Windows 95 was released in 1995, Windows NT in 1996, Windows 2000 in 2000, Windows XP in 2001, Windows Vista in 2007, Windows 7 in 2009 and Windows 10 was released in late 2015.

22.1   Windows Operating System

Microsoft Windows is a family of graphical operating systems developed by Microsoft. The original Windows 1.0 operating environment was introduced in late 1985 as a graphical operating system shell for its command-driven MS/DOS operating system. It was Microsoft's initial response to Apple's GUI operating system.

The Apple Macintosh was released in 1984, and its MAC operating system was GUI based and a paradigm shift for the computer industry. It was friendly, intuitive and easy to use, and it was clear that the future of operating systems was in GUI-driven systems, rather than primitive command-driven operating systems such as MS/DOS.

Microsoft Windows dominates the personal computer market with over 90 % market share. However, Windows has not been as successful on mobile computing platforms such as mobile phones and tablets, where Google's Android operating system is the dominant platform.

The early versions of Windows were not complete operating systems as such and were instead graphical shells in that they ran on top of MS/DOS and extended the operating system. Windows 1.0 used MS/DOS for file system services, and it also included applications such as a calculator, calendar and clock. However, Windows differed from MS/DOS in that it allowed multiple graphical applications to be run at the same time, and this was done through cooperative multitasking.

Windows 2.0 was introduced in 1987 and it was more popular than its predecessor. It included improvements to the user interface and to memory management. Windows 3.0 improved the design of the operating system and used virtual memory and virtual device drivers that allowed arbitrary devices to be shared between multitasked DOS applications. It was introduced in 1990 and it was the first Windows operating system to achieve commercial success. It sold over 2 million copies in the first 6 months.

This was followed by Windows 3.1 in 1992 and Windows 95 in 1995. This was followed by Windows 98 in 1998 and Windows Millennium (ME) in 2000. Windows ME provided expanded multimedia capabilities including the Windows Media Player, and it was the last DOS-based version of Windows. Windows ME was criticised for its speed and instability.

Windows XP was introduced in 2001 and it was marketed into a "Home" edition for personal users and a "Professional" edition for business users. Windows Vista was released in 2006, Windows 7 in 2009, Windows 8 in 2012 and Windows 10 was released in 2015.

22.2   Internet Explorer

Microsoft Internet Explorer is a graphical web browser and it was first released in 1995. It was initially developed for the Windows 95 operating system and later for the Windows NT operating system. There was a small fee for Internet Explorer 1.0 and 2.0, but Internet Explorer 3.0 and all succeeding versions have been free of charge.

Netscape was the most popular browser in the mid-1990s with over 90 % of the market share, and Microsoft enhanced its Internet Explorer product to enable it to compete against Netscape. It bundled Internet Explorer 4.0 as part of its Windows operating system, and this led to what became known as the *Browser Wars* as described later in this chapter. The net result was that Internet Explorer became the dominant browser in the market, and a legal case was brought by the US Department of Justice against Microsoft alleging that it had abused its monopoly position.

Currently, Internet Explorer has approximately 60 % of the web browser market, and its current version is IE 11. It is the default web browser that comes with

Microsoft Windows, and it is likely to retain its strong market position as long as Windows remains a dominant operating system.

22.3   Microsoft Office

Microsoft Office is a suite of office applications for the Microsoft Windows operating system. It includes well-known programs such as Microsoft Word which is a word processor, Microsoft Excel which is a spreadsheet program, Microsoft PowerPoint which is used to create slideshows for presentations, Microsoft Access which is a database management system for Windows and Microsoft Outlook which is a personal information manager.

The first version of Microsoft Word was released in 1983 for the MS/DOS operating system. Wordstar was the leading word processor at the time, and it took some time for Microsoft Word to gain popularity. Word was designed to be used with a mouse, and it provided *what you see is what you get* (WYSIWYG). Microsoft continued to improve the product and it was ported to the MAC operating system in 1985. The first version for Windows was released in 1989.

The first version of Microsoft Excel for the IBM PC was released in 1987, and this spreadsheet program consists of a grid of cells in rows and columns that may be used for data manipulation and arithmetic operations. It includes functionality for statistical, engineering and financial applications. It has functionality to display lines, histograms and charts, as well as support for user defined macros.

PowerPoint was originally developed for the Macintosh computer by Forethought Inc., and its initial release was in 1987. Forethought was acquired by Microsoft for $14 million in 1987, and the first Windows version of PowerPoint was released in 1990.

A Microsoft PowerPoint presentation consists of a number of pages or slides. Each slide may contain text, graphics, audio, movies and so on. PowerPoint has made it easier to create presentations, and it contains many features to enable professional presentations to be made. For example, the user may customise slideshows to show the slides in a different order from the original order.

The first version of Microsoft Access was released in 1992, and this database management system enables users to create tables, queries, forms and reports. It includes a graphical user interface that allows users to build queries without knowledge of the query language.

22.4   Xbox

Xbox (Fig. 22.2) is a series of video game consoles and games developed by Microsoft. The original Xbox console was officially announced at the Game Developers Conference in early 2001, and the audience was impressed with the

Fig. 22.2 Xbox console with "Controller S"

console's technology. It was released to the general public in the United States in late 2001 and to Europe and Asia the following year.

The original Xbox competed mainly against Playstation 2, the Xbox live service was launched in 2002, and this service allowed multiple players to play games against each other online. It is available as both a free or as a subscription service.

The successor to the original Xbox is the Xbox 360, and this was released in 2005. Over 78 million of the Xbox 360 consoles have been sold around the world, and its main competitor is Sony Playstation 3.

The Xbox One is the successor to the Xbox 360, and it competes against Sony Playstation 4. It was released in 2013, and initially there was a controversy with respect to privacy issues. However, these were later resolved.

22.5 Skype

Skype is telecommunications application software that provides voice and video calls from computers, tablets and mobile devices over the Internet to other computers, mobile devices or telephones. The basic service is free and a user may make free Skype video or audio calls to another Skype user, but users require Skype credit or a Skype subscription to make calls to landlines or to mobile phones.

Skype Communications was founded in 2003, and the Skype software was developed in Estonia. The first version of Skype was released in 2003, and by 2005 Skype had a 3 % share of the international call market. Today, its share of the international call market has increased to around 40 %.

Skype was acquired by eBay in 2005 for over $2.5 billion, and Skype was acquired by Microsoft in 2011 for $8.5 billion. It is now a division of Microsoft.

22.6   Microsoft Mobile

Nokia is a Finnish multinational communications and information technology company that provides mobile telecommunications infrastructure to telecom companies around the world.

Nokia was a key player in mobile phone technology, and it played an important role in the development of the GSM standard. Global System Mobile (GSM) is the second generation of mobile technology, and Nokia became a leader in GSM and a leading provider of mobile phones in the mid-1990s.

It remained a leader in mobile phone technology up to the development of Apple's 3G smartphone in 2008. Nokia's smartphone phones were based on the Symbian operating system, and this technology had initially dominated the smartphone market with over a 60 % market share. The introduction of the Android operating system for mobile phones led to a further erosion of market share as well as further losses for Nokia. By 2010 Nokia's market share was down to 30 %.

Microsoft and Nokia announced an alliance in 2011, and they agreed that the Windows Phone operating system would be used instead of Symbian as the primary platform for future Nokia smartphones. This proved to be a strategic mistake, and it led to a collapse in Nokia smartphone sales, with Apple overtaking Nokia to become the largest smartphone maker in 2011.

Nokia began to experience financial difficulties from 2012, and Microsoft acquired Nokia's mobile phone business for over €5 billion in 2013. The new subsidiary is called Microsoft Mobile.

22.7   Microsoft Developer Tools

Microsoft has created a suite of developer tools and programming languages. These include the Visual SourceSafe tool which is a repository that allows code and documents to be placed under configuration management control. Documents or source code modules are checked out for editing, and once a file is checked out, other users are unable to make any modifications until the file is checked back into the repository by the editor. SourceSafe provides a full audit trail of the modifications made to a file, and it also allows files to be labelled as part of a release.

Microsoft Visual Studio is an integrated development environment (IDE) which is used to develop computer programs for Microsoft Windows and websites. It provides support for various programming languages such as C and C++. It also includes a code editor to enable a syntactically correct program to be written and a debugger which is a program that is used to test and debug other programs.

Codeview is a debugger which allows the source code corresponding to the currently debugged code to be viewed in a code window. It allows breakpoints to be set which allows program execution to be temporality halted at a certain position, and the relevant memory locations may then be examined.

Microsoft has developed several programming languages and compilers, and these include Microsoft BASIC, Visual Basic, Visual C++, C#, IronPython, JScript, VBScript, PHP and Axum.

22.8 Microsoft Windows and Apple GUI

Apple Computers took a copyright infringement lawsuit against Microsoft in 1988, with the goal of preventing Microsoft from using its GUI elements in Microsoft's Windows operating system. The legal arguments lasted for 5 years, and the final ruling in 1993 was in favour of Microsoft.

Apple had claimed that the look and feel of the Macintosh operating system was protected by copyright, and this included 189 GUI elements. However, the judge found that 179 of these had already been licenced to Microsoft (as part of the Windows 1.0 licencing agreement) and that most of the 10 other GUI elements were not copyrightable.

This legal case generated a lot of interest as some observers considered Apple to be the villain, as they were using legal means to dominate the GUI market and to restrict the use of an idea that was of benefit to the wider community. Others considered Microsoft to be the villain, with their theft of Apple's work, and their argument was that if Microsoft succeeded, a precedent would be set in allowing larger companies to steal the core concepts of any software developer's work.

The court's judgement seemed to invalidate the copyrighting of the *look and feel* of an application. However, the judgement was based more on contract law rather than copyright law, as Microsoft and Apple had previously entered into a contract with respect to licencing of Apple's icons on the Windows 1.0 operating system. Apple had not acquired a software patent to protect the intellectual idea of the look and feel of its Macintosh operating system, and it was actually Xerox PARC (see Chap. 35) rather than Apple that had first developed the graphical user interface (GUI).

22.9 The Browser Wars

Microsoft was initially slow to respond to the rise of the Internet. It developed Microsoft Network (MSN) to compete directly against America Online (AOL), and it developed some key Internet technologies such as ActiveX, VBScript and JScript.[2] It released a new version of Microsoft SQL Server with built-in support for Internet applications, and it released its first version of Internet Explorer (its Internet browser[3]) in 1995. Internet Explorer 4.0 was released as part of Window's operating system in 1997.

---

[2] Jscript is Microsoft's name for JavaScript which was developed by Netscape.
[3] A browser is a software package with a graphical user interface that allows a user to view the World Wide Web.

This was the beginning of Microsoft's dominance of the browser market. Netscape[4] had dominated the market but as Internet Explorer 4.0 (and its successors) was provided as a standard part of the Windows operating system (and also on Apple computers), this inevitably led to the replacement of Netscape by Internet Explorer.

Netscape launched a legal case against Microsoft alleging that Microsoft was engaged in anticompetitive practices by including its Internet Explorer browser in the Windows operating system and that Microsoft had violated an agreement signed in 1995. The leaking of internal Microsoft company memos caused a great deal of controversy in 1998, as these documents went into detail of the threat that open source software posed to Microsoft, and it hinted at possible legal action against Linux and other open source software.

The Federal Trade Commission and Department of Justice in the United States investigated Microsoft on various antitrust allegations in the early 1990s. The 1991–1994 investigations by the Federal Trade Commission ended with no lawsuits. The 1994 investigation by the Department of Justice ended in 1995 with a consent decree. The 1995 decree imposed restrictions on Microsoft and prohibited the bundling of certain products. The Department of Justice alleged in 1997 that Microsoft violated the 1995 agreement by bundling Internet Explorer with its Windows operating system and requiring manufacturers to distribute Internet Explorer with Windows 95.

The Court of Appeals rejected this violation of the consent decree in 1998 and stated that the 1995 consent decree did not apply to Windows 98 which was shipped with Internet Explorer bundled as part of the operating system. The Department of Justice then filed a major antitrust suit against Microsoft in 1998, and it argued that Microsoft's bundling of Internet Explorer was much more than adding functionality to its operating system and was a deliberate attempt to eliminate Netscape as a competitor in the browser market. It alleged that Microsoft added browser functionality to Windows and marginalised Netscape because Netscape posed a potential threat to the Windows operating system. It alleged that Microsoft feared that since Netscape could run on several operating systems and that this could erode the power of Windows, as applications could be written on top of Netscape.

In other words, the Department of Justice alleged that Microsoft gave away Internet Explorer and bundled it with its operating system to prevent Netscape from becoming a platform that would compete with Microsoft. That is, Microsoft's actions were a defensive move to protect its Windows monopoly. The legal action concluded in mid-2000, and the judgement called the company an *abusive monopoly*.

The judgement stated that the company should be split into two parts. However, this ruling was subsequently overturned on appeal.

---

[4]Netscape was founded by Jim Clark and Mark Andreesen in 1994. Jim Barksdale became the president and CEO of Netscape in 1995.

Chapter 23
Motorola

.

Paul Galvin and his brother Joseph set up the Galvin Manufacturing Corporation in 1928. The company initially had five employees and its first product was a battery eliminator, which is a device that allows battery-powered radios to run on standard household electric current. The company introduced one of the first commercially successful car radios (the Motorola 1 5T71) in 1930 which sold for between $110 and $130. Paul Galvin created the brand name *Motorola* in 1930. The origin of the name is from *Motor* to highlight the company's new car radio, and the suffix *ola* was in common use for audio equipment at the time.

Motorola became a global leader in wireless communications technologies, and it was internationally recognised for its innovation and excellence and its dedication to customer satisfaction. It has played a leading role in transforming the way in which people communicate, and the company was a leader rather than a follower in technology.

Motorola's products have evolved over the years in response to changing customers' needs. Many of its products were radio related, starting with a battery eliminator for radios, to the first walkie-talkies, and to cellular infrastructure equipment and mobile phones. The company was also strong in semiconductor technology,[1] including integrated circuits and the microprocessors used in computers such as the Apple Macintosh and Power Macintosh computers. Motorola had a diverse line of communication products, including satellite systems and digital cable boxes.

The company has played a leading role in transforming the way in which people communicate and especially in changing the paradigm of a phone from that of *a device that connects places to that of a device that connects people.*

The company was renowned for its dedication to quality and it developed the *Six Sigma*™ methodology in 1983. It was awarded the first Malcolm Baldrige National Quality Award by the US Department of Commerce in 1988 in recognition of this

---

[1] Motorola's semiconductor product sector was spun off to become a separate company (Freescale Semiconductor Inc.) in 2003, as Motorola decided to focus on its core activities following a major restructuring of the company.

© Springer International Publishing Switzerland 2015
G. O'Regan, *Pillars of Computing*, DOI 10.1007/978-3-319-21464-1_23

work. Six Sigma is a rigorous customer-focused, data-driven approach to improvement. Its objectives are to eliminate defects from products and processes and to improve the underlying processes to do things better, faster and at a lower cost. It may be applied to every step and activity of the process to improve results, and its core principles include:

- The company needs to be focused on customer satisfaction.
- Data must be gathered to provide visibility into process performance.
- Variation in process performance needs to be eliminated.

23.1 Early Years

The Galvin bothers founded the Galvin Manufacturing Corporation in 1928, and it introduced one of the first commercially successful car radios in 1930. It developed the Motorola Police Cruiser mobile receiver in 1936, which allowed vehicles to receive police broadcasts. Motorola's roots are in radio technology, and its core expertise in radio enabled it to become a leader in mobile phone communications in the mid-1980s.

The company entered the home radio business in 1937, and its products included phonographs (for playing recorded music) and home radios. It developed a lightweight two-way radio system in 1940, which was used for communication during the Second World War. It introduced its first commercial line of Motorola FM two-way radio systems and equipment in 1941.

The Galvin Manufacturing Corporation officially became Motorola, Inc., in 1947, and its well-known logo was introduced in 1955. It introduced its first television for the home entertainment business in 1947. This was the Golden View model VT71 and it was priced under $200.

Motorola set up a research laboratory in 1952 to take advantage of the potential of transistors and semiconductors, and by 1961 it was mass producing semiconductors at a low cost. It became one of the largest manufacturers of semiconductors in the world, and its first mass-produced semiconductor was a transistor intended for car radios. The company introduced a pager in 1956 that allowed radio messages to be sent to a particular individual. It introduced a transistorised walkie-talkie in 1962, and it developed a line of transistorised colour televisions from 1967.

Motorola's radio equipment was used by Neil Armstrong on the Apollo 11 lunar module. A Motorola FM radio receiver was used on NASA's lunar roving vehicle to provide a voice link between the Earth and the moon.

It introduced the 8-bit 6800 microprocessors in 1974 which contained over 4000 transistors, and the 16-bit version of the 68000 microprocessor was released in 1979. The latter was adopted by Apple for its Macintosh personal computers. It introduced the MC68020, the first true 32-bit microprocessor in 1984. This microprocessor contained 200,000 transistors on a three-eighths-inch square chip. Motorola became the main supplier for the microprocessors used in Apple Macintosh and Power Macintosh personal computers.

Motorola made a strategic decision in 1974 to sell off its radio and television manufacturing division. The television manufacturing division produced the Quasar product line. Quasar was sold as a separate brand from Motorola, and all Motorola manufactured televisions were sold as *Quasar*. The Quasar division was sold to Matsushita who were already well known for its Panasonic brand.

Motorola televisions were transistorised coloured models that contained all of the serviceable parts in a drawer beneath the television. However, they had quality problems. The new Japanese management succeeded in producing televisions with significantly higher quality than Motorola, and they had 5 % of the defects of Motorola manufactured televisions. Motorola's executives later visited the Quasar plant near Chicago and were amazed at the quality and performance improvements.

The Japanese had employed the principles of *total quality management* as proposed by Deming and Juran [ORg:14], and they had focused on *improvements to the process*. This had led to major improvements in quality and significant cost savings due to less time spent in reworking defective televisions.

The Japanese quality professionals had recognised that the cost of poor quality was considerable, and their strategy was to focus on the prevention of defects at their source. This led to a dramatic reduction in the number of defects and in the costs of their correction. The Motorola executives were amazed at the correlation between cost and quality, and this provided the motivation for the Six Sigma quality improvement programme in Motorola.

There were allegations that the acquisition by Matsushita of Quasar was a Japanese strategy to avoid paying tariffs on television sets imported into the United States. The "Quasar" brand was considered to be domestically made even though Quasar's engineering and manufacturing division was being scaled down. The Quasar televisions produced consisted of Japanese parts as the company moved away from engineering in the United States and focused on assembly and distribution.

23.2 Development of Mobile Phone Technology

The invention of the telephone by Graham Bell in the late nineteenth century was a revolution in human communication, as it allowed people in different geographic locations to communicate instantaneously rather than meeting face to face. However, the key restriction of the telephone was that the actual physical location of the person to be contacted was required prior to communication, as otherwise communication could not take place, i.e. *communication was between places rather than people*.

The origins of the mobile phone revolution dates back to work done on radio technology from the 1940s. Bell Labs had proposed the idea of a cellular communication system back in 1947, and it was eventually brought to fruition by researchers at Bell Labs and Motorola. Bell Labs constructed and operated a

Fig. 23.1 Martin Cooper
re-enacts DynaTAC call
(Courtesy of Rico Shen)

prototype cellular system in Chicago in the late 1970s and performed public trials
in 1979. Motorola commenced a second US cellular radiophone system test in the
Washington/Baltimore area. The first commercial systems commenced operation in
the United States in 1983.

The DynaTAC (Dynamic adoptive Total Area Coverage) used cellular radio
technology to link people and not places. Motorola was the first company to incor-
porate the technology into a portable device designed for use outside of an automobile, and it spent $100 million on the development of cellular technology. Martin
Cooper (Fig. 23.1) led the team at Motorola that developed the DynaTAC8000X,
and he made the first mobile phone call on a prototype DynaTAC phone to the head
of research at Bell Labs in April 1973. The DynaTAC today is a collectors' item as
most analog networks are now obsolete.

Commercial cellular services commenced in North America in 1983, and the
world's first commercial mobile phone went on sale the same year. This was the
Motorola DynaTAC 8000X, and it was popularly known as the *brick* due to its size
and shape. It weighed 28 oz (almost 2 lbs); it was 13.5″ (over a foot) in length and
3.5″ in width. It had a LED display and could store 30 numbers. It had a talk time of
30 min and 8 h of standby.

The cost of the Motorola DynaTAC 8000X was $3995, and it was too expensive
for most people apart from wealthy consumers. Today, mobile phones are ubiquitous, and there are more mobile phone users than fixed-line users. The cost of a
mobile phone today is typically less than $100, and a mobile phone typically weighs
as little as 3 oz.

Bell Laboratories developed the Advanced Mobile Phone System (AMPS) standard for analog cellular phone service (see Chap. 7). This first-generation mobile

phone system was introduced into North America in the early 1980s, and it used the 800 MHz cellular band. It had a frequency range between 800 and 900 MHz. Each service provider could use half of the 824–849 MHz range for receiving signals from cellular phones and half the 869–894 MHz range for transmitting to cellular phones. The bands were divided into 30 kHz sub-bands called channels and a separate frequency (or channel) was used for each conversation. The division of the spectrum into sub-band channels is achieved by using frequency division multiple access (FDMA).

AMPS allowed voice communication only, and it was susceptible to static and noise. Further, it had no protection from eavesdropping using a scanner. The second generation (2G) of mobile technology was a significant improvement on the older analog technology, and this digital technology encrypted telephone conversations and provided data services such as text and picture messages. The two main second-generation technologies were the Global System for Mobile communications (GSM) standard developed by the European Telecommunications Standards Institute (ETSI) and Code Division Multiple Access (CDMA) developed in the United States. The first GSM call was made by the Finnish prime minister in Finland in 1991, and the first short message service (SMS) or text message was sent in 1992.

The Subscriber Identity Module (SIM) card was a new feature in GSM, and a SIM card is a detachable smartcard that contains the user's subscription information and phone book. The SIM card may be used in other GSM phones, and this is useful when the user purchases a replacement phone. GSM provides an increased level of security, with communication between the subscriber and base station encrypted.

GSM networks evolved into GPRS (2.5 G) which became available in 2000. Third- and fourth-generation mobile UMTS (3G and 4G) provide mobile broadband multimedia communication. Mobile phone technology has transformed the earlier paradigm of *communication between places* to that of *communication between people*.

The signals from a transmitter cover an area called a cell. As a user moves from one cell into a new cell, a handover to the new cell takes place without any noticeable difference to the user. The signals in the adjacent cell are sent and received on different channels to the existing cell's signals, and so there is no interference.

Motorola dominated the analog mobile phone market. However, it was slow to adapt to the GSM standard, and it paid a heavy price with a loss of market share to Nokia and other competitors. The company was very slow to see the potential of a mobile phone as a fashion device,[2] and it was slow to adapt to smartphones.

Motorola played a key role in its design and development of the Iridium satellite system which was launched 1998. The Iridium constellation is the largest commercial satellite constellation in the world, and it provided global satellite voice and data coverage including the oceans, airways and polar regions.

Iridium routes phone calls through space and there are four earth stations. As satellites leave the area of an Earth base station, the routing tables change, and

---

[2] The attitude of Motorola at the time seemed to be similar to that of Henry Ford, i.e. they can have whatever colour they like as long as it is black.

frames are forwarded to the next satellite just coming into view of the Earth base station. The system is used by the US Department of Defence.

23.3 Six Sigma

Motorola defined the *Five-Year Tenfold Improvement Programme* as one of the top 10 goals of the company in 1981. This was a commitment by senior management to achieve significant quality and performance improvements to its products and services over the next 5 years. Motorola developed the Six Sigma programme as a tool to achieve the desired improvements.

The roots of Six Sigma are from the work of the nineteenth-century German mathematician, Carl Friedrich Gauss. He introduced the concept of the normal distribution curve, and this curve is important in probability theory. It is also known as the Gaussian distribution or bell curve.

The Bell curve (Fig. 23.2) has two parameters, and these are the mean (a measure of location or centre of the curve) and the standard deviation (a measure of variability from the mean). The mean is represented by the Greek letter μ (mu) and the standard deviation is represented by the Greek letter σ (sigma). The properties of the standard deviation with respect to the area beneath the curve are given in Table 23.1.

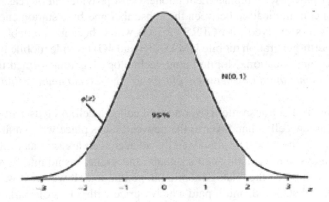

Fig. 23.2 Standard normal bell curve (Gaussian distribution)

Table 23.1 Properties of Sigma levels

σ level	Area of curve within Sigma level (%)
One Sigma	68.27
Two Sigma	95.45
Three Sigma	99.73
Four Sigma	99.993
Five Sigma	99.99994
Six Sigma	99.9999998

Table 23.2 Six Sigma methodology

Activity	Description
Define	Define the process
Measure	Measure the current performance of the process
Analyse	Analyse the process to identify waste
Improve	Improve the process
Control	Measure the improvements made to the process and repeat the cycle

Walter Shewhart was one of the grandfathers of quality, and he worked on quality improvements at Bell Labs in the 1920s. His approach to improving quality was to reduce process variation, and he demonstrated that Three Sigma (or standard deviations) from the mean is the point where a process requires correction.

The term *Six Sigma* was coined by a Motorola engineer named Bill Smith in the early 1980s, and it was used by Motorola both as a measure of process variability and as a methodology for performance and quality improvement. The application of the 6σ methodology in an organisation leads to a change of culture of the organisation.

Motorola engineers realised that the traditional quality levels of measuring defects in thousands of opportunities did not provide sufficient granularity for quality and performance improvements. The new Motorola standard allowed defects per million opportunities to be measured. Six Sigma was a major success for Motorola, and the company made major cost savings following its introduction in the mid-1980s.

The objective of the 6σ programme was to improve the quality and performance of all key operations in the business including manufacturing, service, marketing and support. The goal was to design and manufacture products that are 99.9997 % perfect, i.e. 3.4 defects per million opportunities. The fundamental philosophy of the methodology is that every area of the organisation can be improved. The steps involved in Six Sigma are summarised by the acronym DMAIC[3] in Table 23.2. This stands for *define, measure analyse, improve* and *control*. There is a step zero before you start and it is concerned with Six Sigma leadership.

The methodology is based upon improving processes by understanding and controlling variation. This leads to more predictable processes with enhanced capability and therefore more consistent results.

The participants on a Six Sigma programme have an associated belt (e.g. *green belt, black bet*, etc.) to indicate their experience and expertise with the methodology. A black belt has received extensive training on the Six Sigma methodology and on statistical techniques. Motorola was awarded the first Malcolm Baldrige National Quality Award in recognition of its development of 6σ and its commitment to quality and customer satisfaction.

---

[3] DMAIC was influenced by Deming's "plan, do, check, act" cycle.

The Malcolm Baldrige Award is a performance excellence award that was established by the US Congress in 1987. Its goal was to raise the profile of quality and excellence in the United States and to promote business excellence to enable American business achieve world-class quality and to compete successfully in a global market.

The use of Six Sigma is not a silver bullet to success, as the company also needs to be pursuing the appropriate business strategies. Motorola paid the price for totally misjudging the transition from the analog cellular market to digital cellular, despite its commitment to quality and customer satisfaction.

23.4   Semiconductor Sector

Bell Labs invented the transistor in 1947 and it developed an all-transistor computer in 1954. Motorola set up a research lab in 1952 to take advantage of the potential of semiconductors, and by 1961 it was mass producing semiconductors at a low cost. It introduced a transistorised walkie-talkie in 1962 as well as transistors for its Quasar televisions.

Motorola entered the microprocessor market later than Intel, but, nevertheless, its microprocessors have played an important role in the computing field. These included the influential 68000 and PowerPC architecture, which were used in the Apple Macintosh and Power Macintosh personal computers. The PowerPC chip was developed in a partnership with IBM and Apple.

Motorola introduced its first microprocessor, the 8-bit 6800 microprocessors (Fig. 23.3) in 1974, and this microprocessor was used in automotive, computing and video games. It contained over 4000 transistors. It competed against the Intel 8080 microprocessor, and it was used in some early home computer kits.

It introduced its well-known 68000 16-bit microprocessor in 1979, and this was a hybrid 16/32-bit microprocessor that had 16-bit data buses but could perform 32-bit calculations internally. This microprocessor was considered by IBM for use in its personal computer, but IBM chose the Intel 8088 microprocessor. Motorola introduced its 68020, the first true 32-bit microprocessor in 1984. This microprocessor contained 200,000 transistors on a three-eighths-inch square chip, and the

Fig. 23.3 Motorola 6800

Motorola 68000 family was used on the Apple Macintosh, Sun 3 workstations and Atari computers.

Motorola, IBM and Apple entered a partnership and created the PowerPC microprocessor with a reduced instruction set for use on personal computers. The PowerPC was used on Macintosh computers from 1994 to 2006. Today the PowerPC architecture is used mainly in processors for embedded applications.

Motorola went through a painful adjustment in the late 1990s and decided to focus on its core business of mobile communications. Its semiconductor business was spun off to become a separate company called Freescale Semiconductor Inc. in 2004.

23.5   Motorola and Iridium

Iridium was a global satellite phone company that was backed by Motorola. In many ways it was an engineering triumph over common sense, and over $5 billion was spent in building an infrastructure of low Earth orbit (LEO) satellites to provide universal coverage. It was launched in late 1998 to provide global wireless coverage to its customers, and the coverage included the oceans, airways and polar regions. The existing telecom systems had limited coverage in remote areas, and so the concept of global coverage as provided by Iridium was potentially very useful.

Iridium was implemented by a constellation of 66 satellites (Fig. 23.4). Its original design required 77 satellites, and so the name *Iridium* was chosen since its atomic number in the periodic table is 77. However, the later design required just 66 satellites, and so *Dysprosium* would have been a more appropriate choice of its name. The satellites are in low Earth orbit at a height of approximately 485 miles,

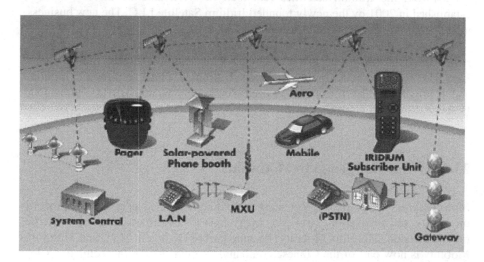

Fig. 23.4 Iridium system (Courtesy of Iridium)

and communication between the satellites is via inter-satellite links. Each satellite contains seven Motorola PowerPC 603E processors running at 200 MHz. These machines are used for satellite communication and control.

Iridium routes phone calls through space and there are several earth stations. As satellites leave the area of an Earth base station, the routing tables change, and frames are forwarded to the next satellite just coming into view of the Earth base station.

The Iridium constellation is the largest commercial satellite constellation in the world, and it is especially suited for industries such as maritime, aviation, government and the military. Motorola was the prime contractor for Iridium, and it played a key role in its design and development. The satellites were produced at a cost of $5 million each ($40 million each including launch costs), and Motorola engineers were able to make a satellite in a phenomenal time of 2–3 weeks.

The first Iridium call was made by Al Gore. However, despite being an engineering triumph, Iridium was a commercial failure, and it went bankrupt in late 1999 due to insufficient demand for its services. It had needed a million subscribers to break even, and as the cost of an Iridium call was very expensive compared to the existing cellular providers, and as the cost of its handsets were much higher and more cumbersome to use than existing mobile phones, there was very little demand for its services. Specifically, the reasons for failure included:

- Insufficient demand for its services (10,000 subscribers)
- High cost of its service ($5 per minute for a call)
- Cost of its mobile handsets ($3000 per handset)
- Bulky mobile handsets
- Competition from existing mobile phone networks
- Management failures

However, the Iridium satellites remained in orbit, and the service was re-established in 2001 by the newly founded Iridium Satellite LLC. The new business model required just 60,000 subscribers to break even.

Iridium was designed in the late 1980s and so it is designed primarily for voice rather than data. This means that it lacks the sophistication of modern mobile phone networks, and it is not as attractive to users. Iridium was later sold for $25 million, and it remains in use today and is used extensively by the US Department of Defence.

23.6 What Happened to Motorola?

Motorola was one of America's greatest companies and it had an outstanding record on quality and innovation. However, today it is a shadow of its former self. Its mobile division (Motorola Mobility) became part of Google in 2011, and Motorola Mobility is now part of the Chinese company, Lenovo. Motorola's semiconductor sector was spun off to become Freescale Semiconductor Inc. in 2004.

Motorola made many mistakes in the cellular area, where it had been the leader of the first-generation analog technologies. By 1994 over 60 % of the mobile phones sold in the United States were made by Motorola, and Motorola had revenues of $22 billion and profits of $2 billion. It was by then the 23rd largest American company.

However, it made major mistakes in the transition to digital technology. It was reasonably fast to support the evolution to digital networks, but it was very slow in producing digital handsets and it paid a heavy price for this. Nokia soon became the largest mobile phone company in the world. Motorola introduced major cost savings from the late 1990s, and it reduced the number of its employees from over 150,000 to 100,000. It introduced a new mobile phone, the Raze, which was a major success for the company.

Motorola made a fatal error in working with Apple in creating a Motorola *i*Tunes phone called the "Rokr" in 2005. Apple learned very quickly how to make mobile phones, and it introduced the *i*Phone in 2007. Motorola phones were way behind and margins fell in a major way. Motorola didn't have a smartphone until late 2009. It entered a partnership with Google and created the first Android phone, the *Droid*. This was initially quite successful but soon other mobile phone companies (e.g. Samsung) were offering Android phones, and Motorola began to fall behind making major financial losses again.

Google bought Motorola Mobility in 2011 for $12.5 billion for two key reasons. First, it allowed Google to move into the mobile phone hardware area and secondly (and more important) it gave Google ownership of Motorola Mobility valuable portfolio of approximately 17,000 patents. This protected Google from patent lawsuits from other players in the telecom field. Google later sold Motorola Mobility (excluding the patents) to Lenovo.

Today, Motorola is a shadow of its former self and is now called "Motorola Solutions". It dominates the market in the United States for emergency communication equipment. For more historical information on Motorola, see [Mot:99].

Chapter 24
Netscape Communications

Marc Andreessen and Jim (James) Clark founded Mosaic Communications (later called Netscape Communications) in April 1994. James Barksdale was the president and CEO of the company from 1995 until the company merged with AOL in 1998. Netscape's headquarters was at Mountain View in California.

Netscape's significance to the computer industry is that it developed the Netscape Navigator web browser, which dominated the web browser market in the mid-1990s. The decline in the usage of Netscape from over a 90 % market share in the mid-1990s to less than 1 % of the market share in 2006 was due to the browser wars with Microsoft's Internet Explorer. The browser wars are discussed later in the chapter.

Netscape also developed important Internet technologies such as secure sockets layer technology (SSL) used for secure payments and the Javascript scripting language for web pages. SSL is a protocol for transferring private information over the Internet, and it creates a secure connection between a client and a server. It uses public and private keys to encrypt and decrypt messages, and SSL is supported by both Netscape Navigator and Internet Explorer.

Andreessen (Fig. 24.1) was a graduate of the University of Illinois and had spent time at the university working at the National Centre for Supercomputing Applications (NCSA). He worked on the Mosaic browser at the NCSA, and he recognised its commercial potential.

Clark (Fig. 24.2) was the founder of Silicon Graphics, Inc. (SGI), a company that specialised in high-performance computing. Many of the new employees of Mosaic Communications were previously employed by NCSA or SGI. There were legal issues with the name "Mosaic" in light of the existing NCSA Mosaic browser, and the company was renamed to Netscape Communications in late 1994.

Netscape Navigator 1.0 was launched in December 1994, and at that time there was no real competition in the browser market. Microsoft was slow to recognise the importance and commercial potential of the web, and it was slow in developing its own web browser. Netscape Navigator was the most advanced browser available,

© Springer International Publishing Switzerland 2015   159
G. O'Regan, *Pillars of Computing*, DOI 10.1007/978-3-319-21464-1_24

Fig. 24.1 Marc Andreessen
at the Tech Crunch40
conference in 2007

Fig. 24.2 Jim Clark

and so it became an immediate success. By early 1995, the Netscape browser was
the dominant player in the browser market, and it was the standard portal for entry
to the web.

Netscape 2.0 was released in 1995, and it transformed Netscape Navigator from
a web browser into an Internet suite. It included new features such as an email
reader called *Netscape Mail* which allowed HTML email to be displayed. Netscape
renamed its Internet suite to *Netscape Communicator* in a later release, and this
consisted of Netscape Mail, newsgroups, an address book and Netscape Composer.

Netscape went public in 1995, and its successful initial public offering valued the
company at over $3 billion. By the late 1990s, the Netscape browser was available
on a wide range of operating systems, including Windows, Mac OS and Linux. It
had a similar appearance and it worked almost identically on each of these platforms, and it provided a standard point of entry to the web.

Microsoft recognised the threat that Netscape posed to its business, and it set out to create its own browser. It licenced the Mosaic browser source code, and it created its first version of Internet Explorer 1.0. This browser was released as an add-on pack to Windows 95. Netscape and Microsoft enhanced their browsers throughout 1995 and 1996, and by the time Internet Explorer 3.0 was released in 1996, both browsers had similar capability.

Microsoft began to bundle Internet Explorer with its Windows operating system from 1997, and Internet Explorer rapidly became the most widely used browser. Netscape took a legal case against Microsoft alleging that it was engaging in anti-competitive practices by giving away Internet Explorer with its operating system. The Department of Justice in the United States later filed a lawsuit against Microsoft alleging that Microsoft gave Internet Explorer away free of charge to prevent Netscape becoming a platform that would compete with Microsoft.

Netscape created the Mozilla project in 1998 with the objective of making the source code of the Netscape Communicator product freely available. The Mozilla Organization was founded to coordinate the future development of the browser product. Mozilla was the original name of the Netscape Navigator, and the Mozilla project initially aimed to create a community that would provide open source software for technology companies. The idea was that the open source software created would then be commercialised by companies such as Netscape. The Mozilla Foundation was set up in 2004, and it is responsible for the development of the Firefox browser.

AOL took over Netscape in 1998 for $4.2 billion, but its acquisition did not lead to any major developments of the Netscape browser. This proved to be a major error, as Netscape began to fall behind Internet Explorer, and this led to further falls in its market share. Netscape 6 was developed on the Mozilla open source code, and it was released in 2000. Netscape 7 was released in 2002.

AOL shut its Netscape department in 2003, and it continued development in-house using Mozilla's Firefox as its code base. The final released version of Netscape was Netscape 9, and AOL ceased development of Netscape Navigator in February 2008. Today, the Netscape browser is no longer supported, but the Mozilla Organization continues to develop the Firefox browser. Today, the browser market is shared between Firefox, Internet Explorer and Google Chrome, with Internet Explorer having close to a 60 % market share. Google Chrome is gaining rapid market share in the tablet and mobile devices market.

24.1 The Browser Wars

Microsoft was initially slow to respond to the rise of the Internet, but it soon recognised the threat that Netscape posed, and it began work on its own web browser. It created its first version of Internet Explorer in 1995. Windows 95 was released later that year, and there was a separate add-on pack to Windows 95 that included Internet Explorer and TCP/IP. It released Internet Explorer 4.0 in 1997, and IE 4.0 was released as part of Window's operating system.

This was the beginning of Microsoft's dominance of the browser market. Netscape had dominated the market up to then but as Internet Explorer 4.0 (and its successors) was provided as a standard part of the Windows operating system (and also on Apple computers), this inevitably led to the replacement of Netscape by Internet Explorer.

Netscape launched a legal case against Microsoft alleging that Microsoft was engaged in anticompetitive practices by including the Internet Explorer browser in the Windows operating system and that Microsoft had violated an agreement signed in 1995.

The Federal Trade Commission and Department of Justice in the United States investigated Microsoft on various antitrust allegations in the early 1990s. The 1991–1994 investigations by the Federal Trade Commission ended with no lawsuits. The 1994 investigation by the Department of Justice ended in 1995 with a consent decree. The 1995 decree imposed restrictions on Microsoft and prohibited bundling of certain products. The Department of Justice alleged in 1997 that Microsoft violated the 1995 agreement by bundling Internet Explorer with its Windows operating system and requiring manufacturers to distribute Internet Explorer with Windows 95.

The Court of Appeals rejected this violation of the consent decree in 1998 and stated that the 1995 consent decree did not apply to Windows 98 which was shipped with an integrated Internet Explorer as part of the operating system. The Department of Justice then filed a major antitrust suit against Microsoft in 1998 and argued that Microsoft's bundling of Internet Explorer and its attempts to eliminate Netscape as a competitor in the browser market was much more than adding new functionality to its operating system.

It alleged that Microsoft added browser functionality to Windows and marginalised Netscape because Netscape posed a potential threat to the Windows operating system. It alleged that Microsoft feared that since Netscape could run on several operating systems, this could erode the power of Windows as applications could be written on top of Netscape.

In other words, the Department of Justice alleged that Microsoft gave away Internet Explorer and bundled it with its operating system to prevent Netscape becoming a platform that would complete with Microsoft. That is, Microsoft's actions were a defensive move to protect its Windows monopoly. The legal action concluded in mid-2000, and the judgement called the company an *abusive monopoly*.

The judgement stated that the company should be split into two parts. However, this ruling was subsequently overturned on appeal.

Chapter 25
Oracle Corporation

Oracle is an American multinational corporation with headquarters in Redwood City, California. It is one of the largest software companies in the world with annual revenue of approximately $37 billion and over 120,000 employees around the world. It is recognised as a world leader in relational database technology, and its software products have changed the face of business computing. Oracle is also involved in the enterprise application market including enterprise resource planning (ERP), customer relationship management (CRM), and supply chain management (SCM).

The company was founded by Larry Ellison, Bob Miner and Ed Oates as Software Development Laboratories in 1977. Ellison (Fig. 25.1) became the chief executive of the company, and he was responsible for sales and marketing, while Miner was responsible for software development.

The company was renamed to Relational Software Inc. in 1979, and it was renamed to *Oracle Systems* in 1982. Oracle became a major success and by the mid-1980s it was the leading provider of relational database management systems (RDBMS). It became a public company in 1986.

IBM dominated the mainframe database market in the late 1970s with products such as DB2 and SQL/DS. However, it delayed entry into the market for relational databases on UNIX and Windows operating systems, and this allowed companies such as Sybase, Oracle and Informix to target this market segment and to become the dominant players in these markets.

Microsoft bought the Sybase SQL Server code base in 1993, and its existing Microsoft Windows database product became known as SQL Server. This product was to become a major competitor to Oracle from the late 1990s. IBM took over Informix in 2001 to complement its DB2 product database product. IBM and Microsoft are major competitors for Oracle on the UNIX, Linux and Microsoft Windows operating systems.

Ellison was familiar with IBM's early work on databases, and the concept of a relational database was described in a paper *A Relational Model of Data for Large Shared Data Banks* by Edgar Codd [Cod:70]. Codd was born in England and he

Fig. 25.1 Larry Ellison
on stage

worked for IBM in the United States. A *relational database* is a database that
conforms to the relational model, and it may be defined as a set of relations (or
tables). Ellison and the other founders realised that relational database technology
had not been commercialised by any company, and they recognised that there was a
major business opportunity to fundamentally change business computing.

The launch of the Oracle database marked a fundamental change in business
computing. The database product was called Oracle in memory of a CIA-funded
project that they had previously worked on. Oracle Version 1 was released in 1978,
and it was written in an assembly language and ran on a PDP computer.

The release of Oracle Version 2 in 1979 was a major milestone in the history of
computing, as it was the world's first commercial SQL relational database management system. Oracle was among the first to offer a portable database management
system (DBMS) that would run on different hardware and operating systems.

Oracle Version 3 was introduced in 1983 and it was highly portable. It was written in the C programming language, and it ran on several operating systems and
hardware platforms. These included mainframes, minicomputers and personal computers. It led to a massive increase in the market share for Oracle's DBMS. Version
5 of Oracle was released in 1985 and it was one of the first relational database
management systems to operate in the client server architecture.

Oracle 7 was a major success for the company on its release in 1992, and it demonstrated the superiority of the Oracle DBMS over competitor offerings. It included
many new performance features, administrative enhancements, tools for application
development and security methods that extended the database directly into the lines
of business. It included technical capabilities such as stored procedures.[1] Oracle was
now the leader of the RDBMS market.

Oracle 8i was released in 1997, and it provided support for the Internet with a
built-in Java Virtual Machine (JVM). Oracle 9i was released in 2001 and provided
support for the Extensible Markup Language (XML). Oracle 10g was introduced in

---

[1] A stored procedure is executable code that is associated with the database. It is usually written in
an imperative programming language, and it is used to perform common operations on the
database.

2003 and provided support for grid computing with features such as resource changing and automatic load balancing. Grid computing allows clusters of low-cost servers to be treated as a single unit. Oracle 10g includes a DBMS and an application server. Oracle 11g was released in 2007.

Oracle is also involved in enterprise application market, and it acquired companies such as PeopleSoft and Siebel Systems in 2005. This had led to it becoming a competitor to SAP in the enterprise resource planning (ERP) and customer relationship management (CRM) market.

This later led to a legal dispute between Oracle and SAP over allegations that an acquired subsidiary of SAP, TomorrowNow, had infringed Oracle's copyrights by illegally downloaded Oracle documents and software. The legal case was taken in 2007, and the court ruled in favour of Oracle in 2010 with the jury awarding Oracle record damages of over $1.3 billion. This was subsequently reduced to $272 million. For more information on Oracle, see [Sym:13].

25.1   The Relational Model

The concept of a relational database was first described in Codd's famous IBM paper [Cod:70]. A relational database is a database that conforms to the relational model, and it may be defined as a set of relations (or tables). The existing database models at the time were the *hierarchical model* and the *network model*.

A binary relation $R(A, B)$ where A and B are sets is a subset of the Cartesian product $(A \times B)$ of A and B. The domain of the relation is A, and the co-domain of the relation is B. The notation aRb signifies that there is a relation between a and b and that $(a, b) \in R$. An n-ary relation $R(A_1, A_2, ... A_n)$ is a subset of the Cartesian product of the n sets, i.e., a subset of $(A_1 \times A_2 \times ... \times A_n)$. However, an n-ary relation may also be regarded as a binary relation $R(A, B)$ with $A = A_1 \times A_2 \times ... \times A_{n-1}$ and $B = A_n$.

The data in the relational model are represented as a mathematical n-ary relation. In other words, a relation is defined as a set of n-tuples and is usually represented by a table. A table is a visual representation of the relation, and the data is organised in rows and columns. The data stored in each column of the table is of the same data type.

The basic relational building block is the domain or data type (often called just *type*). Each row of the table represents one n-tuple (one tuple) of the relation, and the number of tuples in the relation is the cardinality of the relation. Consider the PART relation (Fig. 25.2) taken from [Dat:81], where this relation consists of a heading and the body. There are five data types representing part numbers, part names, part colours, part weights, and locations in which the parts are stored. The body consists of a set of n-tuples. The PART relation is of cardinality six.

Strictly speaking there is no ordering defined among the tuples of a relation, since a relation is a set, and a set is just a collection of objects that may have no inherent order. However, in practice, relations are often considered to be ordered.

P#	PName	Colour	Weight	City
P1	Nut	Red	12	London
P2	Bolt	Green	17	Paris
P3	Screw	Blue	17	Rome
P4	Screw	Red	14	London
P5	Cam	Blue	12	Paris
P6	Cog	Red	19	London

Fig. 25.2 PART relation

Fig. 25.3 Domains vs. attributes

DOMAIN PART_NUMBER	CHARACTER(6)
DOMAIN PART_NAME	CHARACTER(20)
DOMAIN COLOUR	CHARACTER(6)
DOMAIN WEIGHT	NUMERIC(4)
DOMAIN LOCATION	CHARACTER(15)

RELATION PART
    (P#   : DOMAIN PART_NUMBER
      PNAME   : DOMAIN PART_NAME
      COLOUR   : DOMAIN COLOUR
      WEIGHT   : DOMAIN WEIGHT
      CITY   : DOMAIN LOCATION)

There is a distinction between a domain and the columns (or attributes) that are drawn from that domain. An *attribute* represents the *use* of a domain within a relation, and the distinction is often emphasised by giving attribute names that are distinct from the underlying domain. The difference between domains and attributes can be seen in the PART relation (Fig. 25.3) which is taken from [Dat:81].

A *normalised relation* satisfies the property that at every row and column position in the table there is exactly one value (i.e., never a set of values). All relations in a relational database are required to satisfy this condition, and an un-normalised relation may be converted into an equivalent normalised form.

It is often the case that within a given relation that there is one attribute with values that is unique within the relation and can thus be used to identify the tuples of the relation. For example, the attribute P# of the PART relation has this property since each PART tuple contains a distinct P# value, which may be used to distinguish that tuple from all other tuples in the relation. P# is termed the *primary key* for the PART relation, and a candidate key that is not the primary key is termed the *alternate key*.

An *index* is a way of providing quicker access to the data in a relational database, as it allows the tuple in a relation to be looked up directly (using the index) rather than checking all of the tuples in the relation.

The consistency of a relational database is enforced by a set of constraints that provide restrictions on the kinds of data that may be stored in the relations. The constraints are declared as part of the logical schema and are enforced by the database management system. They are used to implement the business rules into the database.

25.2   What Is a Relational Database?

A relational database management system (RDBMS) is a system that manages data using the relational model, and examples of such systems include RDMS developed at MIT in the 1970s; Ingres developed at the University of California, Berkeley, in the mid-1970s; Oracle developed in the late 1970s; DB2; Informix; and Microsoft SQL Server.

A relation is defined as a set of tuples, and it is usually represented by a table, where a table is data organised in rows and columns. The data stored in each column of the table are of the same data type. Constraints may be employed to provide restrictions on the kinds of data that may be stored in the relations. Constraints are Boolean expressions which indicate whether the constraint holds or not and are a way of implementing business rules in the database.

Relations have one or more keys associated with them, and the key uniquely identifies the row of the table. An index is a way of providing fast access to the data in a relational database, as it allows the tuple in a relation to be looked up directly (using the index) rather than checking all of the tuples in the relation.

The Structured Query Language (SQL) is a computer language that tells the relational database what to retrieve and how to display it. A stored procedure is executable code that is associated with the database, and it is used to perform common operations on the database.

25.3   What Is an Oracle Database?

An Oracle database consists of a collection of data managed by an Oracle database management system. Today, Oracle is the main standard for database technology, and Oracle databases are used by companies throughout the world.

An Oracle database is used to store and retrieve related information. It is placed on a server, and the database server manages a large amount of data in a multi-user environment. It allows concurrent access to the data, and the database management system prevents unauthorised access to the database. It also provides a smooth recovery of database information in the case of an outage or any other disruptive event.

Every Oracle database consists of one or more physical data files, which contain all of the database data, and a control file that contains entries that specify the physical structure of the database.

An Oracle database includes logical storage structures that enable the database to have control of disc space use. A schema is a collection of database objects, and the schema objects are the logical structures that directly refer to the database's data. They include structures such as tables, views and indexes.

Tables are the basic unit of data storage in an Oracle database, and each table has several rows and columns. An index is an optional structure associated with a table, and it is used to enhance the performance of data retrieval. The index provides an access path to the table data.

A view is the customised presentation of data from one or more tables. It does not contain actual data, and it derives the data from the actual tables on which it is based.

Each Oracle database has a data dictionary, which stores information about the logical and physical structure of the database. The data dictionary is created when the database is created, and it is updated automatically by the Oracle database management system to ensure that it is an accurate reflection of the status of the database at all times.

An Oracle database uses memory structures and processes to manage and access the database. These include server processes, background processes and user processes.

A database administrator (DBA) is responsible for setting up the Oracle database server and application tools. This role is concerned with allocating system storage and planning future storage requirements for the database management system.

The DBA will create appropriate storage structures to meet the needs of application developers who are designing a new application. The access to the database will be monitored and controlled, and the performance of the database monitored and optimised. The DBA will plan backups and recovery of database information

25.4   Structured Query Language (SQL)

Codd proposed the Alpha language as the database language for his relational model. However, IBM's implementation of Codd's relational model in the System-R project introduced a new data query language that was initially called SEQUEL (later renamed to SQL).

SQL did not strictly adhere to Codd's relational model, but it became the most popular and widely used database language. It was designed to retrieve and manipulate data in the IBM database, and its operations included *insert*, *delete*, *update*, *query*, schema creation and modification, and data access control.

Structured Query Language (SQL) is a computer language that tells the relational database what to retrieve and how to display it. It was designed and developed at IBM by Donald Chamberlin and Raymond Boyce, and it became an ISO standard in 1987.

The most common operation in SQL is the query command, which is performed with the SELECT statement. The SELECT statement retrieves data from one or more tables, and the query specifies one or more columns to be included in the result. Consider the example of a query that returns a list of expensive books (defined as books that cost more than $100.00).

SELECT*[2]

FROM Book
WHERE Price >100.00
ORDER by title;

The *Data Manipulation Language* (DML) is the subset of SQL used to add, update and delete data. It includes the INSERT, UPDATE and DELETE commands. The *Data Definition Language* (DDL) manages table and index structure, and it includes the CREATE, ALTER, RENAME and DROP statements.

There are extensions to standard SQL that add programming language functionality. A stored procedure is executable code that is associated with the database. It is usually written in an imperative programming language, and it is used to perform common operations on the database.

---

[2] The asterisk (*) indicates that all columns of the Book table should be included in the result.

Chapter 26
Philips

Philips is a Dutch multinational technology giant with headquarters in Amsterdam, and its business today includes healthcare, consumer lifestyles and lighting. It employs over 120,000 people around the world, and it has annual revenues of approximately €24 billion.

Philips & Co was founded in Eindhoven in 1891by Gerard and Frederik Philips (Fig. 26.1), and it began as a company making carbon filament lamps. Its first big international order was from the Tsar of Russia who ordered 50,000 light bulbs. By the turn of the century, Philips was one of the largest producers of light bulbs in the world, and it established its first research laboratory in 1914 to study physical and chemical phenomena in order to stimulate product innovation.

This led to innovations in radio and x-ray technology, and it introduced a medical x-ray tube in 1918. It protected its radio and x-ray inventions with patents, and its first patent was granted in 1905. It began producing radios in the mid-1920s, and by the early 1930s, Philips was the largest producer of radios in the world. It launched its first Philips shaver (the Philishave) in 1939.

Most of the Philips family relocated to the United States for the duration of the Second World War, and a number of Philip's factories were bombed by the Allies during the war. Philips Research was active in the post-war years in making important contributions to the recording, transmission and reproduction of television pictures. Philips began selling TV sets in 1949, and it introduced its first vacuum cleaner in 1951. The compact audio cassette was introduced in 1963, and Philips set the standard for tape recording. Philips Semiconductors was founded in 1953, and it produced its first integrated circuits in 1965. Its first integrated circuit was used in a hearing aid.

Philips Research made breakthroughs in the processing, storage and transmission of images, sound and data throughout the 1970s. It launched its home video recorder, the N1500, in 1972, and these bulky video cassettes could initially record for 30 min. This was later improved to over 60 min, but Philips faced competition from Sony's Betamax and the VHS group of manufacturers. Ultimately, the Japanese manufacturers won the video cassette war, despite Philips introduction of the N1700 and Video 2000 systems.

© Springer International Publishing Switzerland 2015
G. O'Regan, *Pillars of Computing*, DOI 10.1007/978-3-319-21464-1_26

Fig. 26.1 Gerard Philips and his father Frederik Philips

Philips cofounded the successful PolyGram music recording label with Siemens in 1972, with Philips and Siemens each owning 50 % of the company. PolyGram was one of the world's largest record companies in the late 1970s.

Philips introduced its first energy saving bulb in 1980. Philips and Sony invented the compact disc in the early 1980s, and this revolutionary device was provided superior sound quality to the existing audio cassettes as well as scratch-free durability. Sony and Philips introduced the Digital Versatile Disc (DVD) in 1997, and DVDs offer greater capacity than compact discs while having the same physical dimensions.

Philips continues to innovate and change to adapt itself to the twenty-first century and to serve its customers better. It sold off its semiconductor business in 2006 to focus on its core areas of business in healthcare, consumer lifestyles and lighting. The former Philips Semiconductors remains in business today and is now known as NXP Semiconductors. Philips moved its headquarters from Eindhoven to Amsterdam in 1997.

26.1 Audio Cassette

Philips invented the compact cassette (Fig. 26.2) for audio storage in 1962, and this device provides a magnetic tape recording format for audio recording and playback. The sound quality was initially quite average, but by the early 1970s, the quality had improved dramatically. The cassette player became a popular alternative to the 12-in. vinyl LP in the late 1970s.

Cassettes are made of a polyester type film with a magnetic coating. The original magnetic material was ferric oxide (Fe_2O_3), and other materials such as chromium dioxide (CrO_2) and magnetite (Fe_3O_4) have also been used to improve sound quality.

Fig. 26.2 Philips cassette
recorder (EL 3302)

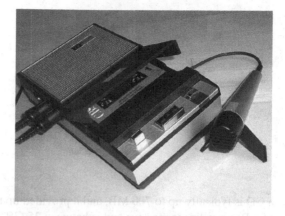

The cassette recorder remained popular in various forms (e.g., Walkman and audio devices in cars) up to the late 1980s. However, the introduction of the compact disc player in the mid-1980s meant that sales of CDs exceeded those of cassettes by the early 1990s.

26.2   Compact Disc

The compact disc (Fig. 26.3) was invented by Philips and Sony, and its invention was a technological revolution in the music industry. Philips demonstrated a prototype compact disc audio player in 1979, and this showed the feasibility of using digital optical recording and playback to reproduce audio signals with superb quality.

The world's first compact disc (CD) was manufactured at a Philips factory near Hannover in Germany in 1982. It provided superior sound quality and scratch-free durability, and it was the beginning of the shift from analogue to digital in music technology.

One of the earliest CDs to be manufactured was *The Visitors* by ABBA which was produced at the Philips PolyGram recording company. Philips introduced its CD 100 CD Player and the first CDs into Europe and the United States in early 1983. One of the earliest fully digital recordings to be brought to market was Dire Straits' *Brother in Arms* album. This was released on CD in 1985, and it sold over a million copies.

The compact disc rapidly became the medium of choice for the music industry. Over 250 billion CDs, 3.5 billion audio CD players, and three billion CD-ROM drives had been sold by 2009. The success of the CD led to the end of the LP era, with most music companies issuing new releases only on CDs from the early 1990s.

The compact disc has played a key role in the shift from analogue music to digital, and it has laid the foundation for an extensive family of optical discs such as CD-ROM, CD-R, CD-RW, DVD, DVD-R, DVD-RW and Blu-ray. The capacity of

Fig. 26.3 Compact disc

a CD is typically up to 700 MB, and it provided up to 80 min of audio. The capacity of a Blu-ray disc is massive and is between 25 GB and 100 GB.

The IEEE Milestone Award was given to Philips in 2009 in recognition of its contributions to the development of the compact disc and in setting the technical standard in digital optical recording systems.

The Digital Versatile Disc (DVD) is a digital optical disc recording format developed by Philips, Sony, Toshiba and Panasonic in the late-1990s. A DVD disc has a similar size to a CD, but it has a much larger capacity (typically 1 and 16 GB). It is used for digital consumer video as a replacement for the VHS video tapes or for digital consumer audio.

26.3   Philips Today

Philips has continued to change and innovate since it was founded back in 1891. It remains a global technology company with a rich heritage of innovation, and it continues to be a leader in healthcare, lighting and consumer lifestyle.

It sold off its semiconductor business in 2006 to focus on its core areas of business, and today the company is focused on being the leading company in health and well-being. Its goal is to make the world healthier and more sustainable through its innovative products. It employs over 120,000 people around the world and its headquarters are in Amsterdam.

Chapter 27
Rational Software

Rational Machines was founded by Paul Levy and Michael Devlin in 1981, with the goal of providing state-of-the-art tools to support modern software engineering practices. Grady Booch (Fig. 27.1) served as chief scientist for the company. One of Rational's earliest products was an integrated development environment (IDE) for the Ada programming language. An IDE provides support to software developers and helps to improve programmer and team productivity.

Rational Machines merged with the Verdix Corporation in 1994, and the new company was called Rational Software. The new company focused on the production of code generators and debuggers for popular architectures such as VAX, x86 and Motorola 68000, as well as integrated development environments for the Ada and C++ programming language.

Booch developed the Booch method of software development at Rational Software [Boo:93], and this technique is used in object-oriented analysis and design. Rational developed the Rose tool to support the Booch notation, and the new tool included functionality for C++ code generation, and it also allowed reverse engineering of C++ code to produce class diagrams.

James Rumbaugh (Fig. 27.3) and Ivar Jacobson (Fig. 27.2) joined Rational Software in the mid-1990s, and they worked together to integrate the Booch method with Rumbaugh's Object Management Technique (OMT) and Jacobson's object-oriented software engineering (OOSE) method to form the Unified Modelling Language (UML). UML is a visual modelling language for software systems which provides a means of specifying, constructing and documenting the object-oriented system.

The *Rational Unified Process* (RUP) [Jac:99] was developed by James Rumbaugh, Grady Booch, and Ivar Jacobson, and it provides a means of specifying, constructing and documenting the object-oriented system. It facilitates an understanding of the architecture and complexity of the system, and it uses UML as a tool for specification and design.

Rational developed a suite of tools to support various software engineering practices. These tools support software design and development and include tools such

© Springer International Publishing Switzerland 2015
G. O'Regan, *Pillars of Computing*, DOI 10.1007/978-3-319-21464-1_27

Fig. 27.1 Grady Booch

Fig. 27.2 Ivar Jacobson

as Rational Software Modeler® (RSM) which is a UML-based visual modelling and design tool used for model-driven development. Rational Rhapsody® is a visual development environment used in real-time or embedded systems. It validates functionality early in development and automates code generation. Other Rational tools include ClearCase, ClearQuest and RequisitePro. Rational Software was taken over by IBM in 2003.

27.1   Unified Modelling Language

The first object-oriented modelling language[1] emerged in the late 1960s, and by the early 1990s, there was a plethora of object-oriented methods. The most popular of these methods included James Rumbaugh's *Object Modelling Technique* (OMT),

---

[1] The first object-oriented programming language to emerge was Simula-67, which was developed in the 1960s at the Norwegian Computing Center in Oslo by Ole Johan Dahl and Kristen Nygaard. This language introduced objects and classes.

the *Booch method* developed by Grady Booch at Rational Software and Ivar Jacobson's *object-oriented software engineering* (OOSE) method. It was clear that there was a need for a single standardised unified modelling language with a formally defined syntax.

Rational Software hired Rumbaugh from General Electric in 1994, and Rational took over Jacobson's company, Objectory AB, in 1995. Booch was the chief scientist for Rational at this time, and this allowed Rumbaugh, Booch and Jacobson to work together to create a unified modelling language.

Their goal was not to create a new modelling language as such, but to integrate the existing Booch method, OMT and OOSE to form a single standardised modelling language. This involved simplifying or expanding the existing diagrams such as class diagrams, use case diagrams, activity diagrams and so on used in several of the object-oriented methods. Their work led to a standardised unified modelling language, as well as an associated formal semantics of the language elements. Today, UML is an industry standard and the Object Management Group (OMG) is responsible for the evolution of the language.

UML is an expressive graphical modelling language for specifying, visualising, constructing and documenting a software system. It provides several views of the software's architecture, which is essential in the development and deployment of systems. It has a clearly defined syntax and semantics for every building block of its graphical notation. Each stakeholder (e.g., project manager, developers, and testers) has a different perspective and looks at the system in different ways at different times over the project's life.

UML is a way to model the software system prior to implementation in some programming language, and the explicit visual model of the system facilitates communication among the various stakeholders. It has been employed in many domains including the banking sector, defence and telecommunications.

A UML specification involves building precise, complete and unambiguous models. Code may be generated from the models in a programming language such as Java or C++. It is also possible to reverse engineer the C++ or Java code to produce UML diagrams. Thus, it is possible to work with the graphical notation of UML or the textual notation of a programming language. UML expresses things that are best expressed graphically, whereas a programming language expresses things that are best expressed textually. The support tools are employed to keep both views consistent.

There are nine key UML diagrams and they are described in Table 27.1 below. They provide a graphical visualisation of the system from different viewpoints. UML is described in more detail in [Jac:05], and it is often used as part of the Rational Unified Process (RUP).

27.2 Rational Unified Process

The *Rational Unified Process* was developed at the Rational Corporation. It uses the Unified Modelling Language (UML) as a tool for specification and design, which provides a means of specifying, constructing and documenting the object-oriented system.

Table 27.1 UML diagrams

Diagram	Description
Class	This shows the set of classes, interfaces and collaborations and their relationships. They address the static design view of the system
Object	This shows a set of objects and their relationships. They represent the static design view of the system but from the perspective of real cases
Use case	This describes the functional requirements from the user's point of view and describes a set of use cases and actors and the relationship between them
Sequence diagram	This diagram shows the interaction between a set of objects and messages exchanged between them. It emphasises the time ordering of messages
Collaboration diagram	A collaboration diagram is a diagram that emphasises the structural organisation of objects that send and receive messages
Statechart	This shows a state machine consisting of states, transitions, events and activities. It addresses the dynamic view of a system and is important in modelling the behaviour of an interface or class
Activity diagram	This is a kind of statechart diagram that shows the flow from activity to activity of a system. It addresses the dynamic view of a system and is important in modelling the function and flow of control among objects
Component diagram	This diagram shows the organisations and dependencies among components. It addresses the static implementation view of a system
Deployment	This diagram shows the configuration of run time processing nodes and the components that live on them

Fig. 27.3 James
Rumbaugh

The origins of the *Rational Unified Process* (RUP) are in Objectory v1.0 (developed by Jacobson's company), Rumbaugh's OMT, and the Booch method. The Objectory's processes were used to define the core processes in RUP (Fig. 27.3), and an early version of RUP was released in 1998. A full description of the RUP process is given in [Jac:99].

RUP is *use case driven*, *architecture centric*, *iterative* and *incremental* and employs a component-based architecture, and it includes cycles, phases, workflows, risk mitigation, quality control, project management and configuration control. Software projects may be very complex, and there are risks that requirements may be incomplete or that the interpretation of a requirement may differ between the customer and the project team.

Requirements are gathered as use cases, and the *use cases describe the functional requirements from the point of view of the user of the system.* They describe what the system will do at a high level and ensure that there is an appropriate focus on the user when defining the scope of the project. *Use cases also drive the development process*, as the developers create a series of design and implementation models that realise the use cases. The developers review each successive model for conformance to the use case model, and the test team verifies that the implementation correctly implements the use cases.

The Rational Unified Process consists of four phases. These are *inception, elaboration, construction* and *transition*. Each phase consists of one or more iterations, with each iteration consisting of several workflows. The workflows may be requirements, analysis, design, implementation and test. Each phase terminates in a milestone with one or more project deliverables.

The inception phase is concerned with the initial project planning and cost estimation, and the initial work on the architecture and functional requirements of the system. It also identifies and prioritises the most important risks. The elaboration phase specifies most of the use cases in detail, and the system architecture is designed. The construction phase is concerned with building the product, where the product contains all of the use cases agreed by management and the customer for the release. The transition phase covers the period where the product moves into the customer site and includes activities such as training customer personnel, providing support and assistance and correcting any defects found after delivery.

The software architecture concept embodies the most significant static and dynamic aspects of the system. The architecture grows out of the use cases and factors such as the platform that the software is to run on, deployment considerations, legacy systems and non-functional requirements.

RUP decomposes the work of a large project into smaller slices or mini-projects, and *each mini-project is an iteration that results in an increment to the product.* The iteration consists of one or more steps in the workflow and generally leads to the growth of the product. *If there is a need to repeat an iteration, then all that is lost is the misdirected effort of one iteration, rather that the entire product.* That is, RUP is a way to mitigate risk in software engineering.

A commercial software project is often a large undertaking that may involve many people. Its duration may be over 1 year to complete, and the work is decomposed into smaller slices or mini-projects, where each mini-project is a manageable chunk. In the Rational Unified Process, each mini-project is an iteration that results in an increment.

The waterfall software development has the disadvantage that the risk is greater towards the end of the project, where it is costly to undo mistakes from earlier phases. With an iterative process, the waterfall steps are applied iteratively. That is, instead of developing the entire system in one step, an increment (i.e., a subset of the system functionality) is selected and developed; then another increment is developed; and so on. The earliest iterations address the areas with the greatest risk. Each iteration produces an executable release and includes integration and testing activities.

27.3   Rational Tools

This section describes various tools that are available from Rational to support the various software engineering activities. These include tools for requirements management, architecture and software design, development and configuration management. A selection of some of the tools that are available to support the various software engineering activities are listed in Table 27.2.

IBM Rational Software Modeler® (RSM) is a UML-based visual modelling and design tool (Fig. 27.4). It promotes communication and collaboration during design and development, and it allows information about development projects to be specified and communicated from several perspectives. It is used for model-driven development, and it aligns the business needs with the product.

It gives the organisation control over the evolving architecture, and it provides an integrated analysis and design platform. Abstract UML specifications may be built with traceability and impact analysis shown. It has an intuitive user interface and a diagram editor to create expressive and interactive diagrams. The tool may be integrated with other IBM Rational tools such as ClearCase, ClearQuest and RequisitePro.

IBM Rational Rhapsody® is a visual development environment used in real-time or embedded systems. It helps teams to collaborate and to understand and elaborate requirements, abstract complexity using modelling languages such as UML, validate functionality early in development and automate code generation to speed up the development process.

IBM Rational Software Architect is a modelling and development environment that uses UML for designing and building architectures.

Table 27.2 Tools for software design

Tool	Description
IBM Rational Software Modeler	This is a UML-based visual modelling and software design tool (Fig. 27.5)
IBM Rational Rhapsody	This modelling environment tool is based on UML and provides a visual development environment for software engineers. It uses graphical models and generates code in C, C++ and Java
IBM Rational Software Architect	This modelling and development tool uses UML for designing architecture for C++ and Java applications
IBM Rational ClearCase	This is a configuration management tool for large and medium companies
IBM Rational ClearQuest	This is a defect management tool

- Use cases driven
- Architecture centric
- Iterative and incremental
- Employs a component based architecture

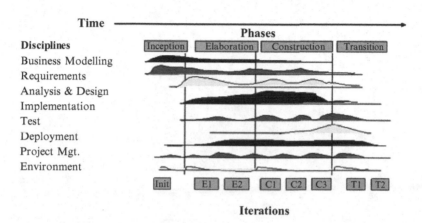

Fig. 27.4 Phases and workflows in rational unified process

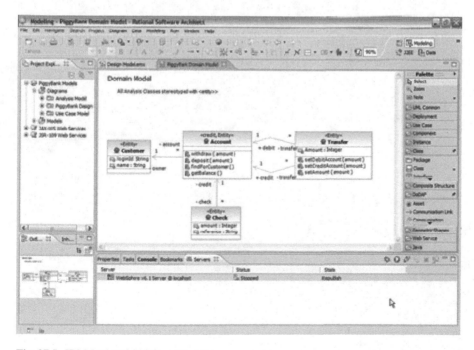

Fig. 27.5 IBM Rational Software Modeler

Chapter 28
Samsung

Samsung is a South Korean multinational conglomerate with headquarters in Seoul, South Korea. The company is involved in many industrial segments such as semiconductors, telecommunications equipment, medical equipment, financial services, information and communications technology services and many more. It has annual revenues of over $300 billion and net income of over $30 billion, and it employs over 400,000 people around the world.

The company has humble beginnings and it was initially founded in 1938 by Byung-chul Lee (Fig. 28.1) as a small grocery and trucking business with just forty employees. It set up a flour mill and confectionary business in the 1940s, and it expanded into other industries such as textiles, insurance and finance, shipbuilding, construction and the media from the 1950s.

Samsung entered the electronics industry in the late 1960s when it established Samsung Electronics in 1969. Today, Samsung Electronics is the flagship subsidiary of the Samsung Group, and it accounts for roughly 70 % of its revenue. It produces semiconductors, memory, batteries, radios, computer components, mobile phones and televisions. The Samsung brand began to expand globally from the 1990s, and today Samsung is a major player in the mobile smartphone and television market.

Byung-chul Lee died in 1987 and his son Kun-Hee Lee (Fig. 28.2) took over as chairman in late 1987. He played a key role in transforming Samsung from a local-thinking South Korean company into a major international conglomerate with an international attitude to doing business. He believed that Samsung was too focused on producing massive quantities of low-quality goods and that the company needed to embrace change to compete globally on quality. He embarked on a major business transformation program which led to Samsung becoming a major international player and one of the most successful Asian brands.

Today, Samsung is one of the largest corporations in the world and one of the leading producers of semiconductors. The company is focused on electronics, engineering and chemicals, and it overtook Nokia to become the largest maker of mobile phones (by unit sales) in 2012.

© Springer International Publishing Switzerland 2015
G. O'Regan, *Pillars of Computing*, DOI 10.1007/978-3-319-21464-1_28

Fig. 28.1 Byung-chul Lee
(Courtesy of Samsung
Corp.)

Fig. 28.2 Kun-Hee Lee
with Korean business
leaders

Samsung Electronics is one of the largest electronics and information technology companies in the world, and its products include computers, digital televisions, mobile phones, monitors, printers, semiconductors and telecommunications networking equipment. It is also one of the world's largest manufacturers of televisions, mobile phones and smartphones.

Samsung C&T is a construction and trading giant. Its engineering and construction group has constructed the Petronas Twin Towers in Kuala Lumpur; the Taipei 101 in Taiwan; and the Burj Khalifa in Dubai. These are three of the world's ten tallest buildings and are 452 m, 508 m and 828 m tall, respectively. Samsung has built industrial plants and large civil engineering infrastructure such as bridges, tunnels, metros and roads. Samsung's trading and investment group is involved in power generation; natural resources such as oil, gas and coal; and industrial materials such as textiles, steel and chemicals.

Samsung Heavy Industries (SHI) is one of the largest shipbuilders in the world, and it constructs various types of ships such as Liquid Natural Gas (LNG) carriers, oil drilling ships, container ships, cruise ships and large passenger ships. SHI has manufacturing facilities in South Korea and in China. For more detailed information about Samsung, see [SoL:14].

28.1   Samsung Smartphones

Samsung Electronics is a key company in the Samsung Group, and it accounts for approximately 70 % of its annual revenue. It is one of the world's largest manufacturers of mobile phones and smartphones, and it is also a major vendor of tablet computers through its Samsung Galaxy Tab range of tablets. Its flagship smartphone handset line is the Samsung Galaxy S which is a competitor to Apple's iPhone.

Samsung's first smartphone was the Samsung SPH-I300 which was released in 2001 (5 years before Apple's iPhone). This Palm-powered smartphone is a distant ancestor of today's smartphones. Samsung introduced the SGH i607 smartphone in 2006. This Windows-powered phone was inspired by Research in Motion's (RIM) Blackberry phone.

The Samsung Instinct was released in 2008 (before the release of Android). It used an operating system developed by Samsung from various Java components, but its touchscreen operating system was not in the same league as Apple's iOS. The Samsung Instinct was a competitor to Apple's iPhone.

The Samsung Galaxy S smartphone was launched in 2010. This touchscreen-enabled Android smartphone is extremely popular, and it is produced in many variations. The Samsung Galaxy SII was released in 2011, and it became a major competitor to Apple's iPhone. The Galaxy SIII was released in 2012 and was a major success. The Samsung Galaxy S has sold over 25 million units, and over 200 million smartphones have been sold in the Galaxy S series of smartphones.

Samsung released the Samsung Focus SGH-i97 smartphone in late 2010, and this phone runs on Microsoft Windows Phone operating system. The Samsung Galaxy Note (Fig. 28.3) was released by Samsung in 2012. This new product category is termed a phablet (pocket tablet/phone), and Samsung is a pioneer in the phablet market.

28.2   Samsung Televisions

Televisions were introduced into South Korea in the early 1960s, and the Korean government's policy was that the European and American manufacturers would need to share their knowledge with Korean manufacturers if they wished to sell their TV technology in South Korea.

Fig. 28.3 Samsung galaxy
note 4

Samsung was one of the companies that benefited from this agreement, and it introduced its first television in 1970. This was a black and white model known as the P-3202, and Samsung's televisions were initially produced for the South Korean domestic market. By the mid-1970s Samsung had produced over a million black and white TVs, and it began to manufacture and sell colour televisions in Asia from 1977. By 1981 it had produced over one million colour TVs, and this figure increased to over 20 million by the late 1980s. Samsung began to export TVs to the rest of the world from the early 1990s.

The company partnered with Sony in the 1990s to create Liquid Crystal Display (LCD) screens, which provided clearer and sharper pictures for its customers. An LCD TV is a television set that uses LCD display technology, and it is much thinner than the traditional cathode ray tube televisions. Samsung began producing flat screen TVs from the late 1990s, and by 1999 it was offering a full lineup of digital TVs and mass producing these for its customers around the world.

Most of the television sets sold in the world today are energy-efficient flat panel TVs such as Plasma displays, LCDs, LEDs and OLEDs. The bulky, high-voltage cathode ray tubes (CRT) screen displays are now largely historical, as they have been largely replaced with these newer technologies. A cathode ray tube is a vacuum tube containing one or more electron guns (electron emitters) and a fluorescent screen that is used to view the images. The CRT may accelerate or deflect the electron streams to create the image.

LCDs come in two types: cold cathode fluorescent lamps which are simply called LCDs and those using LEDs as backlight called LEDs. Today, LCDs and especially LEDs have become the most widely produced and sold display type (Fig. 28.4).

Fig. 28.4 Samsung LED
TV

The growth of digital televisions has encouraged recent innovations such as smart TV, which provides technological convergence between computers and televisions. These devices provide Internet TV, on-demand streaming media and home-networking access. Internet TV allows television content to be received over the Internet. Samsung released its "Smart LED TV" (later renamed to "Samsung Smart TV") in 2007.

Chapter 29
SAP SE

Systems, Applications and Products in Data Processing (SAP SE) is a German multinational corporation that creates enterprise software to manage business operations and customer relations. It is one of the largest software companies in the world, with annual revenues in excess of €16 billion and net income of approximately €3 billion. Its headquarters are in Walldorf, Baden-Württemberg in Germany, and it employs over 70,000 people around the world.

SAP develops software products to help companies to meet their customer needs more effectively. Its products include its Enterprise Resource Planning (ERP) application, its Customer Relationship Management (CRM) applications, its Supply Chain Management (SCM) applications, its enterprise data warehouse product and its Business Warehouse (SAP BW) product.

Today, many corporations (e.g., IBM and Microsoft) use SAP software products to manage and run their businesses, and the SAP applications provide the capability to manage financial, asset and cost accounting; production operations and materials; personnel; plants; and archived documents. The SAP system runs on a number of platforms including a comprehensive Internet-enabled package. The SAP products include e-business applications such as customer relationship management and supply chain management.

SAP was founded as a private company in 1972 by Dietmar Hopp (Fig. 29.1) and four other former IBM employees. These are Hasso Plattner, Hans-Werner Hector, Klaus Tschira, and Claus Wellenreuther. Hopp has served as the CEO and chairman of the board of SAP, and Hasso Plattner (Fig. 29.2) has served as the chairman of the board of the company.

The SAP founders had a background in enterprise software development from their time with IBM, and their first client was the German branch of the former British chemical company, Imperial Chemical Industries (ICI). They developed mainframe programs for payroll and accounting, and they developed standalone software that could be offered to other interested companies.

SAP launched its first product, SAP R/98, in 1973, and this product provided a common system for multiple tasks. It launched SAP R/2 in 1979 to expand the

© Springer International Publishing Switzerland 2015
G. O'Regan, *Pillars of Computing*, DOI 10.1007/978-3-319-21464-1_29

Fig. 29.1 Dietmar Hopp

Fig. 29.2 Hasso Plattner

capabilities of the system to material management and production planning. It released SAP R/3 in 1992, and by the mid-1990s, SAP moved from the mainframe environment to the client server architecture. It responded to the rise of the Internet with mySAP.com which redesigned the concept of business processes with integration via the Internet.

SAP became a public company in 1988, and the company's official name today is SAP SE.[1] Today, SAP is a major player in enterprise software market, and its suite of software products include:

- Customer Relationship Management
- Enterprise Resource Planning
- Supply Chain Management and Logistics Software
- Manufacturing, Warehouse and Industrial Software
- Marketing and Sales Software

SAP has acquired several companies to enhance its product portfolio. These include companies such as Sybase, BusinessObjects, and TomorrowNow. Oracle is a major competitor of SAP, and it filed a case against SAP in 2007 for malpractice with respect to illegal downloading of Oracle software by TomorrowNow (a SAP subsidiary), and it accused SAP of unfair competition. SAP lost the case and it was ordered to pay $1.3 billion in damages to Oracle. However, the judgment was overturned in 2011. For more information about SAP, see [Mir:14].

29.1 SAP CRM

SAP Customer Relationship Management (CRM) is integrated customer relationship management software that enables companies to focus on its customers and on customer satisfaction. SAP CRM helps to manage the customer relationship, and it enables the company to understand their customer needs and business requirements. It has several modules that support key functional areas such as sales, marketing and customer service.

Companies need to be customer focused to be successful in today's competitive environment, and SAP CRM helps companies to do this as well as optimising customer interactions (e.g., in sales, marketing and service). It allows the company to understand the extent of customer satisfaction, and customer satisfaction and loyalty are essential to the success of the company.

SAP CRM is part of SAP Business Suite and it may be integrated with other SAP applications such as Product Lifecycle Management (PLM), Supplier Relationship Management (SRM) and Supply Chain Management (SCM).

SAP CRM Marketing covers the marketing plan and campaign management. SAP CRM Sales covers account and contact management, activity management, sales opportunity management, quotation and order management, and contract management. SAP CRM Service covers service order processing, and complaint and return processing.

---

[1] Societas Europaea.

29.2 SAP ERP

SAP Enterprise Resource Planning (ERP) is enterprise resource planning software developed by SAP SE. It incorporates the key business functions of an organisation, and it includes several modules for marketing and sales, product design and development, production and inventory control, human resources, finance and accounting. SAP ERP combines data from the separate modules to provide the company with enterprise resource planning.

There are potential cost benefits to a company and a return on its investment following the successful implementation of SAP ERP. However, the full implementation of ERP is complex, expensive and time consuming, with the implementation of all modules often taking several years. The average cost of a 3-year implementation is approximately $10 million, and a typical deployment involves consulting, training and software licences. Given these significant costs, it is clear that ERP is normally deployed in large or mid-sized organisations rather than in smaller companies.

The advantages of SAP ERP include that it provides a standard way of working in the organisation and it may create a more efficient working environment for the employees. It enables employees to manipulate data quickly, as well as company-wide access to more information. It may also be customised to meet the specific needs of the company.

The disadvantages of SAP ERP include that it may be inflexible, with SAP's modules not fitting the company's business model, and the customization required to tailor it to the particular business may be expensive. Further the implementation itself is expensive and time consuming with a risk of failure. Further, there may be a long wait for the return on the investment made.

29.3 SAP HR

SAP Human Resource (HR) enables companies to effectively process employee-related data according to business requirements. It includes processes for workforce management (e.g., employee administration, personnel evaluation, benefits management and payroll administration) and talent management (e.g., recruitment, career management, enterprise learning and compensation management).

29.4 SAP SCM

The objective of SAP Supply Chain Management (SCM) is to ensure that the company has the desired products available for its customers at the right time and place and at the minimal cost to the company. This requires an efficient supply chain to enable the company to provide a high level of customer service with as low a stock level as possible and low operational costs.

A physical supply chain exists between the raw material provider and the ultimate customer, and decision management systems are employed to manage and control each of the elements and their interactions. The goals are to provide a high-quality product at the lowest possible cost to the company and to balance demand and supply

The SAP SCM process starts with forecasting future sales (SCM DP, demand planning), and this is used to determine the optimal product quantities to distribute in the company's network (SCM SNP, supply and network planning). The production plan is then derived from the distribution plan (production planning and detailed scheduling), and the production plan is used to source the required components (procurement planning).

The production planning and detailed scheduling are performed for each factory, and the objective is to determine the optimal quantities to produce to meet demand, limit overstocks, and to minimise the time lost when switching from a product to the next. The production planning considers the demand on the factory (sales orders, stock transfers to warehouses) and determines how much is to be produced for each product per period. Detailed scheduling is then performed and the different production orders are scheduled within a period.

Procurement planning determines the components that need to be supplied in order to achieve the production plan.

29.5   SAP SRM

SAP Supplier Relationship Management (SRM) enables a company to coordinate its business processes with its key suppliers and to make them more effective. It involves working in close collaboration with those suppliers that are vital to the success of the company. It enables the company to optimise its procurement strategy, to work more effectively with its pool of suppliers, and to gain long-term benefits from its supplier relationships.

SAP SRM allows the company to examine and forecast purchasing behaviour, shorten procurement cycles, and develop long-term relationships with reliable suppliers.

29.6   SAP PLM

SAP Product Lifecycle Management (PLM) helps the company to optimise its product lifecycle from idea and concept management, to product development, and to the management of all product-related data during the product lifecycle

It provides all needed information about the complete product and asset lifecycle through the extended supply chain. It enables the company to optimise its internal product-related processes and to improve the flow of information. SAP PLM enables the organisation to improve its product development, project management, documents, quality and company-wide collaborative engineering.

Chapter 30
Software Engineering Institute (SEI)

The Software Engineering Institute (SEI) is a federally funded research and development centre located at Carnegie Mellon University (CMU) in the United States. It was founded by the United States Congress in 1984, and it has worked closely with industry and academia in advancing software engineering practices around the world. It opened a European office in Germany in 2004.

It performs research to find solutions to key software engineering problems, and its proposed solutions are validated through international pilots. These solutions are then disseminated to the wider software engineering community through the SEI training programme. The SEI's research and maturity models have played an important role in helping companies to deliver high-quality software consistently on time and on budget.

The early work of the SEI involved working closely with the Department of Defence (DOD), and the objective was to assist the DOD in developing a framework to enable the competence and capability of software subcontractors to be rigorously assessed prior to selection. This research and development evolved into the book *Managing the Software Process*, which was written by Watts Humphrey [Hum:89]. It describes technical and managerial topics essential for good software engineering, and it was influenced by the ideas of Deming and Juran in statistical process control.

Watts Humphrey (Fig. 30.1) was an American software engineer and vice president of technical development at IBM. He made important contributions to the software engineering field, and he is known as the *father of software quality*. He dedicated much of his career to addressing the problems of software development including schedule delays, cost overruns, software quality and productivity.

Humphrey retired from IBM in 1986 and joined the newly formed SEI at CMU. He made a commitment to change the software engineering world by developing sound management principles for the software industry. The SEI has largely fulfilled his commitment, and it has played an important role in enhancing the capability of software organisations throughout the world. Humphrey established the software process program at the SEI, and this led to the development of the software

© Springer International Publishing Switzerland 2015
G. O'Regan, *Pillars of Computing*, DOI 10.1007/978-3-319-21464-1_30

Fig. 30.1 Watts Humphrey
(Courtesy of Watts
Humphrey)

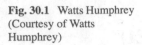

Capability Maturity Model (CMM) and its successors. The CMM is a framework to help an organisation to understand its current process maturity and to prioritise process improvements.

Humphrey introduced software process assessment and software capability evaluation methods, and these include CBA/IPI and CBA/SCE. The CMM model and the associated assessment methods were widely adopted by organisations around the world. Their successors are the CMMI model and the SCAMPI appraisal methodology.

Humphrey focused his later efforts to developing the Personal Software Process (PSP) and the Team Software Process (TSP). These are approaches that teach engineers the skills they need to make and track plans and to produce high-quality software with zero defects. The PSP helps the individual engineer to collect relevant data for statistical process control, whereas the TSP focuses on teams, and the goal is to assist teams to understand and improve their current productivity and quality.

30.1   Software Process Improvement

Software process improvement is concerned with practical action to improve the processes in the organisation, to ensure that they meet business goals more effectively. For example, a business goal might be to develop and deliver a high-quality software product faster to the market, and so there will be a need for performance improvements in key software engineering processes to enable the business goal to be achieved. The origins of the software process improvement field go back to the manufacturing sector and to Walter Shewhart's work on statistical process control in the 1930s (see Chap. 7).

Shewhart's work was later refined by Deming and Juran, who argued that high-quality processes are essential to the delivery of a high-quality product. They argued that the quality of the end product is largely determined by the quality of the processes used to produce and support it. Therefore, there is a need to focus on the process as well as the product itself, and high-quality products need to be built from processes that are fit for purpose.

Deming and Juran's approach transformed struggling manufacturing companies with quality problem to companies that could consistently produce high-quality products. This led to cost reductions and higher productivity, as less time was spent in reworking defective products. Their focus was on the manufacturing process and in reducing its variability in the process [ORg:02].

This work was later applied to the software quality field by Watts Humphrey and others at the SEI, leading to the birth of the software process improvement field. Humphrey asked questions such as:

– *How good is the current software process?*
– *What must I do to improve it?*
– *Where do I start?*

Software process improvement initiatives support the organisation in achieving its key business goals such as delivering software faster to the market, improving quality and reducing or eliminating waste. The objective is to work smarter and to build software better, faster and cheaper than competitors. Software process improvement makes business sense, and it provides a tangible return on investment (ROI).

Humphrey recognised that a software process improvement initiative involves change to the way that work is done, and it therefore needs top management support to be successful. It requires the involvement of the software engineering staff, as they are the process practitioners, and changes to the process are made based on an understanding of the strengths and weaknesses of the process.

Every task and activity can be improved, and change is continuous. Training on new processes is given to all process practitioners, and the process needs to be reinforced with audits to ensure process fidelity. High-quality processes are essential to the delivery of high-quality software products.

The process is an abstraction of the way in which work is done and is seen as the glue (Fig. 30.2) that ties people, procedures and tools together. A *process* is a set of practices or tasks performed to achieve a given purpose. It may include tools, methods, material and people. An organisation will typically have many processes in place for doing its work, and the object of process improvement is to improve the key processes to meet business goals more effectively.

Fig. 30.2 Process as glue for people, procedures and tools

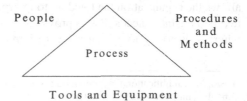

Table 30.1 Benefits of
CMMI implementation

Benefit	Actual saving
Cost	34 %
Schedule	50 %
Productivity	61 %
Quality	48 %
Customer satisfaction	14 %
Return on investment	4:1

The Software Engineering Institute (SEI) developed the Capability Maturity Model (CMM) in the early 1990s as a framework to help software organisations to improve their software process maturity and to implement best practice in software and systems engineering. The SEI believes that there is a close relationship between the maturity of software processes and the quality of the delivered software product. The first version of the CMM was released in 1991, and the first version of its successor, the Capability Maturity Model Integration (CMMI®) [CKS:11], was released in 2001.

The SEI has gathered empirical data (Table 30.1) on the benefits of the implementation of the CMMI [SEI:09]. The table shows the median results reported to the SEI. It includes data for cost, schedule, productivity, quality, customer satisfaction and a return on investment. More detailed information on software quality and software process improvement is in [ORg:10, ORg:14].

30.2   Capability Maturity Model Integrated (CMMI)

The SEI developed the original CMM model in the early 1990s as a framework to help software organisations improve their software process maturity. The CMMI is used to implement best practice in software and systems engineering.

Systems engineering is concerned with the development of systems that may or may not include software, whereas software engineering is concerned with the development of software systems. The model contains extra information relevant to a particular discipline, and this is done by discipline amplification.[1] The SEI and other quality experts believe that there is a close relationship between the maturity of software processes and the quality of the delivered software product.

The CMMI is a process model, and it defines the characteristics (or best practice) of good processes. It does not prescribe how the processes should be done, and it allows the organisation the freedom to interpret the model to suit its particular context and business needs. It also provides a roadmap for an organisation to get from where it is today to a higher level of maturity. The advantage of model-based

---

[1] Discipline amplification is a specialised piece of information that is relevant to a particular discipline. It is introduced in the model by text such as "For Systems Engineering".

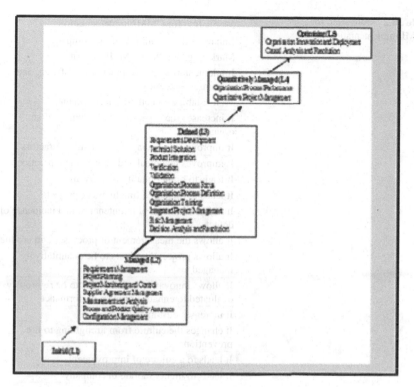

Fig. 30.3 CMMI maturity levels

improvement is that it provides a place to start software process improvement, as well as providing a common language and a shared vision.

The CMMI consists of five maturity levels (Fig. 30.3) with each maturity level (except level one) consisting of a number of process areas. Each process area consists of a set of goals, and these must be implemented by a set of related practices in order for the process area to be satisfied. The practices specify what is to be done rather than how it should be done. Processes are activities associated with carrying out certain tasks, and they need to be defined and documented. The users of the process need to receive appropriate training to enable them to carry out the process, and process discipline needs to be enforced with independent audits. Process performance needs to be monitored and improvements made to ineffective processes.

The emphasis for level two of the CMMI is on maturing management practices such as project management, requirements management, configuration management and so on. The emphasis on level three of the CMMI is on maturing engineering and organisation practices.

Maturity level three is concerned with defining standard organisation processes, and it also includes process areas for various engineering activities needed to design and develop the software. Level four is concerned with ensuring that key processes

Table 30.2 Motivation for
CMMI implementation

Motivation for CMMI implementation
Enhances the credibility of the company
Marketing benefit of CMMI maturity level
Implementation of best practice in software and systems engineering
Well-established path to improvement
It increases the capability and maturity of an organisation
It improves the management of subcontractors
It improves technical and management practices
It leads to higher quality of software
It leads to increased timeliness of projects
It reduces the cost of maintenance and incidence of defects
It allows the measurement of processes and products
It allows projects/products to be quantitatively managed
It allows innovative technologies to be rigorously evaluated to enhance process performance
It increases customer satisfaction
It changes the culture from firefighting to fire prevention
It leads to a culture of improvement
It leads to higher morale in company

are performing within strict quantitative limits and adjusting processes, where necessary, to perform within these limits. Level five is concerned with continuous process improvement.

Maturity levels may not be skipped in the staged implementation of the CMMI, as each maturity level is the foundation for work on the next level. There is also a continuous representation[2] of the CMMI that allows the organisation to focus its improvements on key processes that are closely related to its business goals. This allows it the freedom to choose an approach that should result in the greatest business benefit rather than proceeding on the standard improvement roadmap. However, in practice it is often necessary to implement several of the level two process areas before serious work can be done on maturing a process to a higher capability level.

Table 30.2 presents motivation for the implementation of the CMMI. It helps companies to deliver high-quality software systems that are consistently on time

---

[2] Our focus is on the implementation of the staged representation of the CMMI rather than the continuous representation, as it provides a clearly defined roadmap for process improvement, and it also allows benchmarking of organisations.

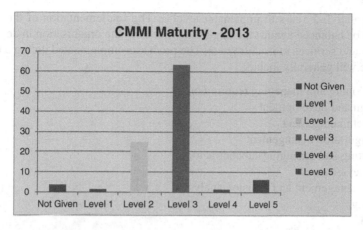

Fig. 30.4 CMMI worldwide maturity 2013

and consistently meet business requirements. The first company to be assessed at CMM level 5[3] was the Motorola plant in Bangalore, India.

The success of the original software CMM led to the development of other process maturity models such as the systems engineering capability maturity mode (CMM/SE), which is concerned with maturing systems engineering practices, and the people capability maturity model (P-CMM) which is concerned with improving the ability of the software organisations to attract, develop and retain talented software engineering professionals.

The CMMI allows organisations to benchmark themselves against similar organisations (Fig. 30.4). This is generally done by a formal SEI SCAMPI Class A appraisal[4] conducted by an authorised SCAMPI lead appraiser. The results will generally be reported back to the SEI, and there is a strict qualification process to become an authorised lead appraiser.

The qualification process helps to ensure that the appraisals are conducted fairly and objectively and that the results are consistent. An appraisal verifies that an organisation has improved, and it enables the organisation to prioritise improvements for its next improvement cycle. Small organisations will often prefer a SCAMPI Class B or C appraisal, as these are less expensive and time consuming.

The time required to implement the CMMI in an organisation depends on its size and current maturity. It generally takes 1–2 years to implement maturity level two

---

[3] Of course, the fact that a company has been appraised at a certain CMM or CMMI rating is no guarantee that it is performing effectively as a commercial organisation. For example, the Motorola plant in India was appraised at CMM level 5 in the late 1990s while Motorola lost business opportunities in the GSM market.

[4] A SCAMPI appraisal is a systematic examination of the processes in an organisation to determine the maturity of the organisation with respect to the CMMI. It consists of interviews with management and reviews with project teams. The appraisers will review documentation and determine the extent to which the processes defined are effective and institutionalised in the organisation.

and a further 1–2 years to implement level 3. The implementation of the CMMI needs to be balanced against the day-to-day needs of the organisation in delivering products and services to its customers. The processes implemented during a CMMI initiative will generally include:

- Developing and managing requirements
- Design and development
- Project management
- Configuration management
- Selecting and managing subcontractors
- Peer reviews
- Risk management and decision analysis
- Testing
- Audits

30.3   SCAMPI Appraisal

Appraisals (Fig. 30.5) play an essential role in the software process improvement programme. They allow an organisation to understand its current software process maturity, including the strengths and weaknesses in its processes. An appraisal is an independent examination of the software engineering and management practices in the organisation and is conducted using the SCAMPI appraisal methodology [SCA:06].

There are three classes of SCAMPI appraisals, and these are termed Class A, B and C. They vary in the level of formality, the cost and duration and the reporting of the appraisal results. Small organisations may not have the budget for a formal SCAMPI Class A appraisal. They may be more interested in an independent

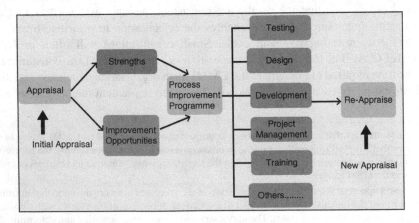

Fig. 30.5 Appraisals

Table 30.3 Phases in a SCAMPI appraisal

Phase	Description
Planning and preparation	This involves identifying the sponsor's objectives and the requirements for the appraisal. A good appraisal plan is fundamental to the success of the appraisal
Conducting the appraisal	The appraisal team interviews the participants and examines data to judge the extent to which the CMMI is implemented in the organisation
Reporting the results	The results of the appraisal are reported back to the sponsor. This will usually include a presentation of the findings and an appraisal report

SCAMPI Class B or C appraisal, which is used to provide feedback on their strengths and opportunities for improvement in the next improvement cycle.

The appraisal will identify strengths and weaknesses in the processes and any gaps that exist with respect to the CMMI practices. An initial appraisal is conducted at the start of the initiative to provide a baseline of its current process maturity and to plan and prioritise improvements for the first improvement cycle. Improvements are then implemented, and an appraisal is typically conducted at the end of the cycle to confirm progress. There are three phases in an appraisal (Table 30.3).

The appraisal leader kicks off the appraisal with the opening presentation, and the leader introduces the appraisal team[5] and presents the activities that will be carried out in the days ahead. These will include presentations, interviews, reviews of project documentation and detailed analysis to determine the extent to which the specific and generic practices have been implemented and whether the specific and generic goals for each process area within the scope of the appraisal are satisfied.

Sample output[6] from a SCAMPI Class A CMMI level 3 appraisal is presented in Fig. 30.6. Each column represents a CMMI process area, and each row represents a specific or generic practice. Colour coding is employed to indicate the extent to which the specific or generic practices have been implemented. The extent of implementation may be:

- Fully satisfied
- Largely satisfied
- Partially satisfied
- Not satisfied
- Not rated

---

[5] The appraisal team could be the CMMI project manager only (if the project manager is a SCAMPI-trained appraiser); alternatively, it could be an external appraiser and the CMMI project manager. A SCAMPI Class A appraisal could involve a large team of 4–9 appraisers (including a SCAMPI lead appraiser) for a large organisation. There is a strict qualification process to become a SCAMPI lead appraiser, and it requires attending the official SEI CMMI and SCAMPI training and conducting two appraisals under the direction of a qualified SCAMPI lead appraiser.

[6] The type of output to be provided is agreed in discussions between the appraisal sponsor and the appraisal leader. The output may just be the strengths and improvement opportunities identified. In other cases, the ratings may just be of the specific and generic goals rather than of the practices.

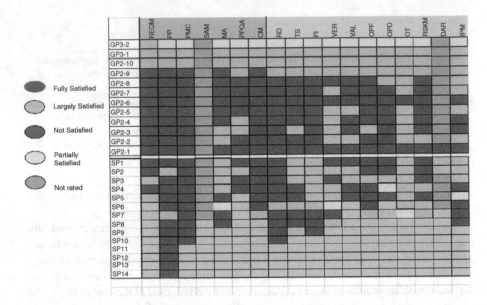

Fig. 30.6 SCAMPI CMMI L3 rating of practices

The appraisal leader will present the appraisal findings, and the appraisal output may include a presentation and an appraisal report. The appraisal output summarises the strengths and opportunities for improvement identified, and ratings of the process areas will be provided (where ratings are a part of the appraisal). The ratings will indicate the current maturity of the organisation's processes and any gaps that exist with respect to the targeted CMMI maturity level.

The appraisal findings allow the CMMI project manager to plan and schedule the next improvement cycle and to continue with the CMMI improvement programme. Appraisals allow an organisation to:

- Understand its current maturity (including strengths and weaknesses of its processes)
- Relate its strengths and weaknesses to the CMMI specific and generic practices
- Prioritise its improvements for the next improvement cycle
- Benchmark itself against other organisations (SCAMPI Class A)

30.4   PSP and TSP

The Personal Software Process (PSP) is a disciplined data-driven software development process that is designed to help software engineers understand and to improve their personal software process performance. It was developed by Watts Humphrey at the SEI, and it helps engineers to improve their estimation and planning skills and to reduce the number of defects in their work. This enables them to make commitments that they can keep and to manage the quality of their projects.

The PSP is focused on the work of the individual engineer, and it includes methods and tools that enable the engineer to produce a product on time, on budget and with the right quality. PSP helps the engineer to get the required data and to focus on statistical process control. The process has three levels with each level offering a different focus. PSP level 1 is focused on estimation and planning (including time, size and defect estimates); PSP level 2 is focused on design, code reviews and quality management; PSP level 3 is focused on larger projects.

The Team Software Process (TSP) was developed by Watts Humphrey at the SEI and is a structured approach designed to help software teams understand and improve their quality and productivity. Its focus is on building an effective software development team, and it involves establishing team goals, assigning team roles as well as other teamwork activities. Team members must already be familiar with the PSP.

The teams are *self-directed* and define their own work processes and produce their own plan. They set their own quality goals and build plans to achieve these goals. They track and report their work (including hours worked, defects found per phase, inspection examination rates and defect densities). The teams share team management responsibilities. The TSP enables teams to adopt a data driven approach to software development.

Chapter 31
Sinclair Research Ltd.

Sinclair Research was founded in Cambridge, England, by Sir Clive Sinclair (Fig. 31.1) in 1973. It was originally called Ablesdeal Ltd., but it was renamed to Sinclair Research in 1981. It was founded as a consumer electronics company, and it entered the home computer market in 1980 with the Sinclair ZX 80. This home computer retailed for £99.95, and it was the cheapest and smallest home computer in the United Kingdom at the time. The Commodore PET had been launched in 1979, but it retailed for £700 which was quite expensive for computer hobbyists.

The ZX 80 was a stepping stone for the Sinclair ZX 81 home computer which was introduced in 1981. The ZX 81 was designed by Rick Dickinson to be a small, simple and low-cost home computer for the general public, and it retailed for an affordable £69.95. It offered tremendous value for money, and it opened the world of computing to those who had been denied access by cost. Most Sinclair computers were bought for educational purposes.

The Sinclair ZX 81 was a highly successful product with sales of over 1.5 million units. It came with 1 KB of memory which could be extended to 16 KB of memory. It had a monochrome black and white display on a UHF television. It was one of the first home computers to be used widely by the general public as distinct from business users, and it led to a large community of enthusiast users. It came with a BASIC interpreter which enabled users to learn about computing and allowed them to write their first BASIC programs. It came with a standard QWERTY keyboard which had some extra keys, and each key had several functions.

Sinclair entered an agreement with Timex, an American company, which allowed Timex to produce clones of Sinclair machines for the American market. These included the Timex Sinclair 1000 and the Timex Sinclair 1500 which were variants of the ZX 81. These were initially successful but soon faced intense completion from other American vendors.

The ZX Spectrum home computer was introduced in 1982, and it became the bestselling computer in the United Kingdom at that time. Its main competitor was the BBC microcomputer produced by Acorn Computers. However, the BBC micro

© Springer International Publishing Switzerland 2015
G. O'Regan, *Pillars of Computing*, DOI 10.1007/978-3-319-21464-1_31

Fig. 31.1 Sir Clive
Sinclair meets young
inventors

was more expensive and retailed for £299, whereas the ZX Spectrum was about half
its price. It led to a boom in companies providing hardware and software for the
Spectrum, and Clive Sinclair received a knighthood for his services to British
industry.

The TV 80 was a pocket television that was launched in 1983, and it used a flat-
tened CRT tube. It was a commercial failure for Sinclair, and it did not cover its
development costs.

The Sinclair QL was released in early 1984 and was a 32-bit microcomputer with
a Motorola 68008 processor. It was targeted at professional users and was priced at
£399. However, it had several design flaws including problems with the reliability
of the hardware and software, and it took several months before fully functional
Sinclair QLs were available. This led to many customer complaints which damaged
the reputation of the company and the *Sinclair* brand.

The company launched several new products in the years that followed including
a FM LCD Wristwatch Radio which was introduced in the United States in early
1985. However, there were performance problems with the product, and it never
went into full production.

Sinclair Research began to experience financial difficulties from the mid-1980s,
and the "Sinclair" brand name and products were sold to Amstrad in 1986 for
£5 million.

Sinclair Research continues to exist today, but it is a shadow of its former self. At
its peak it had revenues of over £100 million, and it employed over a hundred people. It is now a one person company which markets Sir Clive Sinclair's latest
inventions.

31.1 ZX Spectrum

The Sinclair ZX Spectrum (Fig. 31.2) was an 8-bit home computer introduced into the United Kingdom by Sinclair Research in 1982. It used an 8-bit Zilog Z80 microprocessor and it initially came in two models. The Spectrum would eventually be released in eight different models.

The basic model had 16 KB of RAM and retailed for £125, whereas the more advanced model had 48 KB of RAM and retailed for £175. This made the ZX Spectrum significantly cheaper than the existing Commodore 64 home computer and the newly introduced BBC microcomputer. The ZX Spectrum introduced colour graphics and sound, and it included an extended version of Sinclair's existing BASIC interpreter.

The ZX Spectrum was designed by Rick Dickinson and Richard Altwasser who were Sinclair employees. The sleek outward design was created by Dickinson and the internal hardware designed by Altwasser. Clive Sinclair had emphasised the importance in creating a home computer substantially cheaper than the rival BBC microcomputer, and so cost was a key factor in the design of the ZX Spectrum.

Cost forced the designers to find new ways of doing things, and they minimised the components in the keyboard from a few hundred to a handful of moving parts using a new technology. They used the cost-effective 3.5 MHz Z80 processor, a sound beeper, a BASIC interpreter and an audio tape as a storage device.

The demand for the ZX Spectrum was phenomenal, and it caught the imagination of the British general public, and it was embraced by both young and old. It was initially targeted as an educational tool to help students to become familiar with programming, but it soon became popular for playing home video games.

Fig. 31.2 ZX spectrum

The ZX Spectrum was a highly successful home computer with over five million units sold. It was 50 % cheaper than the BBC microcomputer, and this was an important factor in its success. It led to a massive interest in learning about computing, programming and video games among the general public.

The users were supplied with a book from which they could type in a computer program into the computer, or they could load a program from a cassette. This allowed users to modify and experiment with programs as well as playing computer games.

Its simplicity, versatility and good design led to companies writing various software programs for it, and soon computer magazines and books dedicated to the ZX Spectrum were launched with the goal of teaching users how to program the machine.

The ZX Spectrum spawned various clones around the world. Countries such as the United States, Russia and India created their own version of the Spectrum.

The ZX Spectrum remained popular throughout the 1980s, and it was officially retired in 1988. The Spectrum+ was released in 1984, and this was essentially the 48 K version of the Spectrum with an enhanced keyboard. The Spectrum +128 was released in 1986, and it was similar in appearance to the Spectrum +, but it had 128 K of memory.

Sinclair was sold to Amstrad in 1986, and Amstrad created its own models including the ZX Spectrum +2, the ZX Spectrum +2A, the ZX Spectrum +3, the ZX Spectrum +3A and the ZX Spectrum +3B.

There is a large archive of ZX Spectrum-related material available online (http://www.worldofspectrum.org), and it includes software, utilities, games and tools. Today, there are emulators available that allow Spectrum games to be downloaded and played on personal computers. For further information on the ZX Spectrum, see [Woo:13].

Chapter 32
Texas Instruments

Texas Instruments (TI) is an American electronics company that designs and makes semiconductors. It is one of the largest manufacturers of semiconductors in the world, as well as one of the largest manufacturers of chips for cellular handsets. It produces a wide range of other semiconductor products including calculators, microcontrollers, digital signal processors, analog semiconductors and multicore processors. Its headquarters are in Dallas, Texas.

The company was founded in 1951 following the reorganisation of Geophysical Service, a company that was involved in the manufacture of seismic equipment and defence electronics. Shockley and others had developed the transistor at Bell Labs in the late 1940s, and Texas Instruments began research into transistors in the early 1950s. It designed and manufactured one of the first transistor radios in 1954.

Jack Kilby (Fig. 32.1) of Texas Instruments succeeded in building an integrated circuit made of germanium that contained several transistors in 1958. Robert Noyce of Fairchild Semiconductors built an integrated circuit on a single wafer of silicon in 1960, and Kirby and Noyce are considered coinventors of the integrated circuit. Kilby was awarded the Nobel Prize in Physics in 2000 for his role in the invention of the integrated circuit.

Texas Instruments today has revenues of approximately $12 billion and net income of approximately $2 billion. More detailed information on Texas Instruments is in [Pir:05].

32.1 Integrated Circuit

The motivation for the invention of the integrated circuit was the goal of finding a solution to the problems that engineers faced in increasing the performance of their designs as the number of components in the design increased. Each component needed to be wired to many other components, and the wiring and soldering

© Springer International Publishing Switzerland 2015
G. O'Regan, *Pillars of Computing*, DOI 10.1007/978-3-319-21464-1_32

Fig. 32.1 Jack Kilby c.
1958 (Courtesy of Texas
Instruments)

were done manually. Clearly, more components would be required to improve
performance, and therefore, it seemed that future designs would consist almost
entirely of wiring.

An integrated circuit consists of a set of electronic circuits on a small chip of
semiconductor material, and it is much smaller than a circuit made out of independent components. Integrated circuits today are extremely compact and may contain
billions of transistors and other electronic components in a tiny area. The width of
each conducting line has got smaller and smaller due to advances in technology over
the years, and it is now in tens of nanometres.[1]

The electronics industry was dominated by vacuum tube technology up to the
early 1950s. However, vacuum tubes had inherent limitations as they were bulky,
unreliable, produced considerable heat and consumed a lot of power. Bell Labs
invented the transistor in 1947, and transistors were tiny in comparison to vacuum
tubes, and they were more reliable and lasted longer. The transistor stimulated engineers to design ever more complex electronic circuits and equipment containing
hundreds or thousands of discrete components such as transistors, diodes, rectifiers
and capacitors.

However, the problem was that these components still had to be interconnected
to form electronic circuits, and this involved hand soldering of thousands of components to thousands of bits of wire. This was expensive and time consuming, and it
was also unreliable since every soldered joint was a potential source of trouble. The
challenge for the industry was to find a cost-effective and reliable way of producing
these components and interconnecting them.

Kilby joined Texas Instruments in 1958, and he began investigating how to solve
this problem. He realised that semiconductors were all that were really required, as
resistors and capacitors could be made from the same material as the transistors. He

---

[1] 1 nanometre (nm) is equal to 10^{-9} m.

Fig. 32.2 First integrated circuit (Courtesy of Texas Instruments)

realised that since all of the components could be made of a single material, they could also be made in situ interconnected to form a complete circuit.

Kilby's integrated circuit consisted of a transistor and other components on a slice of germanium (Fig. 32.2). His invention revolutionised the electronics industry, and the integrated circuit is the foundation of almost every electronic device in use today. His invention used germanium, and the size of the integrated circuit was 7/16-by-1/16 in. Robert Noyce at Fairchild Electronics later invented an integrated circuit based on silicon, and today silicon is the material of choice for semiconductors.

It took some time for integrated circuits to take off, as they were an unproven technology and remained expensive until mass production. Kilby and others at Texas successfully commercialised the integrated circuit by designing a handheld calculator that was as powerful as the existing large, electromechanical desktop models. The resulting electronic handheld calculator was small enough to fit in a coat pocket. This battery-powered device could perform the four basic arithmetic operations on six digit numbers, and it was completed in 1967.

Today, semiconductors are the foundation of modern electronics, and almost all technology today uses semiconductors with the most important being the integrated circuit (IC). The IC is a set of electronic circuits on a small plate of semiconductor material that is usually made of silicon. An IC may contain several billion transistors in a tiny area.

Fig. 32.3 TI-Nspire CX
(Courtesy of Joerg
Woerner)

32.2   Texas Instruments Education Technology

Texas Instruments is active in the education software market, and it produces the TI-Nspire series of graphical calculators. These include the TI-Nspire CAS, the TI-Nspire CX (Fig. 32.3) and the TI-Nspire CX CAS. These calculators have colour screens, rechargeable batteries and thin designs.

The TI-Nspire series of graphical calculators is quite different from previous versions of Texas Instruments' calculators, in that the new TI-Nspire series includes a user interface that is closer to a PC rather than a traditional calculator.

This series of calculators allows detailed graphs to be drawn, and there is normal calculator functionality as well as functionality for geometry applications, spreadsheets and statistics.

The TI-Nspire Navigator system allows the teacher to connect a network of TI-Nspire calculators to a computer. It allows the teacher to directly monitor the progress and work done by the individual students and to display the student's work on the screen to facilitate class discussion.

Chapter 33
Twitter

Twitter is a social communication tool that allows people to broadcast short messages. It is often described as the *SMS of the Internet*, and it is an online social media and microblogging site that allows its users to send and receive short 140-character messages called *tweets*. The restriction to 140 characters is to allow Twitter to be used on non-smartphone mobile devices. Twitter has over 500 million users with approximately 300 million of these are active users, and it is one of the most visited websites in the world.[1] Users may access Twitter through its website interface, a mobile device app or SMS. The company headquarters are in San Francisco, California.

Twitter messages are often about friends telling one another about their day, what they are doing, where they are and what they are thinking, and Twitter has transformed the world of media, politics and business. It is possible to include links to web pages and other media as a tweet. News such as natural disasters, sports results and so on are often reported first by Twitter. The site has impacted political communication in a major way, as it allows politicians and their followers to debate and exchange political opinions. It allows celebrities to engage and stay in contact with their fans, and it provides a new way for businesses to advertise its brands to its target audience.

As a Twitter user you select which other people who you wish to follow, and when you follow someone, their tweets show up in a list known as your *Twitter stream*. Similarly, anyone that chooses to follow you will see your tweets in their stream.

A *hashtag* is an easy way to find all the tweets about a particular topic of interest, and it may be used even if you are not following the people who are tweeting. It also allows you to contribute to the particular topic that is of interest. A hashtag consists of a short word or acronym preceded by the hash sign (#), and conferences, hot topics and so on often have a hashtag.

---

[1] Twitter has been ranked as one of the ten-most-visited websites in the world.

© Springer International Publishing Switzerland 2015   215
G. O'Regan, *Pillars of Computing*, DOI 10.1007/978-3-319-21464-1_33

A word or topic that is tagged at a greater rate than other hashtags is said to be a trending topic, and a trending topic may be the result of an event that prompts people to discuss a particular topic. Trending may also result from the deliberate action of certain groups (e.g., in the entertainment industry) to raise the profile of a musician or celebrity and to market their work.

Twitter has evolved to become an effective way to communicate the latest news, and its effectiveness for an organisation increases as the number of its followers grows. An organisation may determine what people are saying about it, as well as their positive or negative experience in interacting with it. It allows the organisation to directly interact with its followers, and this is a powerful way to engage its audience and to make people feel heard. It allows the organisation to respond to any negative feedback and to deal with such feedback sensitively and appropriately.

The company was founded in 2006 by Jack Dorsey (Fig. 33.1), Noah Glass, Evan Williams (Fig. 33.2) and Biz Stone. Dorsey initially served as CEO of the company, and Williams later replaced Dorsey as CEO. Dick Costello replaced Williams as CEO, and Dorsey serves as chairman of the board of the company. Twitter initially had eight employees, but it has grown rapidly, and today it has annual revenue of over $600 million, and it employs over 3,000 people.

The company launched its successful initial public offering in late 2013, and the company's share price increased from its initial price of $26 to reach over $44 at the end of the day (over 70 % increase during the day) giving the company a market capitalisation of over $24 billion.

Dorsey introduced the idea of an individual using an SMS service to communicate with a small group while he was still an undergraduate student at New York University. The word *twitter* was the chosen name for this new service, and its definition as *a short burst of information* and *chirps from birds* was highly appropriate.

Fig. 33.1 Jack Dorsey at the 2012 Time 100 Gala

Fig. 33.2 Evan Williams
speaks at XOXO 2013
festival

The first version of Twitter was introduced in mid-2006, and it took the company some time to determine exactly what type of entity it actually was. There was nothing quite like it in existence, and initially it was considered a microblogging and social media site. Today, it is considered to be an information network rather than just a social media site.

Twitter has experienced rapid growth with 400,000 tweets posted per quarter in 2007, to 100 million per quarter in 2008, to 65 million tweets per day from mid-2010, and to 140 million tweets per day in 2011. Twitter's usage spikes during important events such as major sporting events, natural disasters, the death of a celebrity and so on. For such events, there may be over 100,000 tweets per second. For more detailed information on Twitter, see [Sch:14].

33.1 Twitter Business Model

Twitter's main source of revenue is advertisements through *promoted tweets* that appear in a user's timeline (Twitter stream). The first promoted tweets appeared from late 2011, and the use of a tweet for advertisement was ingenious. It helped to make the advertisement feel like part of Twitter, and it meant that an advertisement could go anywhere that a tweet could go. Advertisers are only charged when the user follows the links or retweets the original advertisements. Further, the use of tweets for advertisement meant that the transition to mobile was easy, and today about 80 % of Twitter use is on mobile devices.

Twitter has recently embarked on a strategy that goes beyond these advertisements to sell products directly (including to people who don't use Twitter). Twitter also earns revenue from a data licensing arrangement where it sells its information (fire-hose of data) to companies who use this information to analyse consumer trends. Twitter analyses what users tweet (as Google analyses what users search for) in order to understand their intent.

Chapter 34
Unimation

Joseph Engelberger and George Devol founded the first robotics company, *Unimation Inc.*, in 1956. Engelberger was the entrepreneur and Devol the inventor, and their goal was to develop industrial robots. Unimation was to become the largest robotics company in the world, and it pioneered the worldwide growth of industrial robots.

Devol and Engelberger initially developed a prototype hydraulically driven robot arm that was programmable. It could pick up small metal letters and spell out small phrases. The prototype was introduced at a trade show in Chicago in 1961, and the era of industrial robots was born.

The prototype was demonstrated to the Ford Motor company, and while Ford recognised the potential of robots, it did not see applications of robots to car assembly at that time.

Unimate (Fig. 34.1) was a material handling robot and robots for welding and other applications followed. A prototype of Unimate was installed at a GM die-casting factory in Trenton in 1959, and the first industrial robot (Unimate) was installed on a General Motors (GM) assembly line in New Jersey in 1961. This robot was used to lift hot pieces of metal from a die-casting machine and to stack them. Eventually, over 450 Unimate robots were employed in die-casting.

These robots were very successful and reliable and saved General Motors money by replacing staff with machines. Other automobile companies followed GM in purchasing Unimate robots, and the robot industry continues to play a major role in the automobile sector.

Pullman Inc. (a railroad car manufacturer) took a 51 % stake in Unimation in 1962, and an international branch of Unimation was set up in England in 1966 to focus on international sales in Europe. Nokia was licensed to market robots in Scandinavia and Eastern Europe.

Unimation signed a licensing agreement with Kawasaki Heavy Industries in 1969, and the agreement allowed Kawasaki to manufacture and market Unimate robots for the Asian market. By 1983, over 2400 Japanese-made Kawasaki Unimate robots had been shipped.

Fig. 34.1 Unimate in
1960s

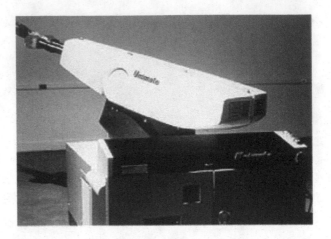

Unimation recognised that the automobile industry had major potential for industrial robots and focused their efforts on overcoming the challenges that robots faced in mastering the skill and intelligence required for the assembly line. They developed a close relationship with General Motors as GM recognised the potential of robot technology. GM rebuilt its plant in Ohio in 1969 for it to become the most automated plant in the world at that time, producing over a hundred cars an hour. The plant revolutionalised automobile making, and robotics became a fundamental part of car assembly. Unimates began to appear in all the major car manufacturers such as Mercedes Benz, BMW, Volvo and so on in the years that followed.

The Unimate family of industrial robots evolved in line with the applications demanded by various industries. The technical innovations resulted in industrial robots with greater capabilities. Unimation began to experience significant completion from Japanese companies from the 1970s.

Unimation made a fatal decision to stay with hydraulic robots rather than embracing electric-driven robots as demanded by the automobile industry. Its partnership with General Motors ended in 1981, and GM developed a partnership with Fujitsu to use their electric robots.

Unimation became a public company in 1981, and it was taken over by Westinghouse in 1982. However, its hydraulic robots were unsuccessful in competing against the new generation of electric-driven robots that were demanded by the automobile sector. Westinghouse entered a partnership with Matsushita Electric, and it sold off what remained of Unimation to Stäubli, a Swiss company.

A Unimate robot appeared on *The Tonight Show* hosted by Johnny Carson in 1966, and the robot poured a beer and sank a golf putt. The Unimate was inducted into the Robot Hall of Fame in 2003. The rise and fall of Unimation Inc. is described in [Mun:11].

Fig. 34.2 George Devol

34.1   George Devol

George Devol (Fig. 34.2) was a prolific American inventor who is regarded (with Joseph Engelberger) as one of the fathers of robotics. He was awarded a patent for the first industrial robot (*Unimate*), and he played an important role in the foundation of the modern robotics industry.

He was born in Kentucky in 1912, and he was interested in electrical and mechanical devices from an early age. He was an avid reader on everything about mechanical devices, and his initial interests were in the practical application of vacuum tubes. He was not strong academically, and he did not pursue a university education.

He formed his own company, United Cinephone, in 1932, and one of his early inventions was the automatic door. His company licensed this invention to Yale & Towne who manufactured the "Phantom Doorman" photoelectric door. His company also developed a bar-code system that was used for sorting packages at the Railway Express Company.

He sold his company at the start of the Second World War and became a manager at the Special Projects Department at Sperry Gyroscope. This department developed radar devices and microwave test equipment.

After the war, Devol was part of the team that developed commercial use of microwave oven technology. He applied for a patent in 1946 on a magnetic recording system for controlling machines and a digital playback device for machines. He licensed this digital magnetic recording device to Remington, and he became manager of their magnetics department. His goal was to develop the device for business data applications, but it proved to be too slow for business data.

He applied for a patent on *programmed article transfer* in 1954, and the goal of this invention was to perform repeated tasks with greater precision and productivity than a human worker. The patent was concerned with automatic operation of machinery, including handling and an automated control apparatus. It introduced the concept of *universal automation*, and the term *Unimate* was coined. This was the first patent for a digitally operated programmable robot arm, and it led to the foundation of the robotics industry.

His Unimate was named by *Popular Mechanics* magazine in 2005 as one of the top 50 inventions of the past 50 years. Devol received various awards for his contributions to robotics. He was inducted into the National Inventor's Hall of Fame in 2011. He died aged 99 in 2011.

34.2   Robotics

The first use of the term *robot* was by the Czech playwright Karel Capek in his play *Rossum's Universal Robots* which was performed in 1921. The word "robot" is a Czech word for forced labour, and the play explores whether it is ethical to exploit artificial workers in a factory and how robots should respond to their exploitation. Capek's robots looked and acted like humans and were created by chemical means. Capek rejected the idea that machines created from metal could think or have human feelings.

Asimov wrote several stories about robots in the 1940s including *I, Robot*, which is a collection of short stories featuring a robopsychologist, Dr. Susan Calvin. She narrates various stories to a reporter describing her work as a robot psychologist and her role in dealing with aberrant robot behaviour. The stories are concerned with the interaction of humans and robots, as well as the associated moral issues. Asimov predicted the rise of a major robot industry, and he introduced a set of rules (or laws) of good robot behaviour. He initially formulated three laws, but these were later extended with a fourth law (Table 34.1).

Robots have been very effective at doing clearly defined repetitive tasks, and there are many sophisticated robots in the workplace today. These are industrial manipulators that are essentially computer-controlled "arms and hands". The term *robot* is defined by the Robot Institute of America as:

Table 34.1 Asimov's laws of robotics

Law	Description
Law zero	A robot may not injure humanity or, through inaction, allow humanity to come to harm
Law one	A robot may not injure a human being or, through inaction, allow a human being to come to harm, unless this would violate a higher order law
Law two	A robot must obey orders given it by human beings, except where such orders would conflict with a higher order law
Law three	A robot must protect its own existence as long as such protection does not conflict with a higher order law

Definition 34.1 (**Robots**) *A re-programmable, multifunctional manipulator designed to move material, parts, tools, or specialized devices through various programmed motions for the performance of a variety of tasks.*

Robots can also improve the quality of life for workers as they can free human workers from performing dangerous or repetitive jobs. They provide consistently high-quality products and can work tirelessly for 24 h a day. This helps to reduce the costs of manufactured goods, thereby benefiting consumers.

Industrial robots can do many different types of work such as spray painting, welding and so on. The precise type of work is determined by its program, which may define relatively simple jobs or more complex tasks. The robot arm may be "taught" a program by moving the robot arm through the desired sequence of operations, and the sequence of operations is recorded in the machine's memory. The robot arm will then follow the prescribed set of actions over and over again.

Early industrial robots include Unimate produced by Unimation in 1961 and Versatran produced by American Machine and Foundry (AMF) in 1967. Initially, there was resistance in the workplace to the introduction of robots, as it was feared that there would be a major impact on employment especially in mass production industries.

There was also a need for a business case to prove that the introduction of automated technology would result in cost savings, as well as guaranteeing the quality of the products. Automation has eliminated many semi-skilled jobs, but it has led to new jobs for personnel to service robots.

Chapter 35
Xerox PARC

Xerox Palo Alto Research Center (Xerox PARC) was founded as the research and development division of Xerox in 1970. It has made important contributions to the computing field, and its inventions include laser printing; Ethernet technology for local area networks; the Xerox Alto which was one of the earliest personal computers and which had a major influence on the Apple Macintosh computer; the graphical user interface (GUI) which included icons and windows for personal computers; Bravo and Gypsy which were the first text formatting WYSIWYG editors; and object-oriented programming with the Smalltalk programming language.

Several Xerox PARC researchers have received the prestigious ACM Turing Award in recognition of their inventions. These include Butler Lampson who won the 1992 Turing Award for his contributions to personal computing and computer science; Alan Kay who received the 2003 Turing Award for his contributions to object-oriented programming and the Smalltalk programming language; and Charles Thacker who received the 2009 Turing Award for his pioneering design and development of the Alto personal computer and for his contributions to Ethernet and the tablet computer.

Xerox PARC's inventions have had a significant influence on developments in the computing field. However, Xerox has been criticised for failing to properly exploit its inventions, as other companies have reaped the benefits of its research. For example, the Xerox 8010 Star, its commercialisation of the Xerox Alto personal computer, was released in 1981, but it was not very successful due mainly to its high price of $16,000. Instead, it was Apple that reaped the benefits of PARC's research in personal computing, when it introduced the Apple Macintosh. This machine revolutionalised the computing field with its bitmap display and mouse-driven graphical user interface, and these were copied from the existing Xerox Alto. The Apple Macintosh was an immediate success following its release in 1984.

Xerox PARC was transformed from a division of Xerox into a wholly owned subsidiary of the company in 2002, and it is now known simply as "PARC". It has

© Springer International Publishing Switzerland 2015
G. O'Regan, *Pillars of Computing*, DOI 10.1007/978-3-319-21464-1_35

several customers including Xerox, Fujitsu, VMware and Samsung, and it remains active in applied research in various areas of the computing field. More detailed information on the history of Xerox PARC is in [Hil:00].

35.1 Xerox Alto Personal Computer

The Xerox Alto (Fig. 35.1) was one of the earliest personal computers, and it was introduced in early 1973. It was designed by Chuck Thacker and others, and it was one of the first computers to use a mouse-driven graphical user interface. It was designed for individual rather than home use, and it was used by a single person sitting at a desk. It was essentially a small minicomputer rather than a personal computer, and it was unlike modern personal computers in that it was not based on the microprocessor. The significance of the Xerox Alto is that it had a major impact on the design of early personal computers and especially on the design of the Apple Macintosh computer.

Butler Lampson wrote a famous memo to management in Xerox [Lam:72] in 1972 in which he requested funds to construct a number of Alto workstations. He made the case for the development of the Alto, and he outlined his vision of personal computing in the memo. His vision described the broad range of applications to which the Xerox Alto could be applied.

He outlined a vision of distributed computing, where several Xerox Alto workstations would form a network of computers, with each computer user having his

Fig. 35.1 Xerox Alto

own files and communicating with other users to interchange or share information. He argued that the development of the Alto would allow the theory that cheap personal computers would be extremely useful to be tested and demonstrated comprehensively to be the case.

This memo led to the development of a network of Altos in the mid-1970s; the development of Ethernet technology for connecting computers in a network; the development of a mouse-driven graphical user interface; the development of a WYSIWYG editor; laser printing; and the development of the Smalltalk object-oriented programming language.

The cost of the Alto machine was approximately $10,000, and this was significantly less than the existing mainframes and minicomputers. The machine was capable of performing almost any computation that a DEC PDP-10 machine could perform.

35.2   Ethernet

Ethernet is a family of computer networking technologies for local area networks (LAN) and larger networks. It was invented at Xerox PARC by Robert Metcalfe (Fig. 35.2) and David Boggs as a standard for connecting computers over short distances. The original idea of the Ethernet technology was described in a 1973 memo (*Alto Ethernet*) written by Metcalfe.

Fig. 35.2 Robert Metcalfe

It was influenced by ALOHAnet which was a wireless packet data network developed at the University of Hawaii and also by ARPANET developed by DARPA (part of the US Department of Defense), which was one of the world's first packet switching networks.

Metcalfe and Boggs's design of the Ethernet emphasised distributed computing, and this was a paradigm shift from the centralised time-sharing systems that dominated the computing field. An early version of the network was running in late 1973, and all of the machines on the local area network (LAN) shared one cable. Each machine had an add-on Ethernet board.

The Ethernet system was deployed in Xerox PARC in the mid-1970s, and it consisted of a network of Xerox Alto computers connected together by a thick coaxial cable. The Xerox 9700 laser printer was linked to the coaxial cable and could be shared among the network of Alto computers.

The coaxial cable was the channel for the communication of data, and Metcalfe described it as *Ether* after the famous luminiferous ether that was postulated as the medium for the transmission of light and electromagnetic radiation in the nineteenth century. The existence of Ether was later disproved by the Michelson Morley experiment in 1887.

Xerox PARC filed a patent on its invention of Ethernet in 1975, with Robert Metcalfe, David Boggs, Charles Thacker and Butler Lampson listed as the inventors. Metcalfe and Boggs published the first paper on Ethernet in 1976.

Metcalfe left PARC to form 3Com in 1979, and Ethernet became an IEEE standard (IEEE 802/3) in 1984. Ethernet today is the dominant LAN technology, and it has evolved over the years to support higher bit rates. The initial speed of Ethernet was just under 3 Mb/s, and today speeds of 100 Gb/s and 400 Gb/s have been achieved.

35.3   Smalltalk Programming Language

Smalltalk is an object-oriented programming language that was developed at the Learning Research Group (LRG) at Xerox PARC. It was designed by Alan Kay, Dan Ingalls and others at Xerox PARC, and the language was influenced by earlier languages such as Lisp and Simula 67. Kay (Fig. 35.3) had become familiar with Simula 67 while a graduate student at the University of Utah, and Simula 67 was the earliest object-oriented language. It was developed by Ole-Johan Dahl and Kristen Nygaard at the Norwegian Computing Centre in Oslo.

Smalltalk's development commenced in the late 1960s, and the first version appeared in 1972. This was Smalltalk-72, and it was used internally within Xerox PARC. The first public version of Smalltalk that was made available to the wider community was Smalltalk-80, and this version was released in 1980.

Smalltalk was an influential programming language, and it influenced later object-oriented languages such as Objective-C and Java. The central concept in Smalltalk-80 is an *object*, where an object is always an instance of a *class*. A class

Fig. 35.3 Alan Kay

describes the properties and behaviours of its members (the instances of the class or objects). A Smalltalk object may hold state information; it may receive a message from another object; or it may send a message to another object.

The early history of Smalltalk is described in a nice article by Alan Kay [Kay:93], in which he describes early object-oriented programming and ideas in computing in the 1960s. The article also describes the work done at Xerox PARC in the 1970s, including the development of Smalltalk-71 and Smalltalk-72, as well as the early applications of Smalltalk and the release of Smalltalk-80.

35.4   Laser Printing

The laser printer was invented at Xerox PARC by Garry Starkweather and others in the early 1970s. Starkweather began thinking about laser printers at a Xerox research centre in the mid-1960s and prior to the creation of Xerox PARC in 1970. He was interested in solving the problem of generalising the work that a facsimile does (i.e., in copying someone else's original) to the use of a computer to generate the original. His idea was to use a laser beam to capture an image of what was to be copied directly onto the copier drum.

He moved to Xerox PARC in 1971 with the goal of building a laser printer. He adapted an existing Xerox 7000 copier to create the first prototype laser printer in early 1972. This machine was named the Scanned Laser Output Terminal (SLOT), and later work with Butler Lampson and others led to the EARS printer. This printer was used with the Xerox Alto computer system and network, and a descendent of this printer became the Xerox 9700 laser printer, which was released in 1977.

The Xerox 9700 Electronic Printing System could print two pages per second (or 120 pages a minute), and it was intended for high-volume applications. This printer was to remain the Rolls-Royce high-volume printer for many years.

Chapter 36
Zuse KG

Zuse KG was founded by Konrad Zuse (Fig. 36.1) at Neukirchen (approximately 100 km north of Frankfurt) in 1949. It was the first computer company in Germany, and it initially had five employees. Zuse KG produced over 250 computers from 1949 to 1969, and by 1964 it had over 1200 employees. The company ran into financial difficulties in the early 1960s, and it was taken over by Rheinstahl in 1964. Rheinstahl was taken over by Siemens in 1967, and Konrad Zuse left the company in 1969.

The initial focus of the company was to restore and improve Zuse's Z4 machine, which had survived the Allied bombing of Berlin, and Zuse's subsequent move to Bavaria. The machine consisted of 2200 relays, a mechanical memory of 64 32-bit words and a processor. The speed of the machine was approximate 1000 instructions per hour. The Henschel Aircraft Company ordered the Z4 machine in 1942. However, the production of the machine was time consuming, and it was never actually delivered to Henschel. The machine was almost complete by the end of the Second World War in 1945.

The Z4 was restored for the Institute of Applied Mathematics at the Eidgenössische Technische Hochschule Zürich (ETH) in Zurich. The restoration was complete in 1950, and it was delivered to the ETH later that year. It was one of the first operational computers in Europe at that time.

It was transferred to the French-German Research Institute of Saint-Louis in France in 1955, and it remained operational there until 1959. Today, the Z4 machine is on display at the Deutsche Museum in Munich.

Zuse KG commenced work on the Z5 in the early 1950s, and this was an extended version of the Z4. The Z5 was one of the first commercial computers in Europe, and it was produced for the Leitz company in Germany. The Z5 followed similar construction principles as the Z4, but it was over six times faster.

The Z11 was sold from 1955 to German companies and universities and to the optical industry. The machine had 654 relays and 28 stepwise relays. It was programmable via a punch tape from 1957.

© Springer International Publishing Switzerland 2015
G. O'Regan, *Pillars of Computing*, DOI 10.1007/978-3-319-21464-1_36

Fig. 36.1 Konrad Zuse
(Courtesy of Horst Zuse,
Berlin)

Several universities ordered computers of the type Z22, which was a cheaper computer based on tubes. The Z23 computer was delivered to 98 universities and companies, and a restored version is now at the Computer History Museum at Mountain View in California.

The market conditions were quite difficult for a new computer company in post-war Germany, and Zuse KG developed international links with the Remington Rand Corporation.[1]

36.1 Konrad Zuse

Konrad Zuse is considered *the father of the computer* in Germany, as he built the world's first programmable machine (the Z3) in 1941. He was born in Berlin in 1910 and studied civil engineering at the Technical University of Berlin. He was talented at mechanical construction, and he won several prizes for his constructions while a student.

He commenced working as a stress analyser for Henschel after his graduation in 1935. Henschel[2] was a German aircraft manufacturer and Zuse stayed in his position for less than a year. He resigned with the intention of forming his own company to build automatic calculating machines.

---

[1] Remington Rand is discussed in Chap. 14.

[2] Henschel manufactured tanks, fighter and bomber aircraft and various missiles during the Second World War.

His parents provided financial support and he commenced work on what would become the Z1 machine in 1936. Zuse employed the binary system for the calculator, and metallic shafts that could shift from position 0 to 1 and vice versa. The Z1 machine was operational by 1938, and it was essentially a binary mechanical calculator with limited programmability.

He served in the German Army on the Eastern Front for 6 months in 1939 at the start of the Second World War. Henschel helped Zuse to obtain a deferment from the army, and it made the case that he was needed as an engineer rather than as a soldier. Zuse re-commenced working at Henschel in 1940 and remained affiliated to Henschel for the duration of the war. He built the Z2 and Z3 machines there. The Z3 was operational in 1941 and it was the world's first programmable computer. The Z4 was almost complete as the Red Army advanced on Berlin in 1945, and Zuse dismantled the Z4 and left for Bavaria.

He designed the world's first high-level programming language between 1943 and 1945, and this language was called Plankalkül. He set up Zuse KG in 1949 and completed the Z4 in 1950. This was one of the earliest commercial computers, and its first customer was the Technical University of Zurich. Zuse KG was taken over by Siemens in 1967.

36.2 Zuse's Machines

Zues was unaware of computer-related developments in Germany or in other countries, and he implemented the principles of modern digital computers in isolation independently of others.

He commenced work on his first machine called the Z1[3] in 1936, and the machine was operational by 1938. It was demonstrated to a small number of people who saw it rattle and compute the determinant of a three by three matrix. It was essentially a binary electrically driven mechanical calculator with limited programmability. It was capable of executing instructions read from the program punch cards, but the program itself was never loaded into the memory.

It employed the binary number system and metallic shafts that could slide from position 0 to position 1 and vice versa. The machine was essentially a 22-bit floating point value adder and subtractor. A decimal keyboard was used for input, and the output was decimal digits. The machine included some control logic which allowed it to perform more complex operations such as multiplications and division. These operations were performed by repeated additions for multiplication, and repeated subtractions for division.

The multiplication took approximately 5 s. The computer memory contained 64 22-bit words. Each word of memory could be read from and written to by the

---

[3] Zuse's machines were originally called V1 to V4. However, he renamed them Z1 to Z4 after the war to avoid the negative association with the destructive V1 and V2 rockets which were launched against London by the Nazis.

Fig. 36.2 Zuse and the reconstructed Z3 (Courtesy of Horst Zuse, Berlin)

program punch cards and the control unit. It had a clock speed of 1 Hz, and two floating point registers of 22 bits each. The machine was slow and unreliable, and a reconstruction of the Z1 machine is in the Deutsches Technikmuseum in Berlin.

Zuse's next attempt was the creation of the Z2 machine which aimed to improve on the Z1. This was a mechanical and relay computer created in 1939. It used a similar mechanical memory, but it replaced the arithmetic and control logic with 600 electrical relay circuits. It used 16-bit fixed point arithmetic instead of the 22-bit used in the Z1. It had a 16-bit word size and the size of its memory was 64 words. It had a clock speed of 3 Hz.

Zuse's Z3 machine (Fig. 36.2) was the first functional tape-stored-program-controlled computer. It was created in 1941 and it used 2,600 telephone relays; the binary number system; and it could perform floating-point arithmetic. It had a clock speed of 5 Hz and multiplication and division took 3 s. The input to the machine was with a decimal keyboard, and the output was on lamps that could display decimal numbers. The word length was 22-bits and the size of the memory was 64 words.

It used a punched film for storing the sequence of program instructions. It could convert decimal to binary and back again, and it was the first digital computer since it pre-dated the Altanasoff-Berry Computer (ABC) by one year. It was proven to be

Turing-complete in 1998, and there is a reconstruction of the Z3 computer in the Deutsches Museum in Munich.

The Z4 was almost complete before the fall of Berlin to the advancing Red Army. Zuse dismantled the Z4 machine and left Berlin for Bavaria. The restored Z4 was one of the first commercial computers when it was introduced in 1950, and it was delivered to ETH, Zurich.

The Z5 was an extended version of the Z4 and it was introduced in the early 1950s. It employed similar construction principles as the Z4, but it was over six times faster. It was one of the first commercial computers in Europe, and it was produced for the Leitz company in Germany.

The Z11 machine was introduced in 1955 and it was sold to German companies and universities. It had 654 relays and 28 stepwise relays, and it was programmable via a punch tape from 1957.

The Z22 machine was an inexpensive computer based on tubes, and it was sold mainly to universities. The Z23 computer was delivered to many universities and companies, and there a restored version at the Computer History Museum at Mountain View in California.

36.3   Zuse and Plankalkül

The earliest high-level programming language was *Plankalkül* developed by Konrad Zuse in 1946. It means *Plan* and *Kalkül*: i.e., a calculus of programs. It is a relatively modern language for a language developed in 1946. There was no compiler for the language, and the Free University of Berlin developed a compiler for it in 2000. This allowed the first Plankalkül program to be run over 55 years after its conception.

It employs data structures and Boolean algebra and includes a mechanism to define more powerful data structures. Zuse demonstrated that the Plankalkül language could be used to solve scientific and engineering problems, and he wrote several example programs including programs for sorting lists and searching a list for a particular entry. The main features of the Plankalkül language are:

- A high-level language
- Fundamental data types are arrays and tuples of arrays
- While construct for iteration
- Conditionals are addressed using guarded commands
- There is no GOTO statement
- Programs are non-recursive functions
- Type of a variable is specified when it is used

The main constructs of the language are variable assignment, arithmetical and logical operations, guarded commands and while loops. There are also some list and set processing functions.

Chapter 37
Epilogue

This book aimed to give a concise account of the contributions of a selection of technology companies that have made important contributions to the computing field. It was not feasible, due to space constraints, to consider all those firms that merit inclusion, and the selection chosen inevitably reflected the bias of the author. We gave a short introduction to each company, as well as a concise account of its key contributions.

The contributions of 35 technology companies were presented, and the discussion proceeded in alphabetical order. The first firm discussed was Adobe Systems and the last company presented was Zuse KG.

The companies may be classified into several categories such as those that produced early computers, firms that produced mainframe and mini-computers, those companies focused on the semiconductor sector, firms that developed home and personal computers, those who were active in the telecommunications field, ecommerce companies, social media companies, enterprise computing companies and so on.

We discussed early players in the computer field such as EMCC/Sperry/Unisys, Leo Computers and Zuse KG. EMCC was founded by John Mauchly and Presper Eckert in 1947. Leo Computers was one of the earliest British computer companies, and it's LEO I computer was based on the EDSAC computer developed at the University of Cambridge. Zuse KG was founded by Konrad Zuse in Germany shortly after the end of the Second World War.

We considered companies such as IBM, Amdahl and Digital that made important contributions to the mainframe and minicomputer fields. IBM has a long and distinguished history, and we discussed the development of SAGE, the System 360 family of computers, and the development of the IBM personal computer. Amdahl became a major competitor to IBM in the mainframe market, and Digital produced the popular PDP minicomputers as well as the VAX series of mainframes.

We presented a selection of companies that made important contributions to the semiconductor field, including Intel, Texas Instruments and Motorola. Intel developed the first microprocessor, the Intel 4004, in the early 1970s, and the microprocessor was a revolution in computing.

© Springer International Publishing Switzerland 2015
G. O'Regan, *Pillars of Computing*, DOI 10.1007/978-3-319-21464-1_37

We discussed companies that were active in developing home and personal computers, as well as those firms that developed applications and games for these machines. Our selection includes Sinclair Research which produced the Sinclair ZX Spectrum; Commodore Business Machines, which produced the Commodore 64 machine; Apple, which developed the Apple I and II computers and it has made major contributions to the computing field; Atari, which was active in developing arcade games and later games for home computers. We discussed the contributions of Digital Research, which developed the CP/M operating system, and the many contributions of Microsoft to the development of operating systems and the computing field.

We discussed some of the important contributions made by research centers such as Bell Labs, Xerox PARC and the Software Engineering Institute. Bell Lab's inventions include information theory and cryptography, coding theory, UNIX and the C programming language, the transistor and the Analogue Mobile Phone System. Xerox PARC's inventions include the Xerox Alto personal computer which was a GUI mouse driven machine which had a major impact on the design of the Apple Macintosh. Xerox PARC also invented Ethernet technology, the smalltalk object-oriented programming language and the laser printer. The Software Engineering Institute has developed state-of-the-art software process maturity models such as the CMMI to assist software development organizations in creating best-in-class software.

We discussed the important contributions of Ericsson and Motorola in the telecommunications field. Ericsson developed the first digital exchange (the AXE system) for fixed line telephony, and AXE's modular design eased Ericsson's transition to the mobile field. Motorola was the leader in first generation Analog mobile telephony, but it failed to adapt rapidly enough to the later generations of mobile.

We considered SAP's contributions in the enterprise software market, and Oracle's contributions to relational database technology. We considered the achievements of ecommerce companies such as Amazon and eBay, as well as the browser wars between Microsoft and Netscape.

We considered the contributions of social media companies such as Facebook and Twitter. Facebook is the leading social networking site in the world, and its mission is to make the world more open and connected. It helps its users to keep in touch with friends and family and allows them to share their opinions on what is happening around the world. Twitter is a social communication tool that allows people to broadcast short messages. It is often described as the *SMS of the Internet*, and it allows its users to send and receive short 140-character messages called *tweets*.

37.1 What Next in Computing?

The technological achievements in computing over the last 100 years are extraordinary. The human race has embarked on an amazing journey from the development of tabulators in the late nineteenth century to the development of analog computers, to the development of the early bulky digital computers, to the development of early commercial computers, to the development of transistors and integrated circuits, to the IBM and Amdahl mainframes and Digital minicomputers, to the revolution in Intel's invention of the microprocessor that led to home computers; to the development of the IBM personal computer and the Apple Macintosh, to the rise of the Internet and World Wide Web, to the rise of the mobile phone, to the development of Smart phones, to the growth of Social Media and so on.

We are living in a rapidly changing world where computer technology has driven innovation in almost all aspects of our world (e.g., communication, the media, medicine, automobiles, banking and so on). These developments have led to major benefits to society, and it is natural to wonder where all of these innovations will lead.

Will robots one day perform much of the work done by humans? Will real progress be made in the artificial intelligence field? Will it be possible some day for machines to achieve human-like intelligence? Will technology assist in the elimination of poverty in the world? Will technology be used for good purposes?

The pace of change with new technology is so relentless, that any predictions made with respect to future trends are likely to be wide of the mark. All that we can say with any level of certainty is that the high levels of innovation associated with technology companies will continue and that new technologies for the benefit of society will continue to be developed.

Test Yourself (Quiz 1)

1. Explain ecommerce and describe how Amazon has evolved to become a major ecommerce company.
2. Explain cloud computing and describe Amazon's implementation of cloud computing with its Amazon Web Services.
3. It is often said that a photograph never lies. Discuss the truth of this statement with reference to Adobe's Photoshop.
4. Explain Postscript and PDF and explain their relevance to the computing field.
5. Discuss Gene Amdahl's contributions to IBM and the Amdahl Corporation.
6. Describe the battle in the mainframe market between IBM and Amdahl.
7. Discuss the relevance of the Apple Macintosh to the computing field.
8. Discuss whether it was appropriate for Apple to receive all of the credit for its development of the Macintosh computer, when many of its user friendly features were taken from the Xerox Alto computer.
9. Discuss the accuracy of the message presented by Apple (i.e., that its competitors such as IBM were stale) in the famous 1984 Superbowl commercial that launched the Apple Macintosh.
10. Discuss the relevance of Atari to game developments and the computing field.
11. Describe the work done on statistical process control by Walter Shewhart at Bell Labs.
12. Describe the work done on Information Theory and Cryptography by Claude Shannon at Bell Labs.
13. Discuss the invention of the transistor at Bell Labs and the relevance of William Shockley to the computing field.
14. Describe Bell Labs contributions to the development of the Analog Mobile Phone System.
15. Discuss the invention of the C programming language and the UNIX operating system at Bell Labs.
16. Discuss the invention of the C++ programming language at Bell Labs.
17. Discuss the importance of the Commodore PET and Commodore 64 home computers.

© Springer International Publishing Switzerland 2015
G. O'Regan, *Pillars of Computing*, DOI 10.1007/978-3-319-21464-1

18. Discuss the importance of the early Amiga computers.
19. Explain the relevance of Cisco to the computing field.

Test Yourself (Quiz 2)

1. Describe how Dell uses lean manufacturing to give it a strategic advantage over its competitors.
2. Discuss the management style of Ken Olsen and Digital Corporation.
3. Discuss the relevance of DEC's PDP and VAX series of minicomputers to the computing field.
4. Explain how eBay pioneered person-to-person auctioning and its relevance to the computing field.
5. Describe eBay's business model.
6. Discuss the relevance of the ENIAC and EDVAC computers to the computing field.
7. Discuss the relevance of UNIVAC and Grace Murray Hopper to the computing field.
8. Describe how Hollerith's work on tabulators for the 1890 population census led to the birth of International Business Machines (IBM).
9. Describe the development of the IBM System 360 and its relevance to the computing field.
10. Explain the relevance of Don Estridge in the history of computing. What errors did IBM make in the introduction of the IBM PC?
11. Explain why Gary Kildall has been described as the "*man who could have been Bill Gates*".
12. What are your views on the controversy between Digital Research and Microsoft?
13. Describe the relevance of Ericsson's AXE system to the telecommunications field.
14. Describe Facebook's business model.
15. What is meant by the Facebook revolution?
16. Describe the Google search engine and Google's suite of products.
17. Describe the core principles of the HP Way.

© Springer International Publishing Switzerland 2015
G. O'Regan, *Pillars of Computing*, DOI 10.1007/978-3-319-21464-1

18. Describe how Intel invented the microprocessor and why this was a revolution in the computing field.
19. Explain the significance of Moore's Law.
20. Compare and contrast the achievements of Bill Gates and Steve Jobs.
21. Compare and contrast the achievements of Thomas Watson Senior and Thomas Watson Jr.

Test Yourself (Quiz 3)

1. Describe LEO's contributions to the early computing field.
2. Describe the browser wars between Netscape and Microsoft and the subsequent legal action between the companies.
3. Discuss Motorola's contributions to the mobile phone and semiconductor fields.
4. Describe Motorola's 6 sigma methodology.
5. Describe the Iridium System.
6. What happened to Motorola?
7. Explain the relational model and relational databases.
8. What is an Oracle Database?
9. Discuss the relevance of Philips to the computing field
10. What are the advantages and disadvantages of SAP's enterprise resource planning software?
11. Discuss the relevance of Sir. Clive Sinclair to the computing field.
12. Explain why Watt Humphries is known as the father of software quality.
13. Describe the Capability Maturity Model Integrated and describe the benefits of software process improvement.
14. Explain the difference between PSP and TSP
15. What is a SCAMPI appraisal and explain how it fits into the software process improvement cycle.
16. Describe the contributions of Rational Software to the software engineering field.
17. Discuss the relevance of Samsung to the computing field.
18. Describe the contributions of Texas Instruments and explain why the Integrated Circuit was a revolution in computing.
19. What is a Tweet? Describe Twitter's business model.

© Springer International Publishing Switzerland 2015
G. O'Regan, *Pillars of Computing*, DOI 10.1007/978-3-319-21464-1

20. Describe the contributions of Xerox PARC to the development of Ethernet technology.
21. Discuss the relevance of the Xerox Alto to the history of computing.
22. Describe the machines developed by Zuse and explain the relevance of the Z3 and Z4 to the computing field.
23. Describe the features of the Plankalkül language and explain why it took over fifty years for a Plankalkül program to be run.

Glossary

ABC	Altanasoff-Berry Computer
ACS	Advanced Computing Systems
AI	Artificial Intelligence
ALGOL	Algoritmic language
AMF	American Machinery Foundation
AMPS	Advanced Mobile Phone System
ANSI	American National Standards Institute
AOL	America On Line
API	Application Programmer Interface
APPN	Advanced Peer to Peer Network
AS/400	Application System / 400
ASCC	Automatic Sequence Controlled Calculator
ASCII	American Standard Code for Information Interchange
ASP	Average Sales Price
ATM	Asynchronous Transfer Mode
AT&T	American Telephone and Telegraph Company
AWS	Amazon Web Services
AXE	Automatic Exchange Electric switching system
B2B	Business to Business
B2C	Business to Consumer
B2G	Business to Government
BASIC	Beginners All-Purpose Symbolic Instruction Code
BIOS	Basic Input Output System
BW	Business Warehouse
C2C	Consumer to Consumer
CAD	Computer Aided Design
CBA/IPI	CMM Based Appraisal/Internal Process Improvement
CBA/SCE	CMM Based Appraisal/Software Capability Evaluation
CCITT	Comité Consultatif International Téléphonique et Télégraphique
CD	Compact Disc
CDMA	Code Division Multiple Access

© Springer International Publishing Switzerland 2015
G. O'Regan, *Pillars of Computing*, DOI 10.1007/978-3-319-21464-1

CEO	Chief Executive Officer
CERN	Conseil European Recherche Nucleaire
CIA	Central Intelligence Agency
CICS	Customer Information Control System
CMM®	Capability Maturity Model
CMMI®	Capability Maturity Model Integration
CMU	Carnegie Mellon University
COBOL	Common Business Oriented Language
CODASYL	Conference on Data Systems Languages
CP/M	Control Program for Microcomputers
CPU	Central Processing Unit
CRM	Customer Relationship Management
CRT	Cathode Ray Tube
CTR	Computing Tabulating Recording Company
DARPA	Defence Advanced Research Project Agency
DB	Database
DBA	Database Administrator
DBMS	Database Management System
DDL	Data Definition Language
DEC	Digital Equipment Corporation
DES	Data Encryption Standard
DMAIC	Define, Measure, Analyse, Improve, Control
DML	Data Manipulation Language
DNS	Domain Naming System
DOD	Department of Defence
DOS	Disk Operating System
DP	Demand Planning
DRAM	Dynamic Random Access Memory
DRI	Digital Research Incorporated
DSL	Digital Subscriber Line
DVD	Digital Versatile Disc
EARS	Ethernet, Alto, Research, character generator Scanned laser output terminal
EDVAC	Electronic Discrete Variable Automatic Computer
EELM	English Electric LEO Marconi
EMCC	Eckert-Mauchly Computer Corporation
ENIAC	Electronic Numerical Integrator and Computer
ERD	Entity Relationship Diagrams
ERP	Enterprise Resource Planning
ETH	Eidgenössische Technische Hochschule
ETACS	Extended TACs
ETSI	European Telecommunications Standards Institute
FDMA	Frequency Division Multiple Access
FTP	File Transfer Protocol
GECOS	General Electric Comprehensive Operating System

GIF	Graphics Interchange Format
GPRS	General Packet Radio Service
GSM	Global System Mobile
GSR	Gigabit Switch Router
GUI	Graphical User Interface
HICL	High Integrity Computing Laboratory
HMD	Head Mounted Display
HP	Hewlett Packard
HTML	Hypertext Markup Language
HTTP	Hyper Text Transport Protocol
IBM	International Business Machines
IC	Integrated Circuit
ICI	Imperial Chemicals Industries
ICL	International Computer Ltd.
IDE	Integrated Development Environment
IE	Internet Explorer
IEEE	Institute of Electrical and Electronic Engineers
IOS	Internetwork operating system
IP	Internet Protocol
ISO	International Standards Organization
ISP	Internet Service Provider
ITU	International Telecommunications Union
JCP	Java Community Process
JDK	Java Development Kit
JIT	Just in Time
JPEG	Joint Photographic Experts Group
JVM	Java Virtual Machine
LAN	Local Area Network
LCD	Liquid Crystal Display
LED	Light Emitting Diode
LEO	Lyons Electronic Office
LEO	Low Earth Orbit
LNG	Liquid Natural Gas
LP	Long Play
LRG	Learning Research Group
LSI	Large Scale Integration
ME	Millennium
MIDI	Musical Instrument Digital Interface
MIPS	Million Instructions Per Second
MIT	Massachusetts Institute of Technology
MITS	Micro Instrumentation and Telemetry System
MS/DOS	Microsoft Disk Operating System
MSN	Microsoft Network
MTA	Mobile Telephone system version A
NACA	National Advisory Committee Aeronautics

NASA	National Aeronautics and Space Administration
NCSA	National Centre for Supercomputing Applications
NMT	Nordic Mobile Telephony system
NORAD	North American Aerospace Defence
NPL	National Physical Laboratory
NR	Norwegian Research
OMG	Object Management Group
OMT	Object Modelling Technique
OOSE	Object-oriented software engineering
OS	Operating System
OSRD	Office Scientific Research and Development
P-CMM	People Capability Maturity Model
PARC	Palo Alto Research Centre
PC	Personal Computer
PC/DOS	Personal Computer Disk Operating System
PDA	Personal Digital Assistant
PDC	Personal Digital Cellular
PDCA	Plan, Do, Check, Act
PDF	Portable Document Format
PNG	Portable Network Graphics
PDP	Programmed Data Processor
PLM	Product Lifecycle Management
PL/M	Programming Language for Microcomputers
PPC	Pay Per Click
PS/2	Personal System 2
PSD	PhotoShop Document
PSP	Personal Software Process
RAM	Random Access Memory
RAMAC	Random Access Method of Accounting and Control
RDBMS	Relational Database Management System
RIM	Research in Motion
RISC	Reduced Instruction Set Computer
ROI	Return on Investment
RUP	Rational Unified Process
SAA	Systems Application Architecture
SAGE	Semi-Automatic Ground Environment
SAP	Systems Applications and Products in data processing
SAT	Stockholms Allmänna Telefonaktiebolag
SCAMPI	Standard CMMI Appraisal Method for Process Improvement
SCM	Supply Chain Management
SDL	Specification and Description Language
SE	Societas Europaea
SEI	Software Engineering Institute
SGI	Silicon Graphics Inc.
SHI	Samsung Heavy Industries

SID	Sound Interface Device
SIM	Subscriber Identity Module
SLOT	Scanned Laser Output Terminal
SMS	Short Message Service
SNA	System Networking Architecture
SNP	Supply and Network Planning
SNS	Social Networking Site
SPC	Statistical Process Control
SQL	Structured Query Language
SQL/DS	Structured Query Language/Data System
SRM	Supplier Relationship Management
SSEM	Small Scale Experimental Machine
SSL	Secure Socket Layer
SWF	Small Web Format
TACS	Total Access Communication
TCP	Transport Control Protocol
TDMA	Time Division Multiple Access
TI	Texas Instrument
TSP	Team Software Process
UCLA	University of California (Los Angeles)
UML	Unified Modelling Language
UMTS	Universal Mobile Telecommunications System
UNIVAC	Universal Automatic Computer
URL	Universal Resource Locator
VAX	Virtual Address eXtension
VCS	Atari Video Computer System
VLSI	Very Large Scale Integration
VM	Virtual Memory
VMS	Virtual Memory System
VOIP	Voice Over Internet Prototcol
W3C	World Wide Web Consortium
WAN	Wide Area Network
WCDMA	Wideband CDMA
WISC	Wisconsin Integrally Sequential Computer
WYSIWYG	What you see is what you get
XML	eXtensible Markup Language

References

[Bag:12]   Bagnall B (2012) Commodore: a company on the edge, 2nd edn. Variant Press, Winnipeg

[BL:00]   Berners-Lee T (2000) Weaving the web. Collins Book, San Francisco

[Blo:04]   Bloomberg Business Week Magazine (2004) The man who could have been Bill Gates, October 2004, http://www.bloomberg.com/bw/stories/2004-10-24/the-man-who-could-have-been-bill-gates

[Boo:93]   Booch G (1993) Object-oriented analysis and design with applications, 2nd edn. Addison Wesley Professional

[Brk:75]   Fred B (1975) The mythical man month. Addison Wesley, Reading

[Brk:86]   Fred B (1986) No silver bullet. Essence and accidents of software engineering, Information processing. Elsevier, Amsterdam

[By:94]   Halfhill T (1994) R.I.P. Commodore. 1954–1994. A look at an innovative industry pioneer, whose achievements have been largely forgotten. Byte Magazine, August 1994

[CKS:11]   Chrissis MB, Conrad M, Shrum S (2011) CMMI. Guidelines for process integration and product improvement, 2011th edn, SEI series in software engineering. Addison Wesley, Boston

[Cod:70]   Codd EF (1970) A relational model of data for large shared data banks. Commun ACM 13(6):377–387

[Coh:03]   Adam C (2003) The perfect store: inside eBay. Back Bay Books, New York

[Dat:81]   Date CJ (1981) An introduction to database systems, 3rd edn, The systems programming series. Addison-Wesley, Reading

[DeF:10]   Dell M, Fredman C (2010) Direct from Dell: strategies that revolutionalised an industry. Michael Dell and Catherine Fredman. Collins Business Series. Harper Business, 2006

[Edw:11]   Edwards B (2011) The history of Atari computers. PC World, April 21st 2011

[Fer:03]   Ferry G (2003) A computer called LEO: Lyons tea shops and the world's first office computer. Harper Perennial; (Reissue) edition (26 Feb. 2010)

[Ger:13]   Gertner J (2013) The idea factory: bell labs and the great age of American innovation. Penguin Books, New York

[Hil:00]   Hilzik MA (2000) Dealers of lightning. Xerox PARC and the dawn of the computer age. Harper Business, New York

[Hum:89]   Humphry W (1989) Managing the software process. Addison Wesley, Reading

[IGN:14]   IGN presents: the history of Atari, March 2014. http://www.ign.com/articles/2014/03/20/ign-presents-the-history-of-atari

[Jac:99]   Jacobson I, Booch G, Rumbaugh J (1999) The unified software development process. Addison Wesley, Reading

© Springer International Publishing Switzerland 2015
G. O'Regan, *Pillars of Computing*, DOI 10.1007/978-3-319-21464-1

[Jac:05]   Jacaobson I et al (2005) The unified modelling language, user guide, 2nd edn. Addison Wesley Professional, Reading

[Kay:93]   Kay A (1993) The early history of smalltalk. HOPL-II. The second ACM SIGPLAN conference on history of programming languages. ACM SIGPLAN 28(3):69–95, March 1993

[KeR:78]   Kernighan B, Ritchie D (1978) The C programming language, 1st edn. Prentice Hall Software Series, Reading

[Lam:72]   Lampson B (1972) Why alto? Xerox inter-office memorandum. December 1972. http://www.digibarn.com/friends/butler-lampson/

[Lev:11]   Levy S (2011) In the plex: how google thinks, works and shapes our lives. Simon and Schuster Publishers, New York

[Mal:14]   Malone MS (2014) The intel trinity: how Robert Noyce, Gordon Moore and Andy Grove built the world's most important company. Harper Business, New York

[MeJ:01]   Meurling J, Jeans R (2001) The Ericsson chronicle: 125 years in telecommunications. Informationsforlaget, Stockholm

[Mir:14]   Mirchandani V (2014) SAP nation: a runaway software economy. Deal Architect Publishers, United States

[Mor:65]   Moore G (1965) Cramming more components onto integrated circuits. Electronics Magazine, 1965

[Mot:99]   Motorola Museum of Electrics and Motorola (1999) Motorola (CB) – a journey through time and technology. Purdue University Press, United States

[Mun:11]   Munson EG (2011) The rise and fall of Unimation Inc. A story of robotics innovation and triumph that changed the world. Robot Magazine, 2011

[ORg:02]   O'Regan G (2002) A practical approach to software quality. Springer, New York

[ORg:06]   O'Regan G (2006) Mathematical approaches to software quality. Springer, London

[ORg:10]   O'Regan G (2010) Introduction to software process improvement. Springer, London

[ORg:11]   O'Regan G (2011) A brief history of computing. Springer, London

[ORg:12]   O'Regan G (2012) Mathematics in computing. Springer, London/New York

[ORg:13]   O'Regan G (2013) Giants of computing. Springer, London/New York

[ORg:14]   O'Regan G (2014) Introduction to software quality. Springer, Cham

[Pac:95]   Packard D (1995) The HP way. How bill hewlett and I built our company. Harper Business, New York

[Pir:05]   III Pirtle C (2005) Engineering the world: stories from the first 75 years of Texas Instruments. Southern Methodist University Press, Dallas

[Pfi:02]   Pfiffner P (2002) Inside the publishing revolution: the adobe story. Adobe Press, Berkeley

[Pug:09]   Pugh EW (2009) Building IBM: shaping an industry and its technology. MIT Press, Cambridge

[Rob:05]   Robbins A (2005) Unix in a nutshell, 4th edn. O'Reilly Media, Sebastopol

[SCA:06]   Standard CMMI Appraisal method for process improvement. Technical Report CMU/SEI-2006-V1.2. Software Engineering Institute, United States

[Sch:04]   Schein E (2004) DEC is dead, long live DEC. The lasting legacy of digital equipment corporation. Barrett-Koehler Publishers, San Francisco

[Sch:14]   Schaefer MW (2014) The tao of twitter. Changing your life and business 140 characters at a time, 2nd edn. McGraw-Hill, New York

[SEI:09]   Software Engineering Institute (2009) CMMI impact. Presentation by Anita Carleton, August 2009

[Sha:37]   Shannon C (1937) A symbolic analysis of relay and switching circuits. Masters thesis, Massachusetts Institute of Technology

[Sha:48]   Shannon C (1948) A mathematical theory of communication. Bell Syst Tech J 27:379–423

[Sha:49]   Shannon CE (1949) Communication theory of secrecy systems. Bell Syst Tech J 28(4):656–715

[Sho:50]   Shockley W (1950) Electrons and holes in semiconductors with applications to transistor electronics. Van Nostrand, New York

[Shw:31]   Shewhart W (1931) The economic control of manufactured products. Van Nostrand, New York

[SoL:14]   Song J, Lee K (2014) The Samsung way: transformational management strategies from the world leader in innovation and design. McGraw-Hill, New York

[Sto:14]   Stone B (2014) The everything store: Jeff Bezos and the age of amazon. Back Bay Books, New York

[Sym:13]   Symonds M (2013) Softwar: an intimate portrait of Larry Ellison and Oracle. Simon & Schuster Publishers, New York

[VN:45]   von Neumann J (1945) First draft of a report on the EDVAC. University of Pennsylvania, Philadelphia

[Woo:13]   Woodcock C (2012) The ZX spectrum on your PC, 2nd edn. Lulu Inc., UK

Index

© Springer International Publishing Switzerland 2015   257
G. O'Regan, *Pillars of Computing*, DOI 10.1007/978-3-319-21464-1

Printed in the United States
By Bookmasters